AN ABODE OF THE GODDESS

KINGSHIP, CASTE AND SACRIFICIAL ORGANIZATION IN A BENGAL VILLAGE

An Abode of the Goddess

Kingship, Caste and Sacrificial Organization in a Bengal Village

MASAHIKO TOGAWA

MANOHAR
2006

First published 2006

ISBN 81-7304-677-8

Published by
Ajay Kumar Jain *for*
Manohar Publishers & Distributors
4753/23 Ansari Road, Daryaganj
New Delhi 110 002

Typeset by
Kohli Print
Delhi 110 051

Printed at
Lordson Publishers Pvt. Ltd.
Delhi 110 007

Distributed in South Asia by
FOUNDATION BOOKS
4381/4, Ansari Rorad
Daryaganj, New Delhi 110 002
and its branches at Mumbai, Hyderabad,
Bangalore, Chennai, Kolkata

Contents

Illustrations

(between pages 112–13)

Maps

Tables

Acknowledgements

Many individuals and institutions helped me during my research work in West Bengal, begun in September 1992, with fieldwork in the village from January 1994 to April 1995. Fieldwork continues intermittently even now.

Most of the data were collected from my observations and from interviews with people in the village of Kshiragram. As I cannot thank everyone who helped, and apologize to those whose names are omitted. At first, I thank the family of Sri Sanat Kumar Chakrabartty who belongs to one of the nine lineages of the priests of the Jogadya temple. He is really an authority on the village rituals. The Sabha-pandit Pranab Bhattacaryya, the Rajkachari Gauri Shankar Mukhopadhyaya, and the Pradhan-purohit Raj Kumar Chakrabartty all occupy the responsible positions in the temple. Sri Jogeswar Chaudhuri is an eminent local historian of Bardhaman (Burdwan) as well as one of the villagers.

The Pradhan, the Kshiragram Gram Panchayat office, Sri Gauri Shankar Datta helped me during my staying in the village. The District Magistrate of Bardhaman, Sri Asim Barman, permitted me to stay in the village and collect data in the District Settlement Record Room.

I thank the members of the Bardhaman Raj and the Deb-seba office in the town of Bardhaman, and am especially indebted to His Highness Sri Pranay Chand Mahatab for his hospitality and helpful advice. He permitted me to use the ritual records in the Deb-seba office and to participate in his family ceremony.

Many scholars helped at every stage of this study. In particular, I owed much to Hitoshi Miyake, Masataka Suzuki and Teigo Yoshida in the graduate school of Keio university in Japan. I am also grateful to Akinobu Kawai, Nariaki Nakazato, Sinkichi Taniguchi and Masayuki Usuda, all eminent historians of Bengal. Masakazu Tanaka and Hiroshi Ishii always encouraged me to write the book. Masao Yamaguchi visited the village and provided intellectual stimulation. In Santiniketan Sri Surajit Sinha always gave me a warm support. Dr. Ajit Kumar Danda gave me continuous encouragement as my guide in India.

This study was financed by the Overseas Student Programme for

Asian Countries, the Ministry of Education, Government of Japan. A part of the research was also supported by the Mitsubishi Foundation for Cultural Promotion.

MASAHIKO TOGAWA

Introduction

This book is about a village society and its relationship with Hindu kingship in the light of the ritual organization of an old temple. In this temple, there are ritual posts and roles that were assigned to the various service castes and lineages. The village, Kshiragram, is famous as one of 51 sakta-pithas or centres of Sakti worship in Bengal, and the village temple (*jogadya-mandir*) prospered under the patronage of the Bardhaman Raj (Burdwan Raj) in the early eighteenth century. The temple organization consists, on the one hand, of the various caste groups and lineages and, on the other, the service tenures granted by the Bardhaman Raj in the late medieval period. The ritual authority of the king is still perceptable, as we shall see. My analysis of the ritual system shows the strong relationship between the village society and the kingship, and indicates how deeply the social life of the village has been influenced by the Hindu kingship through its ritual practices.

Extant Bengali documents indicate that there was a close relationship between the Raj family and the village through the Jogadya temple in the early eighteenth century. Since then, the village temple has enjoyed the patronage of the kings of Bardhaman, and royal influence over the villagers still lives on in the ritual organization of the village temple.

Under the Emperor of Delhi, Kirtichand (the Bardhaman Maharaja, reign 1702–40) was granted zamindari over this area. An ancient Mahapitha, Kshiragram, was one of the villages under its zamindari. It is believed that this sacred place is a dwelling of the goddess Jogadya and her spouse, Kshirkhantak. Kirtichand was extremely delighted with the acquisition of the zamindari of Mahapitha. He built a temple to perform the ritual of the goddess, an annexed building designed for the bedroom of the goddess's night rest (*sayan griha*), and a dance hall (*nath-mandir*) in the village. The inscription on a stone of the altar inside the temple was so damaged that it is now undecipherable. But the old tradition of the temple rituals preserved by the villagers remains intact since the reign of the Bardhaman Raj. (*Bardhamaner rajbsanghaucarita*, 1913, p. 25)

The history of the temple is, however, far older than this if we are to go by the legends and myths about Jogadya recited by the villagers. During the reign of the legendary King Hari Datta, there used to be human sacrifice in front of the image of the goddess. The lineage of Datta, one of nine Kshatriya lineages in the village, is regarded as the descendant of this legendary King. Today a buffalo sacrifice takes the place of human sacrifice to the goddess on the final day of the great festival. At the altar of the goddess a representative of the Dom caste has an important role: he cuts his hand and offers his own blood to the goddess. In this way, the ritual organization involves various caste gruops, according to the historical origin of their office and the right to participate. This system of offices and roles for each caste and lineage is organized hierarchically, but it is the kingship of Bardhaman that has been the ultimate source of the honour of the temple since the late medieval period.

The Village and the Temple

THE SETTING

Of the eighteen castes in the village, the most numerous are (a) the Ugra-Kshatriya, (b) the Bagdi, and (c) the Brahman. The Ugra-Kshatriya is a dominant landholding caste as well as the largest in population. They are the main patrons of the Brahman and the other service castes. They claim the Kshatriya status in the village, and are called *aguri* colloquially. The Bagdi, who constitute the majority among the untouchable castes in the Rarh area (the mid-western part of Bengal), have the second largest population in the village. They provide agricultural labour for the village landholders. In company with the other service castes, they also play an important role in the temple ritual. The village Brahmans are the third largest population strength, engaged mainly in the *jajman-purohit* relationship as household priests of the Ugra-Kshatriyas. In this way, the village society has a caste organization woven by the so-called *jajmani* relationship between the dominant caste and its family priests on the one hand and the patron-client relationship between landholders and service castes on the other.

The organization of the Jogadya temple is based on the system of ritual positions and roles assigned to the various caste groups. These structured hierarchically with the Brahman at the top. Under Brahman supervision calendric rituals are performed in the temple. The Brahmans are always referred to as the highest rank in the village and the authority on ritual. It is the kingship of Bardhaman, however, who is the ultimate authority and source of honour in the temple organization. The royal family is the grantor of the temple service lands and properties. As every temple ritual begins, the priests utter the name of the king of Bardhaman. Moreover, the royal family used to be a zamindar in possession of many estates, including the village, before Independence. In those days, the court of the Bardhaman Raj incurred the expenditure for every temple sacrifie, and control led the temple organization through the superintendent of the temple (*rajkachari*). There are, therefore, four important parties involved in the temple ritual system: (1) the dominant landholding caste, (2) the Brahman priests, (3) service castes, and (4) the Maharaja as the supreme authority. They are interdependent on one another through mutual and sometimes asymmetrical relationships such as *jajman*–priest, patron–service, king–temple, zamindar–*raiyat* and so on. These relationships could be summarized as those of the kingship, caste, and ritual organization.

This book focuses mainly on the following three materials: the ritual organization and its offices in the Jogadya temple; duties and rights both in the temple ritual and in the rituals of the locality; and the ritual processes in which each caste and lineage is assigned its role through the year. It is on these elements that the ritual system of the temple has been based for a long time. For the beginning, we shall overview the village society and the historical accounts on the temple.

HISTORICAL BACKGROUND

During the late Mughal period, the founder of the Bardhaman kingship became a zamindar in the village of Baikunthapur, near the town of Bardhaman. There was a rapid expansion over the present Bardhaman district, and then all over western Bengal. Around the time of the beginning of British rule, this family was the largest zamindar in Bengal in terms of revenues paid to the government. During the British period, the territory of the Bardhaman kingship came under the Permanent Settlement (1793) and the royal family became one of the most powerful zamindars in British India. It continued to be powerful until the Estate Acquisition Act (1953), with two interruptions of direct control by the court of ward of the colonial government. This means that the royal family was in possession of many estates, including the village, and the village landholders of today were engaged in the relationship of zamindar-*raiyat* (landlord and tenant) with the king under the terms of the Bengal Tenancy Act (1885).

The kings of Bardhaman exercised great power as the protector as well as the oppressor of the people [e.g. McLane 1993: 69–95]. The kings annexed the neighbouring territories of the landlords and built more than 48 temples in the kingdom from the 1730s to 1900 [Chaudhuri 1991: 213–214]. The present-day Jogadya temple in the village was rebuilt on the remains of an older temple around 1730 during the reign of the Maharaja Kirtichand (1702–40).

Under the Bengal Tenancy Act (1885), the rights of the owner-cultivators *vis-à-vis* those of the zamindars are stated. This was a prerequisite for the transfer of tenurial rights of the *raiyats* to the direct control of the government. Most of the households of the Ugra-Kshatriyas and Brahmans in the village fall in this category. It is also important that the Bengal Tenancy Act provided for a Survey and Settlement of each district of the Bengal Presidency, the first attempt to survey each plot of the estates systematically and settle the rents on the record book (called *khatiyan* by the British administrators). The rights of the scheduled castes who are mainly small tenants and agricultural labourers, were prescribed by the Government of India Act (1935) through separate seats in the state assembly, and after Independence came a reservation policy in eduation, employment, and election.

In this way, the village society consists of the complex relations between the kingship and the village society, between the dominant caste and the serivce castes, and between the zamindars and the farmers. This is reflected particularly in the ritual of the temple, which occupies the core of the village. The field-data collected from the village seems, therefore, to point to an indigenous political formation. So far the religious aspect of kingship and its impact on village society have been overlooked by the emphasis on Brahmanical values in Hindu society. In this sense, this monograph intends to reconsider the village social form from the viewpoints of kingship, dominant caste, and other service castes in place of the view of village society as one structured on a religious dichotomy between pure and impure. It is important at this stage to outline the recent trends in anthropological studies on South Asia in order to place the topic of this book in perspective.

Anthropology and Village Study

ANTHROPLOGY IN THE 1980s

In *Homo Hierarchicus* L. Dumont (1966) looked at Hindu society, from an unique holistic viewpoint based on the dichotomous relationship between the untouchable and Brahman. However, following the publication in 1970 of the English edition and the revised edition in

1980, many anthropologists presented arguments against the theory of his book. In the 1980s village studies of the social structure model became much fewer in number compared to those of the 1950s, the output of which is represented by the books of Srinivas (1955) and Marriott (1955). Many anthropologists have shifted their attention from village studies to the studies of religion since the 1980s. This fact, however, does not necessarily mean that village studies are any less significant; rather it seems to suggest simply that there is a shortage of the necessary perspective to interpret the village society set in the contexts of broader space and time.

According to Fuller and Jonathan (1990), the issues regarding Hindu society discussed within the 'post-Dumontian framework' of the 1980s were understood through the following three key indicators: Brahman priests, ascetic renouncers, and kingship. Some other facts of the subject could certainly be added, such as the rethinking of the relationship between Hinduism and Hindu society, a topic which C. Fuller himself once discussed (1979).

Concerning Brahman priests, Dumont argued that the status of the Brahman is fundamentally based on his priestly occupation (1980: 47). However, many scholars doubt this. For example, Parry (1980) discusses the relegated status of funeral priests, the Mahabrahmans, at the cremation ground of Benares. Because of their permanent role in the death ritual and the acceptance of *dan* (gift), they are treated 'much like Untouchables'. Fuller (1984) analysed the priestly organizations at the great centre of pilgrimage, the Minaksi temple of Madurai, and presented persuasive data to demonstrate the relative inferiority of the priestly Brahmans compared to their secular caste members.

It was well known that the Kulin-Brahman (*kaulinna-pratha-brahman*) in Bengal holding titles such as *Mukho-upadhyaya*, *Bandyo-upadhyaya*, and *Choto-upadhyaya*, never practised priesthood, and that their superiority was strengthened by their status as bride-takers from the other Brahmans (e.g. Risley 1891). In Hindu society, the bride-taking lineage is superior to the bride-giving lineage. It is ironic that this bride-taking relationship provided a basis for the argument about the marriage alliance theory presented by Dumont (1957). He tried to show the difference between the kinship structures of south and north India on the basis of the kinship terminology regarding affinity. At any rate, as demonstrated by Quigley's theoretical study (1993: Ch. 4), it is now widely acepted that the Brahmans are not always priests in Hindu society and often the 'ideal' Brahman is not seen as a priest at all (also Burghart 1990; Heesterman 1985; van der Veer 1989, etc.).

With regard to asetic renouncers (*sadhu*, or *sanyasin*), Dumont thought that they are only an exceptional element in caste society in his holistic view and correspond to similar individuals in Western society. This comparison is itself interesting as this is certainly a comprehensive attempt to contrast Hindu society with Western society as had been done by Max Weber (1958). However, there is much evidence to suggest that these renouncers are never actually outside Hindu society. On this point, van der Veer (1989) has observed—through an analysis of the organization of priests and 'renouncers' in Ayodhya—that religious ascetics never exist independently and are provided economic assistance from the temple management. Burghart (1983) also argues that there is no simple dichotomy between the Brahman householder and renouncer. Similar studies abound (Bradford 1985; Heesterman 1985, etc.). Despite their idea of egalitarian fraternity among castes, the disciples of the saint Caitanya in Bengal have established a caste ranking within their sect (Dimock 1966). It is also well known that there are caste-like hierarchies in rural Muslim society (Sengupta 1973).

Ethnohistorical studies such as van der Veer's are effective in verifying the so-called 'ethnographical present' as regards the structureal analysis, of which Dumont is representative. However, historical data need to be distinguished from the ethnohistorical synthesis because the latter sometimes leads to an overemphasis on socio-economic factors and overlooks the peculiar religious or ideological factors within the context of Hindu society. Not only South Asian anthropologists but also many contemporary anthropologists commonly share this problem. We have tried to avoid oversimplifying both the ideological and economical factors.

In this respect, I shall mention two studies: *An Anthropologist among the Historians* (Cohn 1987) and *The Hollow Crown* (Dirks 1987). The former is based on the anthropological history or the reconstruction of history under the influence of Hobsbawm and Ranger (1983) and closely corresponds to a series of historical studies called the Subaltern group. The latter is an attempt to synthesize structure and history as done by Sahlins (1985), which leads to the emerging field of colonial studies (Appadurai 1981; Breckenridge and van der Veer 1993; Inden 1986, 1990; Quigley 1993). In both cases, the approach leads inevitably to a rethinking of colonial period history and the colonial impact on indigenous political forms, which leads us to the topic of Hindu kingship.

STUDIES ON KINGSHIP

During the 1980s many anthropologists focused their attention on Hindu kingship, especially the transformations that occurred during British rule. In the beginning, the discussions concentrated chiefly on the concept of power encompassed to religious values by Dumont. In opposition to Dumont's opinion regarding a 'secularized king', the religious functions of the king were pointed out through examples such as the king's role as *jajman* of priests, and his central position in sacrifice (e.g. Derrett 1976; Fuller 1984: 104–6; Heesterman 1995). On the other hand, Biardeau (1989), following the traditions of French sociology, considers the Brahman-Kshatriya relationship to be the core of the structure of Hindu society. According to her the king is the delegate of the gods and goddesses on earth and is there for the protection of the kingdom; he plays the role of *jajman* in the sacrificial rituals performed by the Brahman priests. Thus, Biardeau thinks the king occupies the primary position in Hindu society.

These theoretical questions led to the revaluation of a theory of A.M. Hocart. Quigley (1993: Ch. 6) argues that Hocart's theory is an alternative to that of Dumont and tries to provide a new perspective on caste society. Tanaka (1991) also looks for an alternative slant on Hindu society by focusing on the its sacrificial structure.

Hocart considers the caste system a 'sacrificial organization' in which 'castes are merely families to whom various offices in the ritual are assigned by heredity' (1950: 20). It is worth noting that three aspects of his theory pertain to the subjects discussed in this thesis. First, Hocart suggests that the kings belong to 'the first caste' because they command other castes to play definite roles in the rituals of sacrifice that seek to regenerate the cosmological order and thus ensure the prosperity of the community. An insight into this topic is presented by Hubert and Mauss (1964). The second point in Hocart's theory is his emphasis on initiation for caste membership (ibid.: 56). It seems natural that if the caste system is designed for the sacrificial ritual then initiation is indispensable, because birth into a particular caste is not a sufficient condition for anyone to participate in the ritual. Third point is the concept of reproduced structures of kingship in miniature (ibid.: 68), which is suggestive of later studies on local political structures (Cohn 1962; Stein 1980), and the images of the polities (e.g. Geertz 1980; Tambiah 1976). Regarding these fluid political boundaries, Quigley argues, 'caste results when kingship attempts to assert itself against kinship' (1993: 129). This could explain the relationship between the caste organization and the kingship. It is also connected with the concept of the 'imperial formation' presented by Inden (1990: Ch. 6), which enables us to see the indigenous polity of India as a continual generative process.

Another point made in the study on kingship concerns the changing circumstances around the kingship under British rule. As Fuller (1977) precisely pointed out, the self-sufficient village economy, which has so far been understood to refer to the *jajmani* system, is the result of the permeating influence of the colonial administration. Most field workers overlooked the fact that the colonial government had, through the revenue administrations, taken over the positions formerly held by local kings. It is, therefore, misleading for anthropologists to describe the present villages of South Asia as representing traditional culture, because they only see the villages that have been drastically transformed during the approximately 150 years of British rule. Inden (1990) considers this matter, and describes the formation of Western views about Indian society as a dynamic process of interaction between the West and the East. This forms broadly the argument of Orientalism presented by Asad (1973) and Said (1978).

Some scholars pay attention to the problem of the kingship and the dominant caste in village society. Raheja's (1988a) contribution is most remarkable in this respect. She suggests that the *jajmani* relationship is based on the *dan*, which conveys the inauspiciousness of religious sin from the dominant caste to the village Brahman priests. It is well known that Dumont understands *jajmani* relations to be fundamentally encompassed by the concept of pure and impure (1980). This enables us to reconsider village society as a central and peripheral system that consists of the relationship of the dominant caste and the other service castes based on the idea of auspiciousness and inauspiciousness. This is an attractive point of view for many anthropologists because it presents an alternative to the view of village society as hierarchically structured on an axis between the relationships of the Brahman and the Untouchables, based on the idea of pure and impure; an attempt to reconstruct another holistic view by focusing on the horizontal model of Hindu society.

METHODOLOGICAL PROBLEMS

Apart from these theoretical advancements anthropologists have failed to accumulate sufficient data from the field concerning the organization of local kingships and their influences to the formation of rural societies.

There are indeed some reports on the interviews with an ex-Maharaja (Mayer 1981) and the splendid ritual at the former court of the Raj in Bengal (Ostor 1980). However, during the British period the regional sovereignties were practically handed over to the colonial government and, the process was completed in independent India with the abolition in 1971 of the princely states. With the establishment of modern administrations the indigenous organization of kingship has drastrically changed in rural areas while the ritual systems of the villages, basically controlled by the Brahman priests, have remained relatively unchanged. It is under such circumstances that many anthropologists began their field research in the 1950s (Fuller 1977; Tanabe 1999).

Some anthropologists have no doubt appreciated this matter, but there were very few monographs about it, primarily because of methodological problems. Since the 1980s, many anthropologists began paying attention to this issue and resorted to mainly two methods of analysis. The first is the ethnohistorical approach in which the historical materials preserved in the government offices, such as state archives and the record rooms of the revenue office are used. The analyses of the historical documents of the colonial rule chronicle the changing processes of the local political systems and also throw light on the earlier forms of kingship (Appadurai 1981; Cohn 1987; Dirks 1987).

In the second approach the ritual data preserved at sacred places are used. These data consist mainly of the ritual systems traditionally followed in the old Hindu temples. Formerly, the local kings supported most of the famous temples, which used to function as religious centres in their respective kingdoms. Despite post-Independence changes in royal patronage there remain some old features that are symbolic roles, and kept within the ritual systems of these temples. Many anthropologists have tried to reconstruct an outline of the relationship between the kings and the priests from these. The studies by Fuller (1984), Marglin (1985) and van der Veer (1989) are good examples.

As already discussed, a noticeable trend in the decline of village studies started in the 1980s. Many anthropologists turned to studies of the religious centres belonging to the so-called 'great tradition'. This seems, however, to be confined to descriptions of Hindu society, because these studies have depended on a system specifically formed within the religious traditions, often quite removed from the daily life of rural people. For example, Tanaka (1993) shows that the Brahman priests of the Nataraja temple in Chidambaram form a self-contained community, and are not dependent either economically or ideologically on its patrons. This case is very interesting because it provides a counterargument to the view that the ideal Brahman has to be free from subordinate *jajmani* relations. Simultaneously, it implies that an exceptional case such as the Nataraja temple mainly depends on donations from pilgrims and is separated from rural society. Similar problems can also be pointed out in earlier studies such as those of Appadurai (1981), Fuller (1984) and Marglin (1985): Studies that are mostly on field data concerning the 'great tradition'.

What is discussed so far indicates the importance for further ethnographical analysis of Hindu kingship during and before colonial rule. In this sense, the synthesis in this book between village studies and historical material is neither a functionalistic study regressing to the 1950s nor a structuralistic approach, narrowing objectives into religion. We can construct an analytical perspective using a productive combination with a feasible variety of materials as Dumont through an excellent collaboration of indology and anthropology.

Islam and Rural Bengal

The last topic to be examined here is the ethnography in the context of the history of Bengal, where the various dynasties were conquered repeatedly, and kept under Muslim rule for long periods. Particularly, there is no doubt that Muslim kingships have had strong influence over the local society since the conquest of Nabadwip by Muhammad Bakhtiyar in 1204 which is discussed as a starting point for the process of Islamization in Bengal (Eaton 1994). The population of the Muslims and Hindus in Bengal were balanced for a long time in the rural areas, and we should not overlook the influences brought about by the spread of Islam to the local society as is shown in the extensive study by Roy (1983).

For instance, in the village, the stone image of the goddess Jogadya is installed under water on the bed of the pond Kshirdighi, and this is an essential act in the ritual processes performed in the temple. According to the oral traditions, the villagers suffered repeatedly from the invasions of Muslim and Maratha troops and that is a reason why they have to keep the goddess inside the pond. It suggests that the Bengali folk culture, both Hindu and Muslim have been constructed through mutual interactions, and in this sense the Muslim society has not existed as a separate other from the Hindu society. Because of various taboos regarding worship of the goddess in the village, the

Muslim community was not allowed to dwell inside the village along with several Hindu untouchable castes.

The case of the service lands donated by the Bardhaman Raj to the shrines of Muslim saints during the Mughal period is a good example. We will discuss it further in Chapter 2, and show that the cosmological order of the Hindu kingship, which symbolic analysis tends to describe brilliantly, is not enough to explain why the Muslim peasants in the kingdom so easily accepted the dominance of the Hindu kings. The Bardhaman Raj donated plenty of lands to the shrines of Muslim saints as well as to the Brahman priests. This corresponds to the fact that the Raj family of the Bardhaman privately follows the sect of Vaishnavism (*baishnab*), where there is a taboo on killing, but at the same time, they provided a strong patronage to the Jogadya temple of sakta-cult, which is renowned for being a sacred centre for sacrifices.

This does not necessarily imply that symbolic analysis is not helpful anymore, but rather draws attention to over reliance on it, which static ethnography isolated from the historical process is apt to fall into. The combination of field data and the historical materials enables the researcher to overcome this limitation of the symbolic approaches, and place the Hindu cultures of rural Bengal in the broader contexts of history.

The Village

FIELDWORK IN BENGAL

It was after six months of a pilot survey in West Bengal that I was able to select Kshiragram as a suitable village for the purpose of the present study. It was selected because of three conditions: (1) It is a village isolated from urban settings, thereby representing social and cultural life in rural Bengal, (2) it has an adequate population balance between the dominant landholding caste, the Brahman caste, and the other service castes including untouchables, and (3) it maintains a close relationship with the former zamindar even today, through its religious institution.

It was revealed after I started visiting the village that the village was in many respects related to the kingship of the Bardhaman Raj before the Permanent Settlement, and the temple was under the direct control of the Maharaja until Independence. Further, its relationship with the Maharaja continues in the various ritual processes. It seems, therefore, that it would enable us to understand how kingship was viewed by the villagers and to what extent this has influenced their social life. At the same time, it can provide counter-evidence to Dumontian views of village society based on the Brahman-untouchable axis.

The pilot survey was made from October 1992 to March 1993. Through the survey in various geographical areas from the frontier of Sundarban to the foothills of Jalpaiguri and Purulia I found that ritual traditions preserved from pre-colonial times have remained in more clear forms in the areas where used to be strong political forms such as Radh area and Cooch Behar rather than in frontier villages, because the social and economic supports by the local power are essential conditions, which enable to shape them on the solid basis. I then started to visit those villages having temples of sakta-pithas, one by one. The reasons are as follows.

First, the sakta cult is primarily connected with rituals related to sacrifice, which were in many cases patronized by the Kshatriyas and the kings—the rituals for sacrifice are often concerned with the rituals of kingship. Second, although there are many places where sacrifices are made in the ordinary rituals, the temples of the sakta cult seem to have well organized ritual systems containing of various caste groups in which sacrifices are made throughout the year. The cult of sakta generally belongs to an older tradition than the cult of *baishnab* (Vaisnava) in Bengal, which in contrast strictly prohibits any killing. Finally, it seemed logical to compare all the sakta-pithas in order to select the most suitable village for my research. Chapter 1 discusses the features of sakta-pitha as the sacred place of Hindu culture, and makes a comparative analysis across South Asia.

FIELDWORK IN THE VILLAGE

The village Khsiragram is located at the centre of the Kshiragram Gram Panchayat area, the eastern end of the Mangalkot block in the Bardhaman district. The whole village consists three *mauzas*, namely J.L. Nos. 127, 128 and 129 in the Mangalkote Block. The total area of the village is 1,268.03 hectares (3,133.26 acres) according to 1991 Census. The total irrigated lands amount to 817.86 hectares (2,020.90 acres), unirrigated lands amount to 461.34 hectares (1,139.96 acres), and the rest is 200.17 hectares (494.61 acres). It is accessed about thirty minutes by bus from the local town of Katwa and two hours by bus from Bardhaman town. It takes more than six hours by bus to reach there from Bolpur-Santiniketan. (This includes the time required for changing buses three times and crossing the river Ajoy by boat.)

The population of the village, according to the 1991 Census, is 4,263 (males 2,191, females 2,072) and the number of households is 729. A detailed discussion on the population structure will be presented in Chapter 2. There are three primary schools, a high school, and a rural health centre in the village. On the outskirts is the Gram Panchayat office, within whose jurisdiction there are seven villages.

I began to visit Kshiragram in April 1993. But it was after February 1994 that I started to stay there continuously. Before that I had learnt about the local administration, parties, colleges, and universities concerned with reference to the village and the area, from any persons. The first stage of fieldwork in the village continued till May 1995. After that, I shifted to the university town of Santiniketan, and visited the village at times.

The village temple has undergone drastic transformation, five times in the past due to the following events: (1) the invasions by the Muslims in the medieval period, (2) the rebuilding of the temple by the Maharaja Kirtichand (around 1730), (3) the Maratha invasions (1742–51), (4) the introduciton of the Permanent Settlement by the British (1793), and (5) the abolition of the zamindari system (1953). In this monograph, I have tried to trace developments back to the age of the Maharaja Kirtichand. There is, however, always some doubt about the credibility in the detailed ritual processes, because many parts of them, let alone the social aspect, seem to have been transformed already.

The data on the present situation were collected by direct observation and interviews. Conditions which seem to have changed and in some cases been lost after Independence, were supplemented by the recollections of the villagers and by historical materials. In particular, the data on the land tenures of the village have been collected from the District Settlement Record Room. I also utilized manuscripts and the oral tradition passed down by the villagers.

STRUCTURE OF THE BOOK

In Chapter 1, I have taken a general view of the sakta-pitha in Bengal, and discuss the present structure of each pitha, based on fieldwork. In Chapter 2, I have discussed two points: (i) the religious aspect of the village and its temple, which characterizes the village as a sacred place, and (ii) the social background of the village. In Chapter 3, the ritual organization of the temple has been discussed through an examination of the temple properties and the service lands granted by the Maharaja.

The ritual cycle of the temple has been examined with special emphasis on the rotation system of the Brahman-sebait (temple priests). In Chapter 4 the process of Jogadyapuja, which is the biggest ritual occasion in the village in the lunar month of Baishakh (April–May) is analysed, and the organization of the ritual posts discused. Chapter 5, discusses the annual ritual cycle of the village in three parts, namely the rituals connected with the temple, the temple and the localities, and the localities. Chapter 6 concerns the Durgapuja sponsored by the lineages of the Ugra-Kshatriyas within the dominant caste, and gives a description of a rotation and succession system of the Durgapuja among the dominant caste. Chapter 7 is about the Manasapuja, supported by the village lower castes (Scheduled Castes). The Maharaja grants the Manasa temple in the village to the Bagdi-priests. But the rituals of the goddess Manasa are closely connected with the ritual organization of the Jogadya temple. Finally, a discussion is attempted on the influence of the kingship on the temple rituals and the village social life and the villagers' way of recognition.

CHAPTER 1

The Sakta-Pithas in Bengal

Sakta-pitha is a general term given to certain sacred places in the Indian subcontient[1] associated with the sakti-cult, the cult of the mother goddess. The place is usually called the *pitha-sthan* or *maha-pitha* in Bengali. The word *pitha* means the 'altar' or 'seat' where the body parts of the goddess Sati (another name for the goddess Durga) fell to earth after she had been cut to pieces by the discus (*cakra*) of Visnu. The pithas are believed to be the dwelling places of the goddess (*devi*); these are, therefore, also called *devisthanas* (the abode of the goddess).[2] It is commonly accepted that there are fifty-one places of sakta-pitha (*satir-ekanna-pitha-sthan* in Bengali), but there is disagreement on the exact locations of these pithas. An old manuscript called the *mahapithani-rupana* is a popular text that gives the names of the fifty-one pithas and the scattered body parts of the goddess Sati. It identifies twenty-three pithas in ,greater Bengal and the surrouding areas. Among them are fourteen pithas in West Bengal and seven in what is now Bangladesh. This chapter will discuss the general features of sakta-pitha and attempt a comparative study of the pithas of Bengal.

The Mythology of Sakta-Pitha

The origins of the sakta-pitha are told in a popular myth called *daksha-jagya*, which is part of the magnificent Hindu mythology of *Mahabharata*. It tells of the time when the god Daksha held the ritual ceremony of the sacred fire and summoned all the gods of heaven to attend, except, Siva, the husband of his daughter Sati. At the altar of the sacred fire, the furious goddess Sati, as a protest against the insult to her husband, threw herself into the fire and burned to death. Hearing of the death of his wife, the grieving Siva came and carried her body off on his shoulder. He went nearly mad with grief and wandered the world stamping the ground with his feet. The world could not endure these earth-tremors, and finally the gods of heaven asked Visnu put an end to the wandering of Siva. Visnu threw his discus at Siva and cut the body of Sati, still on Siva's shoulder. The pieces fell and scattered over the world. Wherever one landed, the faithful enshrined an altar to worship the goddess. In the course of time, many places believed themselves to have a piece of Sati's limbs and became centres of pilgrimage for the local worship of the mother goddess. Each pitha having mythological origins regarding the goddess Sati has its own separate name as a *pitha-sthan*, but also bears the names of the goddess (*devi*) and her spouse (*bhairava*). Sati is the goddess wife of Siva, but she is better known in Bengal as Durga. In rural areas great mother godesses such as Durga and Kali have merged with the various other folk goddesses. The great mother goddess Durga, especially, has various names in her incarnations. This is the reason why every pitha is called not only by the name of the deities in her incarnation but at the same time is regarded as an incarnation of Sati through the legend of her dismemberment.

In spite of the popularity of the mythological tradition of sakta-pitha in South Asia, there are many different opinions regarding the actual number and locations of each of the pithas, depending on the interpretations of the various religious texts. D.C. Sircar (1973) discussed comprehensively the various manuscripts of the sakti-cults and conceptualized the idea of *pitha-sthan* as sakta-pitha. It is now widely accepted that there are fifty-one *pitha-sthans* and every name corresponds to an anatomical piece of the goddess Sati. But for the longest time there have been different versions regarding the number and the names of the pitha. Some of the early Tantric texts, such as those of Sahajiaya entitled *Catuspithatantra*, and the famous Tantric text of Buddhism, the *Hevajratantra*, refer to four pithas. The *Kalika-purana*, a popular Tantric text important for its description of the ritual practices of Durgapuja in Bengal, tells of seven pithas. In addition, the *Rudrayamalatantra* mentions ten sites as principal pithas, the *Jnanarnavatantra* lists eight important pithas, and the *Kularnavatantra* refers to eighteen pithas. The *Kubjikatantra*, an important text discovered by Haraprasad Shastri, lists forty-two *siddha-pithas*. To complicate things even further, there is yet another version of sakta-pitha, which counts an additional hundred and eight pitha sites in the classical Sanskrit texts called the *Matsya-purana*. However, the number of pithas accepted by the majority at present is fifty-one: those listed in the *Pithanirnaya* or *Maha-pithanirupana*.[3]

Historical Background

There is general agreement that major sacred places in South Asia such as Varanasi and Kalighat carry the names of the fifty-one sakta-pitha.

The significance of these places as holy ground is rooted in long-established traditions. But there are local minor variations regarding the pitha legends in which people claim their own particular shrine as one of the sakta-pitha. For example, the *Nabajug-Dairektari Panjika*, which is a modern, popular Bengali almanac printed in Dhaka, recognizes thirteen pithas as actually existing in West Bengal, and seven pithas as existing in Bangladesh. On the other hand, the *Sri Madan Gupter Phul Panjika*, printed in Kolkata, reports only ten pithas existing in West Bengal and just five pithas in Bangladesh. Following an inquiry by Sircar into the historical places mentioned in the *Mahapitha-nirupana*, it was determined that there are fourteen pithas which can be linked to present-day places in West Bengal, and seven in Bangladesh. There are twenty-three pithas in total in the eastern part of the Indian subcontinent, which account for more than forty-five per cent of the total in South Asia. So, there remains the question why so many such places are located in Bengal.

One explanation is the popularity of the cult of the mother goddess and the Tantric religion among the Bengali people. The Bengali culture has kept to its Tantric tradition of commingled Buddhism and Hinduism since medieval times, and this is still observable in the cult of Sahajiya and in the ascetic practices of the folk singers of Baul. The Bengali Hindu developed a unique cult that worships the indigenous mother goddess, and follows a fertility and agricultural rite in its primordial form—this is best observed during the splendid autumnal festivals such as Durgapuja and Kalipuja. Lynn Gatwood (1991) referred to the cult of the great mother goddesses of Durga and Kali that developed in Bengal by the term 'Mahadevi'. The worship of the mother goddess is represented by the female principle called '*sakti*', which symbolizes the fertility of women and crops, an idea inherited from the indigenous culture of the pre-Aryan races (e.g. Kinsley 1987; Wadley 1977). This religious idea of a dichotomy between the female principle (*sakti*) and the male principle (usually *purusa*) is represented by conjugal deities such as Siva and Durga, or Krishna and Radha. These deities are often referred to in the religious texts of Purana and Tantrism, and in Vaisnava literature in Bengal.

Sociological Background

There is another reason that explains the great number of sakta-pitha in Bengal. The validity of the sacred places of the fifty-one sakta-pitha is based on the myth of the Hindu goddess, which combines the various local deities into the so-called 'great tradition' of the South Asian civilization.[4] At the same time, people consider their local shrines as part of the great tradition of the Hindu sacred places mentioned throughout the mythology.

In reality, no classical text ever referred to any actual geographical location that might be found in a modern atlas, and simply mentions the names of the dismembered pieces of the goddess Sati and the names of the goddesses who were her incarnations. Hence, the assertion that a shrine believed to be a sakta-pitha by the local people, is supported by the sacred scriptures cannot be refuted. For example, the temple of the goddess Melai Chandi, by the town of Amta in the Howrah district of West Bengal, is regarded as a sakta-pitha on which the left shank of the Sati fell. However, this body part is widely thought by the people of eastern Bengal to have landed at the Bamjanga-Mahapitha temple in the village of Baurbhag, which is in the Kanaighat thana of the Sylhet district of Bangladesh. It was very famous as a sacred place under the Khasiya Raj, and during the time of the British rule its fame was well established because it was described by Edward Gait (1905) as the brutal shrine of human sacrifice.

The list of fifty-one sakta-pithas is important as a source helping one understand the popularity of the folk cult of the mother goddess. It is, therefore, important to distinguish between two epistemological categories of pithas: the *maha-pitha* and the *upa-pitha. Mahapitha* is a major place of sakta-pitha and is recognized as such by the majority of people throughout South Asia. Most of the historical palces that are recognized as sacred places of the mother goddess and have been pilgrimage centres in South Asia for hundreds of years are counted as sakta-pithas such sites as Varanasi, Kanchipuram, and Kanyakumari. However, these sites usually belong to the older tradition of the various religious cults: the indigenous cult of the mother goddess, Buddhism, Jainism and the sakta-cult. It could be said that most of the major sacred places of South Asia were considered sakta-pithas at one time or other.

On the other hand, the *upa-pitha* is of minor importance and so recognized only by the local people is not validated by the classical Sanskrit texts. It is, therefore, sometimes difficult to enumerate the actual number of *upa-pithas,* because the distinction between these categories is one of which only the local people are aware; even so they take every opportunity to promote their local shrine as one of the major sakta-pithas. It rather depeds on how popular the temple is in the local society; if it gained a certain favour with the loca people at some time in the past it might have become a major centre of worship and pilgrimage afterwards.

Beyond its importance as a religious centre each pithas has integrated with the socio-religious life of the local society and connects it through pilgrimage and trade to the outside world. During the annual festivals a large number of people come to visit from outside the region. The annual trade fair or *mela* is also organized to coincide with this religious occasion, and various commodities from the prosaic to the exotic are traded. In this way, these places have developed multi-dimensional functions as religious centres that are deeply-rooted in the everyday lives of the local inhabitants. The local society can connect to the outside world by way of a network of sacred places, and these places encourages local people to travel to distant regions. The local royalty also regarded these shrines as an influential religious authority separate from secular power. Since medieval times, many Bengali rulers and landlords avidly patronized the shrines and donated lands to them.

The Distribution of the Sakta-Pithas in Bengal

Table 1.1 gives a list of the sakta-pithas that are commonly acknowledged in Bengal. The information is extracted from various religious Bengali texts and almanacs. This table is attached to Map 1.3, which shows the geographical sites of these pithas. The list mentions most of the popular places that are recognized as sakta-pitha in present-day Bengal, although there still remain other interpretations of where the sites should be. This list, then, shows the major places accepted by the people in Bengal is that appear in the religious manuscripts of the early eighteenth century and in the printed Bengali almanacs of today.

The map shows a larger concentration in West Bengal than in Bangladesh as a whole; and there is especially a concentration in the historical region of Rarh. The reason for this is that there are many pithas in West Bengal that appeared in the later versions of the *Mahapithanirupana* (to be discussed later). But it is not correct to attribute this dispersal to the modern border line separating eastern and western Bengal that was established under colonial rule. The central towns of Islamic culture in the medieval period, such as Gaur and Pandua, were situated in western Bengal, and the district of Birbhum was part of the frontier region at that time; yet this is where most pithas were concentrated.

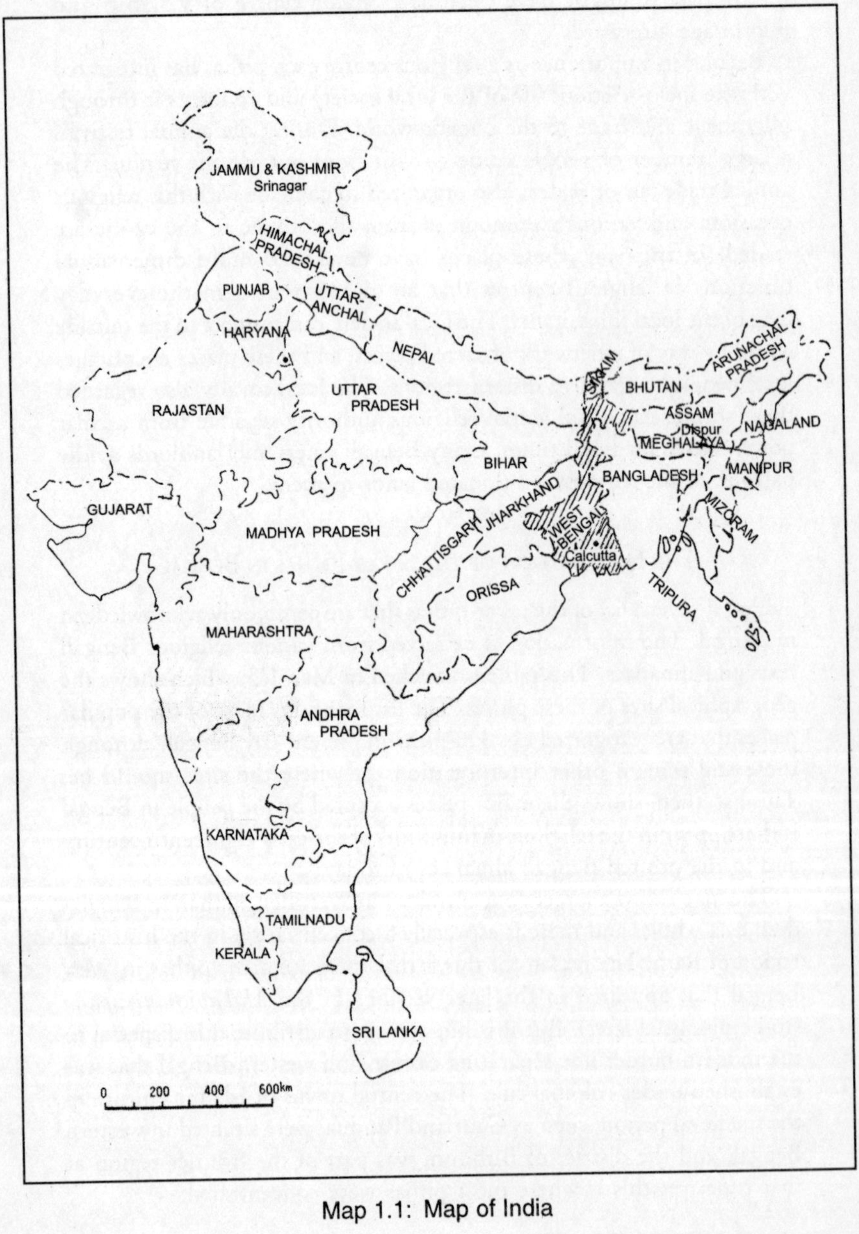

Map 1.1: Map of India

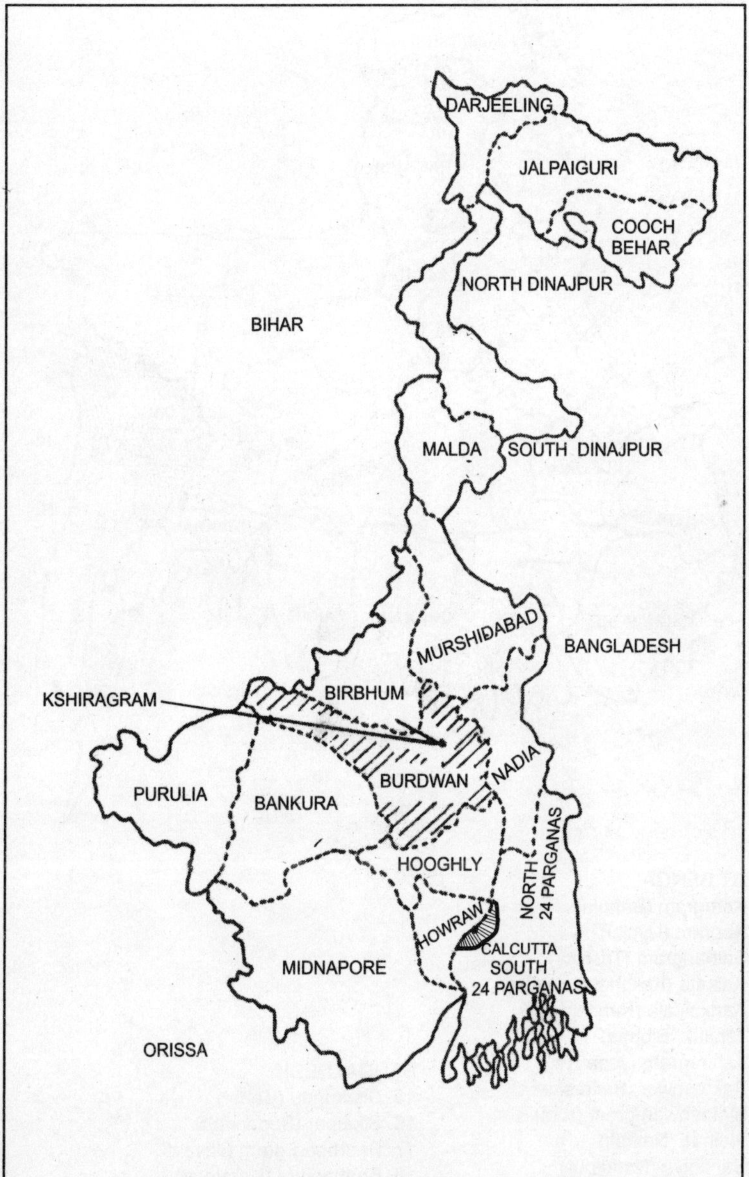

Map 1.2: Map of West Bengal

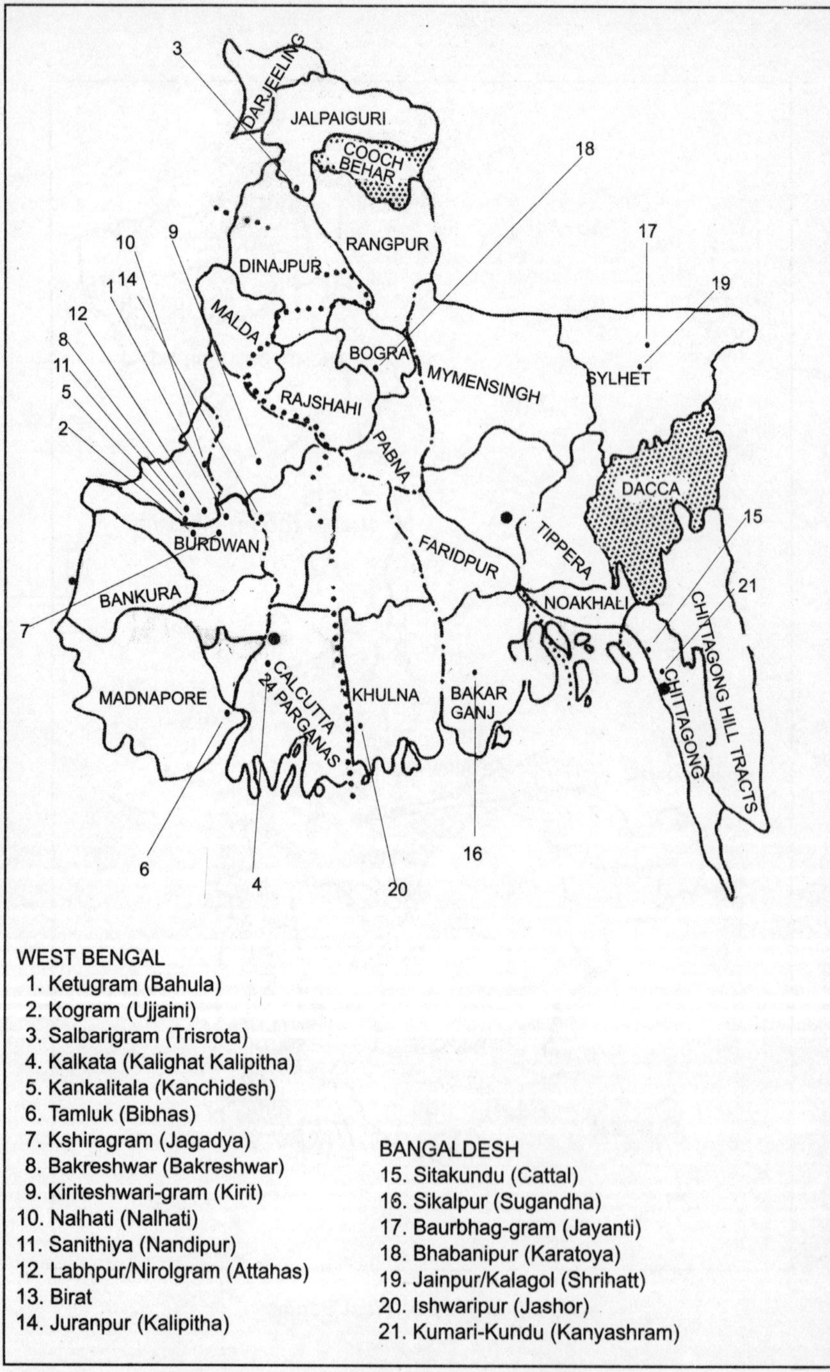

Map 1.3: Distribution of Saka-Pithas in Bengal

TABLE 1.1: LIST OF SAKTA-PITHAS IN BENGAL

Sakta-Pitha in Texts	Geographical Location	Fallen Body Parts	A	B	C	D	E	F	G	H
Bangladesh			7	6	7	6	6	6	5	5
Cattal	Sitakundu	Right arm	O	O	O	O	O	O	O	O
Sugandha	Sikalpur	Nose	O	O	O	O	O	O	O	O
Jayanti	Baurbhag-gram	Left shank	O	O	O	O	O	O	O	O
Karatoya	Bhabanipur	Bedding	O	O	O	O	O	O	O	O
Shrihatt	Jainpur/Kalagol	Throat	O	O	O	O	O	O	O	O
Jashor	Ishwaripur	Right plam	+	–	O	O	O	O	O	O
Kanyashram	Kumari-Kundu	Back	O		O		?	?	×	×
West Bengal, India		14	13	13	12	12	12	11	10	
Bahula	Ketugram	Left arm	O	O	O	O	O	O	O	O
Ujjaini	Kogram	Right elbow	O	O	O	O	O	O	×	×
Trisrota	Salbari-gram	Left leg	O	O	O	O	O	O	O	O
Kalipitha (Kalighat)	Kolkata	Right foot four fingers	O	O	O	O	O	O	O	O
Kanchidesh	Kankalitala	Skeleton	O	O	O	O	O	O	O	×
Bibhas	Tamluk	Left ankle	O	O	O	O	O	O	O	O
Jagadya	Kshiragram	Right foot thumb	O	O	O	O	O	O	O	O
Bakreshwar	Bakreshwar	Eye brow (mind)	+	O	O	O	O	O	O	O
Kirit	Kiriteshwari-gram	Crown	O	–	O	O	O	O	O	O
Nalhati	Nalhati	Tubular bone	+	–	O	O	O	O	O	O
Nandipur	Sanithiya	Necklace	+	–	O	O	O	O	O	O
Attahas	Labhpur/Nirolgram	Lower lip	+	–	O		O	O	O	O

Contd.

TABLE 1.1. (contd).

Sakta-Pitha in Texts	Geographical Location	Fallen Body Parts	A	B	C	D	E	F	G	H
Birat		Left foot four fingers	+		×	O	?	?	×	×
Kalighat (Kalipitha)	Juranpur	Head	+	–	O					
Other parts of eastern India										
Tripura	Udaypur	Right foot	O	O	O	O	O	O	O	O
Kamarupa	Kamakhya	Vagina	O	O	O	O	O	O	O	O

Sources:

A: The *Mahapithanirupana.* Cf. D.C. Sircar, 1973.
B: The *Sivacarita.* Cf. D.C. Sircar, 1973.
C: *Nabajug-Dairektari Panjika,* Dhaka.
D: *Gupta Press Dairektari Panjika,* Calcutta. Cf. pp. 152–3, Indrani Basu Roy, 1993.
E: *P.M. Bagcir Dairektari Panjika,* Calcutta, 1401.
F: *Benimadhab Shiler Fhul Panjika,* Calcutta, 1401.
G: *Benimadhab Bhattacaryyer Fhul Panjika,* 1404, Calcutta.
(It is new version of *Benimadhab Shiler Fhul Panjika.*)
H: *Sri Madan Gupter Phul Panjika,* 1400, Calcutta: Rajendra Library.

Abbrivations:

O: Maha-Pithasthan, ×: Different place outside Bengal ?: Supposition
–: Upa-pitha, +: Supplemented names in the later version

THE SAKTA-PITHAS IN WEST BENGAL, INDIA

Kalighat in Kolkata has been very popular since the medieval period and there is no doubt that its temple has grown with the commercial development of the great city of Kolkata (Ray 1993). It has become a great centre of pilgrimage for Hindus from all over India. Also, its attractions are much more diverse and plentiful than those of the other places on the list.

For example, the Bakreshwar temple in the Birbhum district is well known for its hot-spring therapy spa as well as its thriving pilgrimage centre. In contrast, the Kalipitha, the Jaydurga temple near the town of Katwa, in the Kaliganj block of the Nadia district, and the Mangalchandi temple in the village of Kogram, in the Mangalkote block of the Bardhaman (Burdwan) district, are visited only by the neighbouring villagers, and visitors from outside are rare. However, these places were prosperous during the medieval period under the patronage of the Hindu rulers of Natore Raj and Bardhaman Raj. As is the nature of things, during the modern period the most popular places are the ones that have invested in the development of their commerical and transportation infrastructure and other facilities for attracting people from distant places.

There are a few pithas that share the same name and are thought by many to be the same sakta-pitha. For example, there are two Attahas temples regarded as a sakta-pitha. One is near the town of Labhpur, in the Labhpur block of the Birbhum district, and the other is in the village of Dakshindhihi, near the Nirolgram village of the Ketugram block in the Bardhaman district. Both attract devout worshippers from the neighbouring areas and were, before Partition, under the patronage of the local rulers and landlords. The temple of Kankalitala near the town of Bolpur in the Birbhum district is identified as a pitha with the name *kanci*. Kancipuram near the city of Chennai (Madras) in the Tamil Nadu state of India, is a very famous sakta-pitha in southern India. Furthermore, the *Sri Madan Gupter Dairektari Panjika* identifies *Ujani* (*ujjayni*) with the famous pilgrimage place of Ujjain in Madhya Pradesh, famous for the great triennial Kumbha Mela. This name, however, is usually associated in Bengal with the village of Kogram, near the town of Natunhat in the Mangalkote block of the Bardhaman district. This place was also called *ujani* in the medieval period and mentioned in Bengali folk literature called the *Manglkabya*. This place is especially famous as the scene of the marriage ceremony of the heroine Behula depicted in the *Manasamangal*.

Not surprisingly, there are many places in West Bengal that lay claim to be pithas simply because they share the same name as a place that has had a long established pitha. It doesn't seem, however, to be a matter of controversy, but rather the site is accepted by the local peoples as a religious centre deeply rooted in the social life of the populace. This duplication of pitha identities is the main reason that there are more pithas in West Bengal than in eastern Bengal.

According to Sircar (1973: 24) the *Mahapithanirupana*, written in 1690–1720, named a number of pithas in rural Bengal, and afterwards they became popular with the spread of the Tantric philosophy in eastern India. Sircar assumes that the fifty-one pithas in the original text of the *Mahapithanirupana* are soon followed by those of the *Kubjikatantra*, which refers to forty-two sites as *siddha-pithas.* Through the influence of another text, the *Sivacarita*, verses 48–55 of the *Mahapithanirupana* were added to the original text at a later date. These verses included the names of eight sakta-pithas: Nalahati, Kalighata (Kalipitha), Vakresvara, Yasora, Attahas, Nandipura, Lanka, and Virata, which are on the whole the famous sakta-pithas in West Bengal today. Their names correspond to the present-day place names of Nalhati, Bakreshwar, Attahas, and Nandipur in Birbhum district, and Kalipitha near the town of Katwa in Nadia district. Yasora (Jashor) is situated in the Satkhira district, near the town of Jashor (Jessore) in Bangladesh, close to the border with India. As is shown in the development of the Kalighat temple in Kolkata, Sircar concludes that the sakta-pithas in Bengal 'rose to eminence in the medieval period and became a great rival of the north western school'.

Yet, there are places that have been established as pithas for so long that they developed a reputation as such throughout the pan-Hindu world. These sacred places belong to the older tradition of Bengal, and, in fact, most of them are mentioned in various historiacal texts as important shrines. For example, the town of Tamluk in the Midnapore district of West Bengal, where the temple of Garba Bhima is situated, was well known by the name of Tamralipta in the old days. In the seventh century Tamralipta was a Buddhist centre with a thousand monasteries and is considered an indispensable point of reference in the medieval history of Mahayana Buddhism. Both Xuan Zang (602–64) and Yi Jing (635–715) visited it. The hillock and valley of Sitakundu in the Chittagong district of Bangladesh was established as a *pitha-sthan* by the Hindu raja of Tripura in the beginning of the sixteenth century. But, it is also famous as a pilgrimage centre for the Buddhists, because there still remains a foot print of the Buddha at the top of the mountain of Chandrashekhar. This will be discussed in the next section. In any case, these places had prospered as centres of Buddhism for hundreds of years.

The name of the village of Kshiragram, can be traced back to the verses of the *Kubjikatantra*, preserved in the Asiatic Society at Kolkata. Besides this, we also find references to the village and the goddess in other Sanskrit literary compositions, such as the *Niltantra*, the *Rudrayamalatantra*, the *Saktananda-tarangini*, and the *Mahapithanirupana*. Also in the *Mangalkabya*, such as the *Candi-mangal* by Mukundram Chakrabartti, references to both the village and the goddess appear. The present temple in the village was built around 1730 by the Raja Kirtichand (1702–40) of Bardhaman. These materials show that the name Kshiragram has become more popular since the medieval period.

Kiriteshwari-gram is famous as the land of the ascetic practice of Tantrism by the prince of Natore, Ramkrishna. This place is also well known for the Bengal Nawab, Alivardi Khan (1725–39) who poured coloured powder (*abir*) over himself together with the Hindus every year on the occasion of Holi (*daul-jatra*). Because of these various associations these historical places are recognized by most of the people as *mahapithas* and are indisputably pitha-sthans.

THE SAKTA-PITHAS IN BANGLADESH

Seven pithas in the *Mahapithanirupana* lie in Bangladesh. As already mentioned, the name of Jashor (Yasora) is added to the later version of the Mahapithanirupana, but the temple of Jashoreshwarikali, in the village of Ishwaripur in the Satkhira district has been very popular since the medieval period. It is said that the name of the town of Jashor (Jessore) is taken from the goddess of the same name. Sircar maintains that the temple of Kanyashram in the suburb of Chittagong city is one of the pithas, but this opinion is supported mainly by the local people because the *Benimadhab Shiler Fhul Panjika* refers to this name in connection with a different village, in Rajasthan.

Since the British period two temples have kept the ritual relationship with the family members of the local royalty and the landlords. The temple of Ma-Bhabani in the village of Bhabanipur in the Bogra district had prospered under the patronage of Natore Raj in the eighteenth century; this was one of most influential Hindu kingships in northern Bengal. The temple was given the name of the well-known benevolent queen, the Rani Bhabani of Natore. After the abolition of the zamindari system, the descendants of this house migrated to India and the title to its private estate was transferred to the office of the State Manager. At the time of the annual festival the family members now resident in Kolkata, send offerings for the altar. However, the ritual of the Bhabani temple is now under the supervision of a caretaker (*nayeb*) who is appointed by the estate manager of Natore.

The legendary king of Pratapaditya in the jungle area of Sundarban is supposed to be the founder of the temple of Jashoreshwarikali in Satkhira. Ishwaripur village is regarded as the capital of this legendary kingdom. There are some ruins of the old capital around the area. The zamindar family of Chaterjee built the present temple—a splendid two-storey building—at the side of the ruin. It has come down through oral tradition that the zamindar family of Chaterjee migrated to this part of the country during the time of the Raja Pratapaditya and served as his family priests. The family members living in Dhaka still oversee the management of the annual festival.

The other four temples are managed by temple committees. All of them had been prosperous under the strong patronage of the local rulers and landlords. The local Hindu community organized most of these temple committees after the abolition of zamindar. For example, the temple of Ugratara in the Sikalpur village of the Ujirpur thana in the Barishar district, was under the patronage of the great landlord Narayan Gupta, who migrated to India after Partition. The residents organized a trust board for temple management and now the *debottar* (donated land to the temple) belongs to the temple trust. The temple of Bamjyanga in the village of Baurubhag in the Kanaighat thana of the Sylhet district, was famous in the eighteenth century under the patronage of the Khasiya rulers, as mentioned. After Partition most of the royal family migrated to Meghalaya in India. The local Hindus organized the temple committee in 1996 for the management of the temple festivals and the *debottar*. The temple building and surrounding wall with its fine terracotta work shows the splendour of those days. The temple of Mahalakshmi near the town of Sylhet, was also under the patronage of the local zamindar during the British period and after their migration to India the Hindus organized a committee in 1960 to manage the temple. The temple has a distinctive shape in that the building is uncovered, and the altar is a large exposed rock on earth.

The sacred place of Sitakundu has a more ancient historical background. The place is indeed a huge religious complex with many temples, sacred ponds, and other facilities surrounded by hills with waterfalls. It is sometimes mentioned as 'the first of all the Hindu sacred places' in Bengal, and is actually older than even the Hindu tradition. Since a long period, this place was popular as the sacred place of a Buddhist monastery and the Arakhan Raj (*c.* 1785) is believed to have dedicated the Buddha's ashes to the temple here. The oldest record referring to this place is one that recounts the pilgrimage by the Raja Biswambhar Sur, a descendant of the Adisur of Gaur, to Sitakundu sometime around AD. 1203–4 (Adhikary 1927: 5). Yet, the Tripula Raja of Dharmamanikshya is most famous as the founder of the present Hindu temple at Sitakundu. During 1423, Shyaka, the Raja Dharmamanikshya, constructed the temple buildings and donated *debottar* land of more than 400 acres for it. Since the medieval period, the sacred place of Sitakundu has been famous as a pilgrimage centre for Buddhists as well as Hindus. Every spring festival at the end of the lunar month of Chaitra, thousands of pilgrims and ascetics (*sadhu*) used to come to visit the place from all over India. However, the temple management faces continuous conflict over the numerous properties owned by the temple and the pilgrim donatoins. During the British period, the high court of Kolkata ordered the formation of a temple committee and appointed the District Commissioner as its head in order to avoid further conflict over management.

DISCUSSION

In its own way, each temple in Bengal seems to have prospered as a sakta-pitha under the strong patronage of the local rajas and landlords. This patronage by the local elite seems to have been indispensable for the establishment of these temples as sakta-pitha. However, many pithas pre-date the emergence of the local power structure. Some pithas, such as those of Sitakundu and Tamluk, go as far back as the Buddhist era, In some cases, these famous pithas, which had already been well recognized as religious centres by the community, attracted the local rulers and landlords, who helped to legitimize their power through the donation of land and the construction of temples. We should avoid jumping to conclusions here as to whether the local elite's patronage made the establishment of the sacred places possible or if the religious centres attracted local powers in search of legitimation. For the time being, we can point out that the list of fifty-one sakta-pitha shows the locations of religious centres that have been accepted as such by the people of Bengal long ago. Nowadays, in Bangladesh, it is not the private donations of the local elite but the voluntary efforts of the ordinary people that make it possible to maintain temple managements.

After Partition and the Liberation (1971), most of the sakta-pitha temples lost patronage and endured various hardships, and many social changes went on around them. Instead of patronage from the local elite, voluntary efforts by ordinary people managed to maintain the unkeep of these sacred places. In spite of the many problems, the temples enjoy such widespread popularity at present that their continued existence and importance appear to be assured.

THE VILLAGE AS A SAKTA-PIHTA

FROM MANUSCRIPTS

The sample village is widely accepted as one of the fifty-one sakta-pithas scattered all over the Indian subcontinent. According to Sircar, the fifty-one pithas in the original text of the *Mahapithanirupana* is, as is already discussed, partially followed by the *Kubjikatantra* which refers the name of forty-two as *siddha-pithas.* With the influence of another text, the *Sivacarita,* the verses 48–55 of the *Mahapithanirupana* were added.[5] These verses included eight names of sakta-pithas, later modified: Nalahati, Kalighata (Kalipitha), Vakresvara, Yasora, Attahas, Nandipura, Lanka, and Virata. It is noteworthy that through the name of the village Kshiragram is not included in this additional list, it is mentioned in the original text of the *Kubjikatantra* as a *siddha-pitha.* The oldest mention of Kshiragram is in verses in the *Kubjikatantra* preserved in the Asiatic Society, Kolkata as follows:

Kshiragramang Baidyanathang Janiyadbamalocane
Kamarupang Mahapithang Sarbbakamaphalapradam

Besides in the *Kubjikatantra,* we also find references to the village and the goddess in the other Sanskrit literary compositions, such the *Niltantra,* the *Rudrayamalatantra,* the *Sivacarita,* the *Saktananda-tarangini,* and the *Mahapithanirupana.*[6] In the *Tantracuramani,* the names of Jugadya and of Kshirkanthak as the Bhairabha of the goddess have been mentioned. Also in the *Mangalkabya,* a series of medieval Bengali folk compositions, viz., the *Candi-mangal* by Mukundram Chakrabartti, the *Candi-mangal* by Ramanand Jatir, the *Shri-dharma-*

mangal by Ghanaram Chakrabartti, the *Dharma-mangal* by Ruparam Chakrabartti, the *Kalika-mangal* by Balaram Chakrabartti, the *Abhaya-mangal* by Ramdas Adak, the *Manasa-mangal* by Ketakadas Kshemanand, the *Dharma-mangal* by Manik Ganguli, and the *Ananda-mangal* by Bharatchandra Ray Gunakar, references to both the village and the goddess occur.

According to a popular account in the village the *Kubjikatantra*, discovered in Nepal by Haraprashad Shastri, was compiled in sixth century.[7] It is regarded as doubtful to infer the year of the manuscript so old; but we have discussed already that among the popular names of fifty-one of sakta-pithas in the *Mahapithanirupana*, forty-two are believed to have originated from the *Kubjikatantra* and eight have been added later under influence from the *Sivacaritra*. In the original text of the *Mahapithanirupana*, the names of sakta-pithas corresponding to the present pithas in Bengal are Kalighat (Kolkata), Cattala (Chandrasekhar in Chottagram), Vibhasa (Tamluk), and Kshiragram.[8] It is thus clear that the name Kshiragram inherits at least the older tradition along with Kalighat and Tamluk and had aquired more popularity since the medieval period than the other eight names of the pithas, in spite of their present popularity in Bengal.

THE HISTORY OF THE TEMPLE

The most popular epic of the goddess Jogadya is the *Jogadya-bandana*, which tells that the toe of Sati's right foot fell on to the place where the Jogadya temple (*Jogadya-mandir*) of today is located. The temple was rebuilt around 1730 during the rule of Kirtichand, the Maharaja of Bardhman. According to Jogeshwar Chaudhuri, the construction of the temple Jogadya is the first main achievement in the temple making venture of the Maharaja Kirtichand.[9] The succeeding monarchs followed his example as shown in Appendix 4. In 1732, the Maharaja Kirtichand built the temple of Gopeshwar Siva in the village Baikunthapur (which is the original place of the royal family in Bardhaman) and the temple of Sarbamangala near the Raj palace in Bardhaman town. It is said, however, that the broken pieces of bricks of the former temple which are now buried beneath the present temple can be traced back to eleventh or twelfth century.[10]

The Jogadya temple building consists of a stepped designed tower (*ratna*), the main temple (*ardhamandap*) and a dance hall (*natmandir*); however at the altar inside the temple, there is no symbol to show the presence of the goddess. The image of the goddess is enshrined in the bed of the pond Kshirdighi usually in the western part of the village as will be discussed later. According to the *Joagadya-bandana*, when Hanuman saved Rama from underground in Sri Lanka, he returned, carrying the goddess Durga on his back and reached the village of Kshiragram.[11] In another version of the *Jogadya-bandana* of the famous poet Krittibas Ojha, it is described that Hanuman went around the whole world with the goddess on his back to find a suitable place to perform her ritual at last found the place where now the Jogadya temple is situated.[12] The same story is recorded also in the *Candi-mangal.* It is interesting to note that a popular belief in the village is that Kshiragram is the centre of the world and that is the reason Hanuman selected the village for the ritual.

Every year, the priests of the villages of Gobardhanpur and the Ittya pay a visit to the altar of the goddess Jogadya on the ritual occasion. At the time of *guya-dak* ritual, a representative of the Datta lineage addresses the five names of the neighbouring villages and their representatives of the Ugra-Kshatriya. These five villages are the Ugra-Kshatrya dominant villages scattered over the present Mangalkote block. Besides centering the village Kshiragram, there are four shrines in the neighbouring villages on every side. In the north, Shitalgram has a temple called Shiddeswari; in the south, Parashi has the temple Patareshwari; in the east, Gidagram has a Giddeshwari temple in the west, Nigongram has the Ringeshwari temple. In this way, the Jogadya temple is recognized as a centre of the local network of the deities and ritual practice by the neighbouring villages.

THE VILLAGE CUSTOMS

As the inhabitants of the sakta-pithas (the abode of the goddess), the villagers observe a few special customs in addition to the usual ones followed by the Hindu in general. These customs mainly consist of various kinds of taboos observed during the lunar month of Baishakh, the period of the biggest ritual occasion of Jogadyapuja in the village. There were some other taboos observed permanently: not allowing the Karmakar, Kumbhakar, Tody, and Muslims to stay in the village; not making brick houses (*pakkā-bari*) higher than the second floor, and so on. It is very difficult to observe these customs in these days of socail change such as transportation facilities and cement houses in rural area. But in the month of Baishakh, many villagers try to observe the special village customs prescribed for this period. Table 1.2 is a list of these customs.[13]

TABLE 1.2: LIST OF TABOOS REGARDING THE GODDESS JOGADYA

1 using sandals and umbrellas when walking in the village,
2 grinding turmeric with mortar,
3 using wooden spatulas in cooking of boiled rice,
4 twisting wicks for lights,
5 using the potter's wheel and the wringer for mustard seed oil,
6 threshing rice,
7 Tilling the fields with a plough before the ritual of *hal-nagal* (on the 29th day of Baishakh),
8 staying of the pregnant women in the village,
9 sexual intercourse between husband and wife in the village,
10 holding any marriage ceremony before the ritual of *lagna-utsab* (on the 15th day of Baishakh),
11 living in rooms with doors on the north,
12 writing with pens during the first five days, the last five days as well as on the fifteenth of Baishakh; and on the other days of Baishakh, writing in any colours of ink except in red ink,

Let us consider these taboos in the light of the following points. First, some items such as No. 1 are basically observed to show their respect for the goddess Jogadya. People usually do not enter the temple with their shoes on, or visit sacred places with open umbrella. Shoes would bring the pollution to the temple and it is only over the seat of the deity that an umbrella is put up inside the temple. It may be assumed that the whole area of the village becomes a sacred palce, a temporary temple ground, during the month of Baishakh. Durkheim [1915 (1912)] is one of the eminent scholars, who discuss the dichotomy of the sacred and profane in the rituals. The sacred becomes conspicuous all the more for emphasizing the contrast with the profane. In this sense, the taboo to build the brick house inside the village is due to the contrast with the three-storied brick temple of the goddess. It is, therefore, possible to assume that it enables to show their respects to the goddess through restriction to build brick house or to put umbrella on their heads in the village.

The second point to notice is the item connected with agricultural affairs such as Nos. 6 and 7. Baishakh is the preliminary season for the cultivation of *aman* rice. It is a vital question in rural areas to decide the suitable time to start cultivation in fields. It was, therefore, common in rural Bengal to perform the various agricultural rituals such as *halakarshan* and *briksharopan* and to hand down the oral traditions about agricultural affairs such as Khanar-bachan. The ritual of *hal-nagal* in the 29th of Baishakh includes the typical characters of this ritual for cultivation. The ritual of traction of the plough and making a round of the village admits to its interpretation as a ritual of fertility, to be discussed in Chapter 4. In the village, there is another occasion prescribed to start cultivation, which is the ritual of *makari-saptami* on the seventh of the bright fortnight in the month of Magh. The day after the ritual of *makari-saptami* is the beginning day of traction of ploughs for rice. Numerous such examples show the connection between the religious customs and the agricultural affairs in the village. It could be supposed that these ritual taboos consisted of an element of trditional culture regarding the agriculture of Bengal, along with the oral traditions and the ritual systems, most of which are nowadays lost in rural area.

The third point to notice in this connection is the taboo on sexual activity. Hindus usually restrict weddings to certain suitable months and auspicious days of the ritual almanac. Phalgun, for example, is a suitable month for weddings, but not Chaitra.[14] The villagers say that the ritual of Jogadyapuja of Baishakh means the occasion of marriage of the goddess and so they never allow their weddings to occur before the goddess marriage. This could be a way of showing respect to the goddess.

There is another reason which might be more important. Sexual activity is always connected with the ritual of fertility. It goes without saying that the cultures in many countries prescribe restrictions on sex according to the agricultural calendar and its rituals (e.g. Frazer 1911–36; Levi-Strauss 1962). It is supposed that control over sexuality would mean fertility of the field. In agricultural societies this would bring the blessing of the goddess of crops, propitiated through abstinence. In this respect, the restriction on sexuality prescribed in Nos. 9 and 10 correspond to the sexuality of the goddess in a symmetrical relationship. In other words, various taboos regarding the goddess Jogadya practised by the villagers are related to each other, and based on the religious ideas of the separation of the sacred and profane, the ritual of fertility, and the restriction on sexuality.

THE RITUALS IN THE VILLAGE

On the altar inside the temple, there is only a small hole which is, according to the villagers, for connection with the under world, from where Hanuman rescued the goddess. The people worship the altar without any idol. Only in the month of Baishakh do they put a copper pot on the altar, filled with water from the pond called Kshirdighi. The stone image of the goddess Jogadya is usually kept at the bottom of the Kshirdighi on the western side of the village. It is only once in a year that the image is pulled up from the bottom of the pond and is placed on the special altar called *utthan-mandir* so as to open the image to the public. Except on that day, the village people are prohibited acsess to the stone image. There are many anecdotes telling how someone fell sick or even died as a result of an unintented approach to the image under the water.

On the occasions of the temple rituals, many caste groups in the village occupy various posts in the ritual organization and play diverse roles. The Brahman-sebaits (temple priest) who are divided into nine lineages naturally play important roles. Not only the Brahman-sebait, the general as well as the Scheduled Caste also have their own roles and posts in the temple rituals severally. The dominant caste, the Ugra-Kshatriya (*Aguri*), is assigned the role of fetching a pot of water of Kshirdighi on his head to purify the altar and to perform the ritual dance called *mayurnac* (the dance of peacock). A lineage of the Bagdi caste assumes the role as the holder of the Maharaja's flags in processions in front of the altar and also the role for preparing the buffalo for sacrifice. The representation from the Dom caste is to offer a few drops of blood from one's finger by slicing it in front of the image of the goddess before dawn of the final day of Baishakh. Besides, the Malakar, the Karmakar, and the Baiti also have definite roles in the ritual system. It would, therefore, be possible to suppose that the system of the roles and the practices of the temple ritual represents the social structure as well as the ritual organization of the village.

It is the ritual of sacrifices that form the nucleus of the ritual system of the Jogadyapuja. On the last day of Baishakh, the buffalo sacrifice is held in front of the image of the goddess at the Utthanmandir by the people of the Bagdi caste. In days gone by, it is believed that human sacrifices were performed every year instead of buffalo sacrifice.

NOTES

1. D.C. Sircar, *The Sakta Pithas* [Delhi: MLBD, 1973 (1948)], p. 3, Monier-Williams, *Sanskrit-English Dictionary* (Oxford, 1899), translates *pitha* as seat, chair, and 'names of various temples erected on the 51 spots where the limbs of Parvati fell after she had been cut to pieces by the discus of Vishnu'. p. 629.

2. S.G. Bagchi, *Eminent Indian Sakta Centres in Eastern India: An inter-disiplinary study in the background of the pitha of Kalighata, Vakresvara and Kamakhya* (Calcutta: Punthi Pustak, 1980), pp. 1–3.
3. It is estimated by Sircar (1973: 24) that the *Mahapithanirupana* was written around AD 1690–1720.
4. Marriott (1955) defines the concept of 'great tradition' as a polar concept contrasting with 'little tradition'. The former signifies the high culture preserved in the written text such as the Sanskrit, and the latter is the folk culture handed down orally. Srinivas (1952, 1955) applies it to the concept of 'Sankritization' so as to describe the dynamism of culture change in rural society.
5. Sircar, *The Sakta Pitha*, p. 39. See, also Niguranand, *Mahatiirth Ekanna-pither Sandhane.* 1978.
6. Jogeshwar Chaudhuri, *Bardhaman: Itihas O Sanskriti*, Tritiya Khanda (Bengali), Calcutta: Pustak Bipani, 1991, pp. 80–91.
7. Satya Narayan Mukhopadhyaya, 'Kshiragramer Pracin Oitijjya', *Pashcim-banger Puja-Parban O Mela*, Pancham Khanda (Bengali), ed. Ashok Mitra, Govt. of West Bengal, 1961.
8. Sircar, *The Sakta Pitha*, pp. 35–7. It is very difficult to conclude that the names on manuscripts have to be related with the places which are believed currently as actual sakta pithas such as a case of Kanci (No. 28).
9. Jogeshwar Chaudhuri, *Bardhaman: Itihas O Sanskrit*, Dwitiya Khanda, pp. 213–14.
10. N.B. Sanyal, 'A Tale of a Pilgrimage', *Kalna College Magazine*, 1961. This article is reprinted in *Kshiragram Sri Jogadya-banipitha Patrika, Platinam Jayanti Sankhya*, 1969, pp. 41–6.
11. *Jogadya-bandana*, Sri Bancharam Bidyaratna Bhattacaryya (compiled).
12. *Jogadya-bandana* attributed to Sri Krittibas Ojha. This *bandana* is compiled by Sri Sanat Kumar Chakrabartty (resident in Kshiragram) from the manuscripts in the Punthi-Bibhag, Visva-Bharati University. See, Jogeshwar Chaudhuri, *Bardhaman: Itihas O Sanskriti*, Dwitiya Khanda, pp. 443–8.
13. These customs are described on every *Jogadya-Bandana* or *Jogadya-akhyan*, though there are some differences in the selection among them. In this respect, see also, Jogeshwar Chaudhuri (1991: 80–91).
14. It is a custom for Hindus to have marriage ceremonies in the months of Baishakh, Jyaistha, Asar, Sraban, Agrahayan, Magh and Phalgun. It is inauspicious to have marriage ceremonies during Bhadra, Aswin, Karttik, Paus and Chaitra.

CHAPTER 2

Village Society and Ritual Organization

THE SOCIAL BACKGROUND

The population of the village of Kshiragram, according to the 1991 Census, is 4,263 and the number of households is 729. The population of the Scheduled Castes is 1,930 (990 males, 940 females), and the Scheduled Tribes is 28 (10 males, 18 females). The tribal people are Santals who migrated to the village after Independence, and even have few roles in the temple ritual. The village society consists of eighteen caste groups. Table 2.1 shows the population composition of the village with respect of caste. The largest group is the Ugra-Kshatriya, followed by the Bagdi, and then the Brahmans. The number of households of these three groups counts 480, 73 per cent of the village total. The Ugra-Kshatriyas possess most of the agricultural land. They claim to be the Khsatriyas of Bengal. They are divided into two sub-castes, namely *jana-aguri* and *suta-aguri*, and into nine lineages distinguished by their titles, viz., Datta, Samant, Malla, Sani, Ray, Josh, Chota-Ray, Chota-Samant, and Chaudhuri. The Datta and Samant lineages belong to the sub-caste of *jana-aguri*, and the others are *suta-aguri*. Each lineage sends a representative to participate in the temple ritual, and occupies an important role in the annual village ritual. Thus, the Ugra-Kshtriyas can be considered as the dominant caste of the village with respect to population, landholdings, and the ritual status.[1]

The Bagdi caste is the largest Scheduled Caste in Bardhaman district. They are mostly landless and engage in agricultural labour. In Kshiragram, the Bagdi belong to the lower class. Nevertheless, they have been entrusted with important ritual roles in the temple and are regarded of relatively higher rank in the caste hierarchy of the village than the Bauri and the Dom. They are divided into two endogamous sub-castes, the Kusmethi-Bagdi and the Tetuliya-Bagdi.

The Brahman occupies the highest rank, and are divided into three

TABLE 2.1: CASTE COMPOSITION OF KSHIRAGRAM

Caste/Sub Caste	Traditional Occupation	Present Occupation	No. of Households
Ugra-Kshatriya	Warrior/Landholder	Farmer	217
Jana-Aguri			(84)
Suta-Aguri			(133)
Bagdi	Labourer	Agricultural Labourer	178
Brahman	Priest	Priest/Farmer	85
Muci	Leather work	Agricultural Labour	71
Gaela	Cow breeding	Cow breeding/Labourer	50
Bauri	Labourer	Agricultural Labourer	11
Tanti	Weaver	Weaver/Labourer	7
Dom	Bamboo work	Agricultural Labourer	6
Santal	Scheduled tribe	Agricultural Labourer	6
Sutradhar	Carpenter	Carpenter	4
Kayastha	Clerk	Farmer	3
Bene	Spice merchant	Agricultural Labourer	3
Hari	Sweeper/Midwife	Midwife/Agricultural Labourer	3
Napit	Barber	Barber	3
Baiti	Drummer	Drummer	3
Maera	Confectioner	Shopkeeper	2
Malakar	Gardener	Temple Servant	2
Sunri	Brewer	Brewer	1
Total			655

hierarchical groups as is generally observed in rural Bengal. The highest status group is called 'Kulin-Brahman' (*kaulinna-pratha Brahman* in literary) who never serve as priests for other castes. The number of the Kulin-Brahman in the village is relatively small and they have few roles in the temple service. It is said that they are late migrants into the village. The second highest are the Brahman-sebait, who are perform religious services for the Jogadya temple and are family priests of their patrons (*jajmans*) of the Ugra-Kshatriya caste.[2] They are divided into two clans which have the titles of Chakrabartti and Bhattacaryya. The clan of Chakrabartti is the priests (*pujari*), who serves various temple rituals. They are divided into nine lineages and share the daily shifts for the temple services through the year as will be discussed in Chapter 3. Only a lineage of the director of the ritual organization (*sabha-pandit*) is granted the title of Bhattacaryya by the Maharaja. The Bhattacaryyas are the priests for the *Caidipathak*. They are divided into two lineages. The third highest is the so called Varna-Brahmans, who have the *jajman* of the Scheduled Caste people in the village. They sometimes engage in minor work for the Brahman-sebaits. Some priests come from other villages for the family ritual of the lower castes in the village. They perform the ritual services for their *jajmans* which they inherited for generations.

These three groups are closely interdependent. The Brahmans and the Ugra-Kshatriyas are linked by *jajmani* relation and the Bagdis labour for the landlords. The Ugra-Kshatriya is the main patron of the village rituals, and Durgapuja is the biggest function for them. The Bagdi caste has its own priest (*deyasin*) for their temple of the goddess Manasa. Manasa-puja is the biggest festival for the Bagdi caste.

In its geographical layout, the village is constituted around the Jogadya temple, as is shown in Map 2.1. The Brahman caste occupies the central part of the village. The other castes occupy concentric circles around the temple, the Ugra-Kshatriya, the Gaela, the other service castes, and the Bagdi caste located in this order. The Bauri, the Dom, and the Santal occupy the outer fringe of the village. Thus, the higher the socio-ritual position of a group, the closer is its location to the temple. It is obvious from the evidence of the geographical setting that the village temple is the most important landmark of the village society.

Temple Institutions

Before going into discussion on the ritual organization, it is necessary to give an outline of the temple institutions. The temple building consists of the three main structures, viz., the stepped designed tower (*ratna*), the main temple (*ardhamandap*), and the dance hall (*natmandir*). The altar of the goddess Jogadya is enshrined inside the tower, which has two stairs of the steeple. The main temple, attached to the tower, is covered with a big dome and people worship the goddess inside the domed hall. The Natmandir (dance hall) is a stage with surrounding pillars, designed for various ritual performances. Map 2.2 shows the other building in the temple ground. The Bhogmandir is the temple kitchen for everyday service to the goddess and worshippers. Inside, an offering of sundried rice (*anna-bhog*) is served to the goddess by the priest at noon. The Shyamsundar-mandir is the temple for Krishna and his spouse Radha. At the time of spring festival, the villagers gather here and perform songs (*kirtan*) in praise of the Krishna. The office of the temple management is called *kacharibari*, because it was the office of the superintendent of the temple (*rajkachari*, or *daroga-babu* in

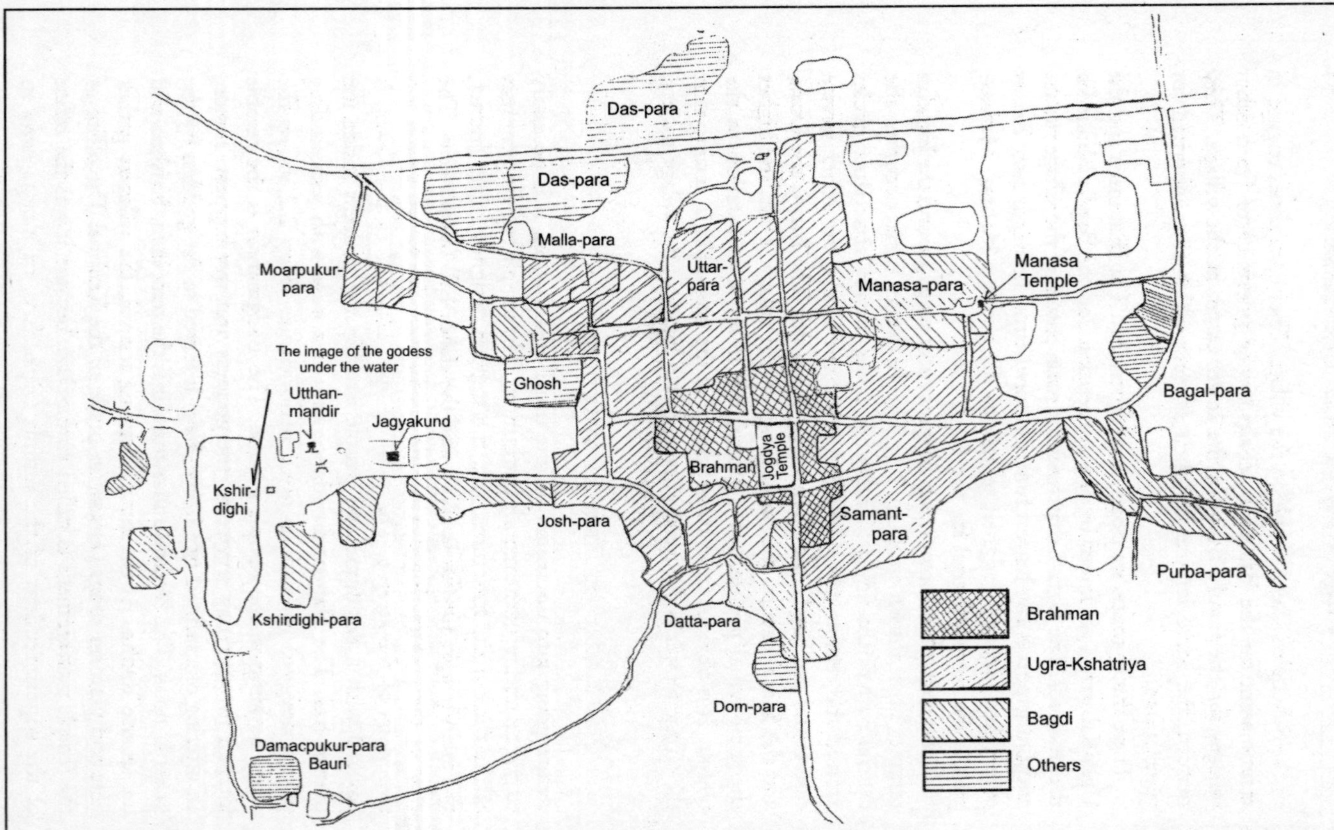

Map 2.1: Distribution of Caste Groups

1 Main temple (*ardhamandap*), 2 Stepped designed tower (*ratna*), 3 Natmandir (dance hall), 4 Jagyasthan, 5 Ganesmund, 6 Bhogmandir, 7 Shyamsundar-mandir, 8 Kachari-bari, 9 Guya-beti, 10 Eastern gate, 11 Western gate, 12 Kshireshwari-mandir,

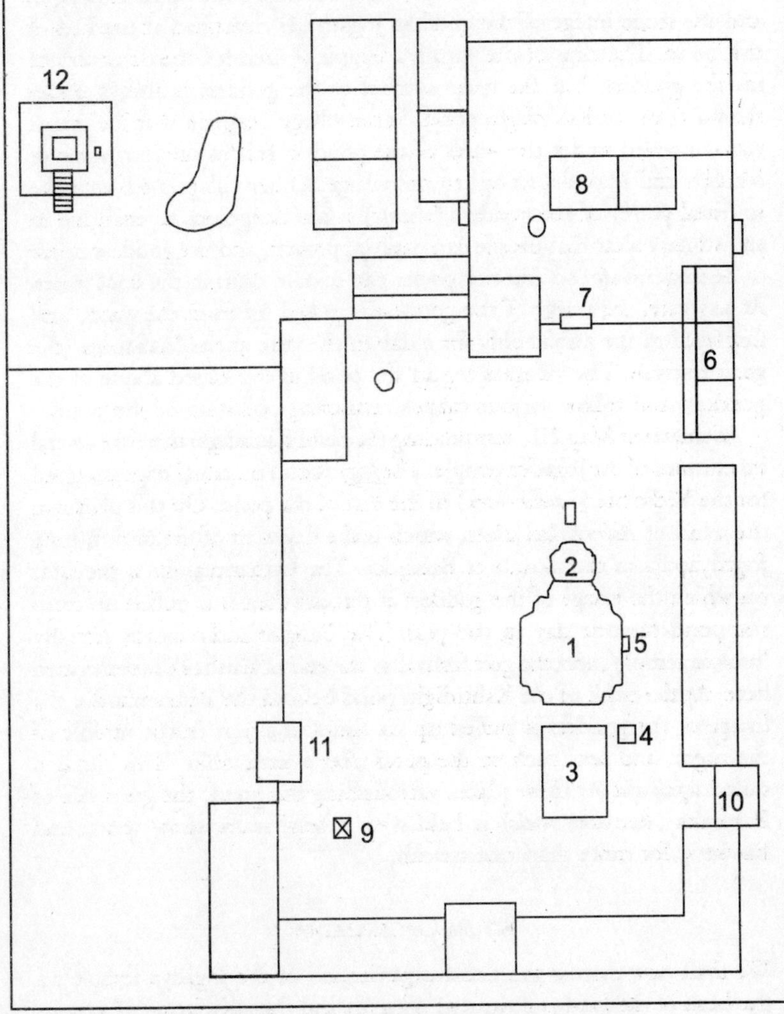

Map 2.2: The Jogadya Temple (grand plan)

colloquial), who used to supervise the temple organization in the name of the Bardhaman Raj. The Kshideshwari temple is the three-stair temple for Kshirkantak (another name of Siva) as the spouse of Jogadya. The Siva-linga is enshrined at the altar of the top stair, but this icon is now broken, and the villagers say that it was damaged by the intrusion of the Muslim troops in the past.

In the western part of the village, there is a large pond called *kshirdighi*, and the stone image of the goddess Jogadya is enshrined at the bed of this pond. The altar of the Jogadya temple is used for the daily service for the goddess, but the main symbol of the goddess is always under the water of the Kshirdighi pond. Some villagers explain that the image was concealed under the water of the pond in fear of the intrusions of Muslim and Maratha troops to the village. Other villagers tell that the spiritual power of the goddess (*shakti*) is too dangerous to enshrine in an ordinary altar that people can easily approach, and the goddess needs to be under water so that her power can remain calm in the cool water. At any rate, the image of the goddess is pulled up from the water, and displayed to the public only for a day in the year, at the Mahapuja (the great festival). The villagers regard the pond as the sacred abode of the goddess, and follow various taboos restricting pollution of the pond.

As shown in Map 2.1, surrounding the pond Kshirdighi there are several institutions of the Jogadya temple. The Jagyakund is a ritual stage designed for the Vedic fire (*baidik-hom*) to the east of the pond. On this platform the ritual of *Kshirkalasi* starts, which is the first step of the month-long Jogadyapuja in the month of Baishakh. The Utthanmandir is the altar on which the image of the goddess is placed when it is pulled up from the pond for one day in the year. The Bangamandir means literally 'broken temple', and the gret festival in the end of Baishakh is performed here. At the bank of the Kshirdighi pond behind the Bangamandir, the image of the goddess is pulled up six times in a year in the middle of the night, and sent back to the pond after a little while. This ritual is called *ugalpuja*. At these places surrounding the pond, the great fair of Baishakh (*baishakh mela*) is held with several stalls, show tents, and hawkers, for more than one month.

Ritual Organization

We shall now discuss the ritual organization of the Jogadya temple on the basis of the land endowment patterns and the association of various castes and lineages for ritual services. The first is the fixed properties attached to the temple Jogadya, which consist mainly of the sacred pond and the sites for various institutions of the temple. Since the Settlement Record by the British Government, these lands were classified as 'lakheraj lands', exempt from tax. The second is the 'cakran lands' (service land), which the various castes and lineages were granted by the Maharaja in return for ritual services. They provide the main basis of the ritual organization. Cakran land is usually meant as the service land such as caukidari cakran in Bengal, which is granted in return for maintaining the order of the village; however the cakran land in the temple is not necessarily the same as the caukidari cakran, because each cakran land is not always corresponding to a specific ritual duty, but rather the ritual orgaization consists of the various castes and lineages, and is based on the cakran lands as a whole. It is neither the donated land to temple (*debottar*) in general meaning, nor the donated land to Brahman priest (*brahmottar*), despite the fact that it is occupied in return for religious services. The third is the allowance of the court of the Maharaja of Bardhaman paid to the temple servants.

Lakheraj Land

The landlord properties attached to the temple institutions of the goddess Jogadya are regarded as granted lands by the Maharaja of Bardhaman. There are some other lands for other religious institutions which belonged to the Pattanidar (intermediary land holders) under the zamindari system of the British period.[3] We will first survey the historical material, the Cadastral Survey Record (C.S. Record) of the village, even though it comprises a vast amount of land data, too voluninous to examine here.

The purpose of the Survey and Settlement Operations in Bengal was prescribed under the Bengal Tenancy Act (1885) it was to extend the system of 'records-of-rights' to all kinds of estate.[4] The settlement officer in each district recorded the mutual rights and liabilities of landlords and tenants in detail and connected them with the Plot No. (Dag No.) in the *mauza* map in a unified standard. The operation began in 1898 in Bengal. In the district of Bardhaman, it was practised from 1927 to 1934, and on the village Kshiragram, which consist of three *mauzas*, namely Ksharija Kshiragram, Kshiragram and Cak Ksharija Kshiragram (J.L. Nos. 127, 128 and 129), the operation was done in 1927/8 under the supervision of the settlement officer. Table 2.2 gives a list of the plots belonging to the Jogadya and Kshideshwari temples which are picked up from the cadastral records of the *mauzas*. Most of the plots

TABLE 2.2: LAKHERAJ LAND OF THE VILLAGE RELIGIOUS INSTITUTIONS

Institutions	Dag No. (J.L. No.)	Land type	Area (acre)	Owner	Owner	Use
Jogyakund	8 (127)	Bhiti	0.11	Bharat Samrat (B.S.)	Maharaja	Public
Utthanmandir	10 (127)	Mandir	0.01	B.S.	Maharaja	Public
Kshirdighi	22 (127)	Pukur	13.5	B.S.	Maharaja	Public
Kshirdighi	29 (127)	Danga	0.04	B.S.	Maharaja	Public
Kshirdighi	9 (127)	Danga	0.54	B.S.	Maharaja	Public
Kshireshwari temple	7 (129)	Mandir	0.07	B.S.	Maharaja	Public
Kshireshwari temple	9 (129)	Bhiti	0.03	B.S.	Maharaja	Public
Kshireshwari temple	18 (129)	Path	0.03	B.S.	Maharaja	Public
Jogadya temple	20 (129)	Basta	0.10	B.S.	Maharaja	Kachari
Jogadya temple	24 (129)	Basta	0.88	B.S.	Maharaja	Public
Jogadya temple	25 (129)	Mandir	0.03	B.S.	Maharaja	Public
Jogadya temple	42 (129)	Bhiti	0.02	B.S.	Maharaja	Public
Jogadya temple	108 (129)	Danga	0.05	B.S.	Maharaja	Public
Altar of *grahapuja*	6261 (128)	Bagan	0.03	B.S.	Maharaja	Kathali
Altar of Jogadya	4995 (128)	Danga	0.15	B.S.	Maharaja	Public
Jogadya temple	5611 (128)	Shali	0.57	B.S.	Maharaja	Public
Altar of Gajan	45 (129)	Basta	0.08	B.S.	Maharaja	Public
Altar of Panchanan	84 (129)	Bhiti	0.02	B.S.	Maharaja	Bagdi
Shrine of Sib-narayan	78 (129)	Basta	0.07	B.S.	Maharaja	Karmakar
Shrine of Sib-narayan	79 (129)	Basta	0.10	B.S.	Maharaja	Bhattacaryya
Manasa temple	83 (129)	Bhiti	0.02	Maharaja	Bagdi	Debattar
Shrine of Dharmaraj	66 (129)	Bhiti	0.01	Pttanidar	Bagdi	Debattar

Abbreviations:	Bagan	Garden	Do	Double-cropping land
<Land Type>	Bhiti	Raised land	Garlayek	Unculturable land
	Basta	Homestead	Mandir	Temple
	Doba	Marshy ditch	Pukur	Pond
	Dokan	Shop	Path	Street
	Danga	Upland	Shali	Rice land
			Suna	Rice land

were recorded as owned by the Maharaja of Bardhaman. There are only a few plots which were under the other *pattanidar* and the *raiyats* (owner farmers) outside the village for religious use.

For the present, we shall draw attention to four points about the land holdings in the list. First, most of the lands connected with the rituals of Jogadya are registered under the ownership of the Maharaja of

Bardhaman. In the Settlement Record, it was as a matter of form that the rights of supreme ownership over the estates were endowed by the British Emperor (*barat samrat*) to the ultimate owner. It is, however, the family of the Maharaja of Bardhaman who is still regarded by the villagers as the owner of these plots. For example, the superintendent of the temple (*rajkachari*) supervised the temple management in the name of the Maharaja before Independence. It is still the name of the Maharaja that the priests proclaim at the beginning of the ritual process called *sankalpa*. This corresponds with the fact that the name of the Maharaja is placed as the prime servant (sebait) for the ritual on each page of the land register (*khatiyans*) on the Settlement Record. These things signify that the name of the Maharaja is placed in the ultimate position in the stratified organization of the temple service in the village, which included the nine lineages of the Brahman-sebait and the other service castes serving the temple.

Secondly, the British Government classified these lands as 'lakheraj land' simultaneously under the settlement operation. Lakheraj means simply tax-exempted land registered for the purpose of some public welfare and service in the Settlement office. According to the definitions in the Settlement Record, the lakheraj means 'lands held revenue-free' and 'sometime used loosely also for rent-free land'.[5] As shown in Table 2.2, these plots were mostly held revenue-free by the Maharaja. On the other hand, the purpose of these plots on the land register was defined in the additional section as follows: 'for the general use by all the Hindu'. Actually, most of the lands of the temple institutions and the alters of the goddess Jogadya are immovable estates. The lands to the temple institutions are usually called *debottar* in Bengal. On the Settlement Record, such land was defined as 'a form of rent-free tenure or revenue-free property'.[6] A grantor of debottar land could be entitled to resume it. In other words, only the right of the tenure was granted by the higher-ranking owner without taxation.[7] On each page of the land register of these plots, however, the purpose of the land was clearly prescribed as for the general use by all Hindus, although owner was registered as the Maharaja. These lands were, therefore, explicitly for public interests. In this regard, it could be said that all the villagers had a usufruct without rent over the estates, which were assured and/or donated to them by the Maharaja. Many villagers regarded them as lands of rent-free tenure. As a public institution, the temple was open to all Hindus for worship, without restrictions on the basis of caste or sect.

Only a family of the Bagdi caste who were prescribed as the servants of the god Panchanan can perform the ritual service at the altar called *panchanan-tala*. In the same way, a family of Kathali-Brahmans exclusively performed the ritual service to the deity Grahathakur. As with the *debottar* land, the Maharaja grants them land so far as they continue their ritual duties at each plot. Hence, it can be said that this relationship is equivalent to the relationship between a Bagdi priest and the Maharaja in terms of the *debottar* land of the Manasa temple, or the relationship between a Brahman family and the *pattanidar* of the Dharmaraj temple given in the table.

Third, only the temple organization could restrict access to the deities on particular occasions according to custom. The villagers observed religious taboos, as is often the case in such sacred places and even in an ordinary altar. There are the other customs of the village, such as fishing in the Kshirdighi pond and the gathering of the fruits from the trees of tamarind (*tetul-gach*) on the bank of the pond. It is the temple servant who is allowed to gather the fruits from the branches of the tamarind tree in season for sale. The profits thus accrued go to the temple management. If some villagers catch fish in the pond, the temple and the fishers share the haul. They dedicate the caudal fin to the goddess at first and then divide the catch into two halves between the temple and the fishers. They keep aside these sale proceeds for the temple management. At this point we can appreciate that the land of the temple is not merely a public property opened to all, but an estate controlled by the temple ritual organization.

Another example is the field surrounding the Kshirdighi pond, where *baishakh mela* is held with several stalls for more than one month. The ownership of this area was subinfudated from the Maharaja to the *pattanidar* (intermediary land holder) under the zamindari system and the occupancy right over the area was subdivided and shared by the several *raiyats* (tenant farmers) in the village. Subsequently, this area for the annual fair has subdivided into small plots in the course of succession in the households of the *raiyats* over the generations. It is interesting that the occupancy rights over each plot are now practically dealt with not merely as the nominal possessory right, but rather as the customary right over setting the stalls during the time of the fair, which includes the right of collection of the fixed share to the earnings from the commercial stalls. In other words, the occupancy right over the plots of the annual fair is regarded as a part of commercial privilege over the annual fair by the villagers.

Finally, it is interesting to see the composition of land types of the Jogadya temple in the list. There are no cultivated lands belonging to the temple which ordinarily constitute a large part of the donated lands. The size of the pond of Kshirdighi is the largest. The second largest is that allotted for the residence of the service castes. The pond is itself a sacred place and constitutes one of the temple institutions. The villagers have many customs to restrict the entry and use of the pond water. They also relate many stories of the evil consequences for violation of the associated taboos.

In this way, the rights over the estates of the religious institutions are not prescribed in a simple interest as in the case of ordinary transferred lands. The village maintained the customary rights with nominal ownership, tenure, and rights of usufruct along with the various customary rights as well as taboos, which are organized into a stratified relationship as a whole in relation to the Jogadya temple. It could be ironically said that the operation of the Settlement Record by the British Government, instead of creating individual property rights according to the unified standards over Bengal, brought about a complicated system of interests.

Cakran Land and the Ritual Posts

THE POSTS ASSIGNED BY THE MAHARAJA

The Maharaja's cakran land (service land), which is generally called *maharaja cakran sampatti*, ensures the occupancy right of the land owned by the Maharaja in exchange for service to the temple. The types of cakran include agricultural field, residential land, pond and wasteland. The sizes of these plots are not fixed. The usufruct of the cakran lands are also varied—from a household to a large lineage in the village. It could be supposed that the succession rule over the inseparable rights over the lands from their duties for the temple services brought about this diverse types of land holdings, and simultaneously the division of succession of their lands, the share of the duties among the lineages, and the rotation of the services and privileges over the temple rituals.

First, we have prepared a list of the cakran lands, the occupiers, and their roles in the temple services. The list is made from the Settlement Records of 1927/8 of this area. In the village, it is said that before 1927/8 there were a few more lineges who occupied the cakran lands and performed the temple duties, except for the names on the list. But the names and the descriptions regarding the cakran lands exclusively depend on the Settlement Record.[8] The items on the list follows this order: (a) concerned group for each duty, (b) duty for the temple service, (c) rule for the sharing duty at present. The descriptions of the duties are directly translated from the records on each page of the land register in Bengali. The performances in the actual ritual context at the temple have complicated impressions. This is the direct quotation so as to enable us to compare with the analysis of the ritual processes discussed in the later chapters.

The duties of the Occupiers of the Cakran Lands of the Maharaja

The priest for the Vedic fire ritual (*baidik-purohit*)
(a) two lineages having the title Bhattacaryya in the village Nigan
(b) the vedic fire ritual on every last day of months
(c) a priest according to the shift of the two lineages

The Grahacarya (the specialist for reading the ritual almanac)
(a) the lineage having the title Bhattacaryya in the village Ramdaspur (the block Katwa)
(b) proclamation of the royal almanac of the new year in the ritual of *lagna-utsab*
(c) the *pradhan-purohit* perform the ritual on behalf of the Grahacarya

The Brahman-sebait (the priests for the temple services)
(a) nine lineages of the Brahman priests in the village Kshiragram having the titles Cakrabartty and Bhattacaryya
(b) daily service and the special rituals for the goddess Jogadya
(c) daily shift for the temple service among the nine lineages

The Candi-*pathak* (the reciter of the Candi, viz., the *Devimahatmya*)
(a) two lineages in the village Kshiragram having the title Bhattacaryya
(b) recitation of the Candi at the daily service and the special rituals
(c) at the daily service the Brahman-sebaits perform their duty; and at the special rituals a priest of the lineages performs it

The priest for the Shyamsundar temple
(a) the lineage in the village Kshiragram holding the title Bhattacaryya
(b) the daily service in the temple of Shyamsundar
(c) a priest of the lineage performs it

The decorator for the daughter in *makari-saptami*
(a) the lineage of Babataran Bhattacaryya in Kshiragram
(b) the decoration and the reception of foods for the daughter in *makari-saptami*
(c) suspension

The Datta
(a) the lineage of the Datta in Kshiragram
(b) the ritual of *mayurnac* (dance of peacock), to carry the pot of *kshirkalasi*, and the procession in the *hal-nagal* in the month of Baishakh
(c) a family of the Datta continues the duty

The Samant
(a) the lineage of the Samant in Kshiragram
(b) *mayurnac* in the month of Baishakh
(c) a family of the Samant continues the duty

The Ghosh
(a) two lineages of the Ghosh, namely Raghunath Ghosh and Bhushan Candra Ghosh in Kshiragram
(b) the preparation of the buffalos in the rituals of *nabami* in the month of Ashwin and the Mahapuja in Baishakh
(c) a family of the Ghosh continues the duty

The *Paik*
(a) the lineage of the sub-caste of Kusmethi-Bagdi in Kshiragram
(b) *paik* (preparations for the rituals)
(c) two lineages of the lineage have a shifts to do their duty

The *Patakadhari*
(a) the lineage of the Kusmethi-Bagdi in Kshiragram
(b) to draw water for ablution from bank of the Ganga in Katwa, upholding the flags of the Maharaja, and guard the goats for sacrifice
(c) three families of the lineage continue the duty

The Dom
(a) the lineage of the Dom in Kshiragram
(b) guard of the altar of the goddess, to make the bamboo basket in the Jogadyapuja, and the sacrifice in the ritual of *meryakhata*
(c) three families of the lineage continue the duty

The Malakar
(a) the lineage of the Malakar Kshiragram
(b) the preparation of flowers for the daily service and arrangements for rituals in the temple
(c) the family of the lineage continues the duty

The *Jharudar*
(a) the lineage of the Hari caste Kshiragram
(b) sweeping the temple ground
(c) three families of the lineage continue the duty

The *Badyakar* (*dakhi*)
(a) the lineage of the Baiti caste
(b) playing drum
(c) shift among three families of the lineage

The Muci
(a) the lineage in the village Gobardanpur and Bhuichi
(b) the leatherwork on the drum of *madals*
(c) the families of the lineage continue the duty

The Karmakar
(a) the lineage of the title Pramanik in the village Nigan
(b) sacrifice on the western Bank of Kshirdighi for a zamindar
(c) the lineage continues the duty

The Cakran Lands Granted to the Posts Outside the Village

The priest to carry a basket
(a) the lineage having the title Acaryya in the village Gobardhanpur
(b) carrying a bamboo basket to the Jogadya temple on the day of the Mahapuja
(c) the family continues the duty
(d) Bastta land of 0.06 acre

The preparation of goats for sacrifice
(a) the lineage having the title Ray in the village Jobagram
(b) dedication of goats to the goddess on the day of the Mahapuja
(c) a family of the lineage continues the duty
(d) Shali land of 0.54 acre

The Baiti
(a) the lineage of Baiti in the village Gobardanpur
(b) the daily service at the goddess temple in Gobardanpur
(c) a family of the lineage continues the duty
(d) Shali land of 3.91 acres and Do land of 0.35 acre

The Cakran Lands and the Ritual Organization

Cakran land is a kind of service tenure in Bengal. In south India, it is known as *inam land*, to signify various kinds of service tenures. In Bengal, landlords usually assigned cakran land to village *caukidars* for guarding the village, or to *gamasta* (rent collector in the local office) in the Toshildhar system of the British local administration, though the British government until in the early twentieth century abolished most of them.[9] In the village, cakran lands, however, were allotted to varoius caste groups for religious purposes and these were closely connected with the temple ritual organization. Because of this, most of the lands remain virtually in the village as service tenure despite the repeated reforms of land administration since Independence. Below, I show the cakran lands classified by each ritual post held by the caste groups compiled from the list on the previous pages and the share of cakran lands classified by the caste groups. We shall try to highlight three issues through this analysis.

First, unlike the untouchable at the temple rituals in the south India, it is intersting that the lower castes of the village such as the Bagdi and the Dom were assigned important posts and engaged in the indispensable roles in the temple ritual. The untouchables in south India were generally not allowed to enter the temple, and were deprived of land in rural areas. But it is important to indicate that in Bengal a system of land holding involving the lower castes was legitimized by the Maharaja through direct endowments to the temple servants. The Brahman-sebait certainly occupies the largest percentage of the holdings of the cakran lands. It is rather easy to explain their high proportion because, first they are the largest group, consisting of nine lineages; second, only they perform the various kinds of worship to the deities (*puja*) in occasional rituals as well as daily services, and third, the lineage of the director of the ritual organization (*sabha-pandit*) who is the supervisor of the ritual performances is included as the Brahman-sebait. But, in spite of their high proportion, they do not cover more than half of the total cakran lands of the temple: precisely, it is 43.6 per cent.

TABLE 2.3: THE CAKRAN LANDS CLASSIFIED BY THE RITUAL POSTS

Post/Type	Caste	Shali	Suna	Do	Basta	Bhiti	Pukur	Doba	Danga	Total	% of total
Brahman-sebait	Brahman	20.51	0.17		0.27	0.30			0.29	21.54	43.60
Candi-*pathak*	Brahman	4.24								4.24	8.60
Baidik-purohit	Brahman	0.54								0.54	1.10
Shyamsundar	Brahman				0.17					0.17	0.30
Grahacarya	Brahman				0.06					0.06	0.10
Makari-saptami	Brhaman					0.02				0.02	0.04
Datta	Kshatriya				0.57		1.23	0.06		1.86	3.80
Samant	Kshatriya				0.19					0.19	0.40
Ghosh	Goera				0.08					0.08	0.20
Chief servant	Bagdi	5.81			0.24					6.05	12.20
Flag holder	Bagdi	0.37			0.24	0.06				0.67	1.40
Badyakar	Baiti	5.88			0.12					6.00	12.10
Malakar	Malakar	2.60			0.10		0.80			3.50	7.10
Hari	Hari	1.24			1.39					2.63	5.30
Muci	Muci	0.86								0.86	1.70
Dom	Dom	0.15		0.06	0.27		0.35			0.83	1.70
Karmakar	Bene							0.15		0.15	0.30
Total		42.2	0.17	0.06	3.70	0.38	2.38	0.21	0.29	49.39	100

Abbreviations:

<Post> Candi-*pathak*: The reciter of the Candi
Baidik-purohit: The priest for the Vedic fire ritual
Shyamsundar: The priest for the Shyamsundar temple
Makari-saptami: The decorator for the daughter in *Makari-saptami*
Badyakar: The drummer

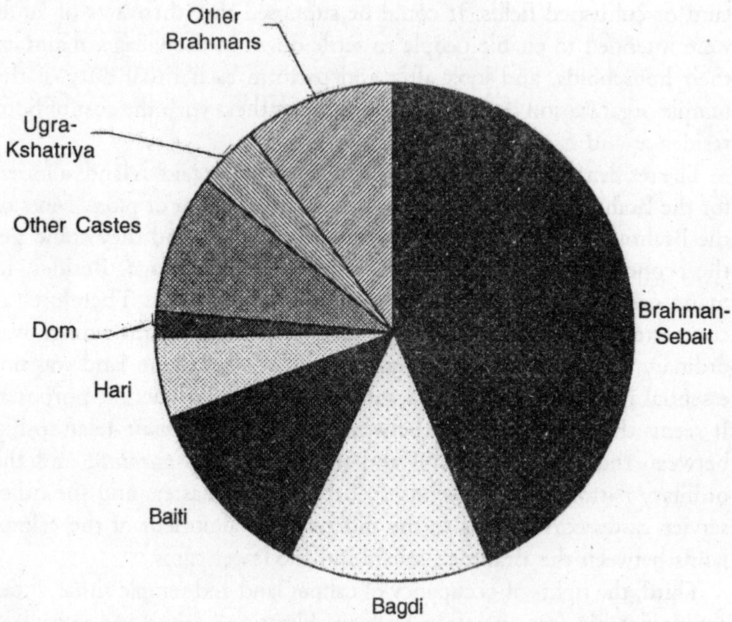

Chart 1: Pie Chart of Cakran Land by Caste Groups

The sum total of land holding by the so called *chota lok* in Bengal which is the caste groups of the Bagdi, the Dom, the Baiti, and the Hari, amounts to 34.4 per cent. As contrasted with the case of the untouchables in south India who were alienated from the temple ritual performances in most cases, the greater part of the ritual organization here was dependent on such lower caste groups. It is supported also by the distribution of the sort of the cakran lands that the productive double-cropping lands are allotted for the Dom, and the irrigation ponds are distributed for the Dom and the Malakar. These facts indicate that the lower castes were not necessarily handicapped in relation to the upper castes in respect of distributed lands.

Second, under the form of the land use, it is interesting that residential plots are not included in the holdings of lineages dweling outside the village. They visit the village only on the occasion of temple rituals. Most of their lands consisted of cultivated lands of the village, and in practice these were sublet to tenant farmers of the village. Meanwhile, the land held by the village lower castes is always either the residential land or cultivated fields. It could be supposed that these sets of lands were intended to enable people to settle down in the village, maintain their households, and look after and perform each ritual duty of the temple organization by way of the providing them with the cost of both residence and earning.

The residential lands are comparatively few in the cakran lands allotted for the Brahman-sebait, but consist of a large number of plots. Most of the Brahman-sebait have their own patron *jajman*, and they could get the economical support from patrons inside the village. Besides, in many cases they even had their own cultivated lands. Therefore, as contrasted with the lower castes, their settlement in the village was ordinary and easy. For many Brahman-sebait, the cakran land was not essential for subsistence, but a surplus for their production purposes. It seems that the distinction between the so-calld *jajmani*-relationship between the patron (*jajman*) and the priest (*kula-purohit*), and the ordinary patron-client relationship between the masters and the other service castes corresponds to the difference of allotment of the cakran lands between the Brahman-sebait and the lower cates.

Third, the rights of occupancy of cakran land and temple ritual duties are inseparable. It is, therefore, both an obligation (*daitya*) and a privilege (*adhikar*) of each caste to engage in the services of the temple organization. It is regarded as the indispensable obligation for the beneficiaries of the cakran lands to render service for temple ritual. In other words, each cakran plot is severally assigned, and the occupancies for the plots by the households of each caste groups automatically lead to the engagement for the ritual services classified by the caste statuses of the village. At the same time, the successions by the households of the specified caste groups legitimate their exclusive engagement in the temple services. It is a matter of course that the attributions of their caste groups assure their engagement in the specified roles in the ritual organization, but what is more important is that patrilineal groups, who inherit the cakran lands of the temple, inherit simultaneously the exclusive right to engage in temple services. Because of the inseparable relation of the rights of occupancy and the obligations for ritual services, they could maintain the basis of the ritual organization of the temple, notwithstanding the successoin and fragmentation of inheritance in the larger lineages. Before the Estate Aquitisiion Act (1953), they were prohibited from the disposal of the lands at will under the supervision of the *rajkachari*. Each post and role in the temple ritual are, therefore, sustained for generations, as each plot of the cakran lands remains in the village in spite of the migration of any caste group.

Each household holding cakran lands is indispensable to the division of labour in the ritual system at the same time their caste identities result in a hierarchical structure of the ritual organization. These identities apparently have no association with the concepts of pure and impure. It is the supremacy of the Maharaja that assures the legitimacy of ritual positions by means of grant of cakran lands, and organizes a hierarchical system for management of the temple rituals.

THE JOGADYA TEMPLE AND THE LAND SETTLEMENT

The form of temple management and maintenance of households, and the influence through the granted properties by the kingship, raise a complicated question concerning land management at the time of the British Land Settlement, which intended to standardize the land register all over Bengal. Table 2.4 gives a list of the land distribution classified by the type of the land use, which includes all kinds of land categories, in the whole area of the *mauza*, Cauk Ksharija Kshiragram (J.L. No. 129). Table 2.5 shows the distribution of the land types regarding to the cakran lands in the village for the temple service granted by the Maharaja to the villagers. Table 2.6 is the distribution of the land types of the lakheraj lands actually endowed by the Maharaja. This brings out a few facts about land distribution.

First, the lakheraj lands directly belonging to the Jogadya temple mainly consist of the estates of the temple institutions, the sacred pond, and the lands of the residences for some temple servants, but are not the means of productoin. On the other hand, the cakran lands belonging to the various temle servants mainly consist of the cultivated lands and in addition the residential lands for the cultivators of these lands. It is noteworthy that the percentage of cultivated lands and residential lands in the cakran lands is high as compared with land types in the entire *mauza* Chauk Ksharija Kshiragram. Besides, Table 2.7 shows the abstracted composition from the sum total of the lakheraj lands and the cakran lands, which means the total land of the Jogadya temple rituals in the village. The land types of the temple estates bear a resemblance to the general composition of the whole land of this *mauza* as shown in Table 2.4.

These suggest that the resistered lands in the Settlement Record as

TABLE 2.4: LAND DISTRIBUTION OF THE CHAUK KSHARIJA KSHIRAGRAM CLASSIFIED BY LAND TYPE

Land type	Acre	%
Shali	140.23	69.90
Pukur	27.33	13.60
Do	11.39	5.70
Suna	7.28	3.60
Basta	4.67	2.30
Pkp	4.44	2.20
Rst	1.97	1.00
Bhiti	1.92	1.00
Doba	0.83	0.40
Bagan	0.29	0.10
Danga	0.15	0.07
Mandir	0.10	0.05
Dakan	0.09	0.04
Garlayek	0.06	0.03
Total	200.75	100

TABLE 2.5: DISTRIBUTION OF THE CAKRAN LANDS CLASSIFIED BY LAND TYPE

Land type	Acre	%
Shali	42.20	85.4
Basta	3.70	7.5
Pukur	2.38	4.8
Bhiti	0.38	0.8
Danga	0.29	0.6
Doba	0.21	0.4
Suna	0.17	0.3
Do	0.06	0.1
Total	49.39	100

Lakheraj land and/or cakran land composed of a part of the donated lands to the temple, namely the *mauza* Chauk Ksharija Kshiragram (J.L. No. 129) and Ksharija Kshiragram (J.L. No. 127). It is very difficult now to ascertain the details about the temple estate at one time but one could conjecture that the total land belonging to the Chauk Ksharija Kshiragram and the Ksharija Kshiragram was donated to the temple for a religious purpose. Ksharija means 'transferred', and this indicates

TABLE 2.6: DISTRIBUTION OF LAKHERAJ LANDS CLASSFIED BY LAND TYPE

Land type	Acre	%
Pukur	13.50	82.00
Basta	1.23	7.50
Danga	0.78	4.70
Shali	0.57	3.50
Bhiti	0.21	1.28
Mandir	0.11	0.67
Path	0.03	0.18
Bagan	0.03	0.18
Total	16.46	100

TABLE 2.7: SUM OF DISTRIBUTIONS OF CAKRAN LAND AND LAKHERAJ LAND CLASSIFIED BY LAND TYPE

Land type	Acre	%
Shali	42.77	65.00
Pukur	15.88	24.10
Basta	4.93	7.50
Danga	1.07	1.60
Bhiti	0.59	0.90
Doba	0.21	0.30
Suna	0.17	0.30
Mandir	0.11	0.20
Do	0.06	0.09
Path	0.03	0.05
Bagan	0.03	0.05
Total	65.85	100

this conjecture that the estates named Ksharija Kshiragram were separated from the estate of Kshiragram at one time and made over to the Jogadya temple.[10]

Before the Settlement, lands donated for religious purposes were generlaly called *debottar* or *brahmottar* in the case of Hindu estates, which means the land belonged to some deity and the Brahman. In the Survey and Settlement Records in Bengal the Settlement Officers put the land category cakran, which means service land for specified duites such as *gamasta* or chaukidar. However, in the village, they registered the estates directly attached to the temple as lakheraj land under the ownership by the upper landholding of the Maharaja. And again they simultaneously prescribed the purpose of them as public use. It is not sure that they understood well the customary arrangements concerned with the rights of temple management, although the customary interests were settled in written form.

After the abolition of the zamindari system and the Estate Acquisition Act (1953) and the Land Reform Act (1955), paradoxically, most of the cakran lands for temple services were taxed and registered as private properties under the Revenue Settlement Records. In contrast, the lakheraj lands attached to the temple were registered as the tax-exempt land in the name of the Maharaja. This caused some confusoin in the management of temple organization. For example, the residential land for the *rajkachari* was originally attached to the ground of the Jogadya temple, where the lineage of the *rajkachari* have dwelled for generations. On the Settlement Records the land type of this plot was included in the lakheraj lands under the name of ownership by the Maharaja, but it corresponded in practice with residential land within the cakran lands for the temple servants. The settlement officers, however registered this residential land for the *rajkachari* as lakheraj land along with the temple estates. Another example is a plot for a general store next to the temple ground, where the shopkeeper was allowed customarily to do business only during the annual fair. But at the time of the Revenue Settlement, he stayed on until the registration was completed, and finally succeeded in getting the plot registered for permanent commerical use. This sort of confusion on the register regarding the customary rights in the village occurred variously during the Land Settlement in the 1920s and around Independence.

THE ALLOWANCES GIVEN BY THE COURT OF THE RAJ

Before the abolition of the zamindari system, the deb-seba-office attached to the court of the Maharaja of Bardhaman, supervised directly some aspects of the temple management through the local *kacharibari.* They allotted the budget for the temples in the kingdom each year, and received reports about the settlement of accounts from the temples at the end of year. In the village of Kshiragram, all the service castes who were assigned cakran lands for the temple ritual were under the supervision of the *rajkachari.* He usually controlled the temple organization for the ritual in the office at the temple, and on the other hand owed a duty to report about their temple management regularly to the deb-seba-office in the town of Bardhaman. In the final three days of the lunar month of Baishakh, the superintendent of the court of the Raj vistied the village to attend the buffalo sacrifice in front of the the Utthanmandir by a deputy of the Maharaja once in a year. In addition to the cakran lands for the service castes, the court sent monthly allowances to the principal officiants. The *rajkachari* received it directly from the deb-seba-office and kept the records. The heads of every service caste received it monthly in the office in the temple.

In this way, the court of the Raj in the town of Bardhaman supervised the temple ritual in the village through the allotment of budget and the directions at times. The budget was divided mainly into two parts, the daily service and occasional dedicatoins of goats and buffalos for sacrifice. The distribution and content of these offerings will be discussed in the next chapter in detail. The following list shows the official posts in the temple which got the monthly allowances from the *rajkachari* for their duties. The items on the list are (a) concerned group for each duty, (b) their assignment to the cakran lands, and (c) the contents of the main duties for the temple service.

Posts Receiving Monthly Allowances from the Court

The *Rajkachari*

(a) a head of a lineage having the title Mukhapadyaya in the village Kshiragram
(b) no cakran land by the Maharaja
(c) (i) supervisor on the all kind of works in the Jogadya temple
 (ii) keeping accounts the budget for the temple management and the payment for the specified posts
 (iii) annual report to the court of the Raj

The *Sabha-pandit*

(a) a head of a lineage having the title Bhattacharyya in the village Kshiragram
(b) shared with the other Brahman-sebaits
(c) (i) supervisor on the ritual processes of the Jogadya temple
 (ii) assistant priest (*trantradarak*) in the major rituals in the temple
 (iii) declaration to begin the Jogadya puja in the name of Maharaja

TABLE 2.8: ALLOWANCE OF THE JOGADYA TEMPLE SERVANTS

Post	Allowance	Number of persons
The superintendent of the temple (*rajkachari*)	17 *taka* (50 after rise)	1
The director of the ritual organization (*sabha-pandit*)	3.5 *taka*	1
The chief priest (*pradhan-purohit*)	4 *ana*	1
The storekeeper (*bhandari*)	4 *ana*	1
The chief servants of Bagdi (*mula-paik*)	2 *ana*	2
The clerk (*piyan*)	2 *taka*	1
The guardian of the pond	25-30 *taka* (seasonally)	1
The sacrificer	2.5 *taka*	1

The *Pradhan-purohit*
(a) a head of a lineage having the title Cakrabartty belonging to the lineage of Shat-bhai in the village Kshiragram
(b) shared with the other Brahman-sebaits
(c) the representative of the Brahman-sebait

The *Bhandari*
(a) a head of a lineage
(b) the residential land was allotted as the cakran land, which is now included in the temple estate
(c) the preparation for the ritual utensils for the temple services

The *Mula-paik*
(a) *paiks* belonging to a lineage of Kusmethi Bagdi holding the title Dhara in the village Kshiragram
(b) shared with the other *paiks*
(c) the preparation for all the ritual services

The Piyan
(a) a family
(b) no cakran land
(c) assistant works for the *Rajkachari*

The guardians of the pond
(a) lineages of the Kusmethi-Bagdi in the village

(b) no cakran land
(c) regularly guard on the bank of Kshirdighi

The sacrificer
(a) a lineage of the Karmakar in the village Nigon
(b) the total area of cakran land is 0.15 acre
(c) the sacrifice in the temple rituals by the goddess sword.

NOTES

1. The term 'dominant caste' was first defined by M.N. Srinivas (1987). This signifies in the original definition the caste group being superior to the other caste groups in terms of population, landholding, and ritual status in the village.
2. In the village, they are called *sebait*, but usually the word of *sebait* means temple servants including the other service castes in Bengali. So that, the Brahman priests for the temple ritual services are referred as 'Brahman-sebait' in this thesis.
3. In this respect, see MacLane, *Land and Local Kingship in Eighteenth-century Bengal*, 1993, pp. 287–305. See also Ray, *Change in Bengal Agrarian Society, c. 1760–1850,* 1979.
4. Government of Bengal, *Guide and Glossary to Survey and Settlement Records in Bengal*, 1917 (rpt. 1938) p. 2.
5. Government of Bengal, *Guide and Glossary to Survey and Settlement Records in Bengal*, 1917 (rpt., 1938), p. 39. In the Bengal Tenancy Act, 'Lakheraj' is described as follows: 'The word of lakheraj is often used loosely: in strictness, it indicates a freedom from liability to revenue, but it is constantly used as indicating exemption from liability to pay rent.' Sen, 1925, p. 25.
6. Government of Bengal, *Guide and Glossary*, p. 32.
7. In this respect, the Bengal Tenancy Act prescribes it as follows. 'Where there has been a rent-free grant by a proprietor there is a relationship of landlord and tenant between the grantor and the grantee' Sen, 1925, p. 24.
8. It is known that there was a family of *bhandari* (storekeepers) who had cakran lands and a residence beside the temple. They had emigrated before 1920. Becasue of this, their lands have not been recorded on the pages of *khatiyan* at the time of Settlement operation.
9. In this respect, see in particular, Palit, *Tension in Bengal Rural Society: Landlords, Planters and Colonial Rule, 1830–60,* 1975, pp. 26–59. See, also, Sinha, *The Law of Service Tenures in Bengal*, 1911, pp. 74–80.

10. On the pages of the Settlement Records the word *kharija* is explained as follows, 'separated independent taluk' and is 'one separated from the zamindari under Regulation VII of 1793 and now a separate estate. A tenant is *kharija* when the landlord allows him to pay rent separately from his co-sharers for which he has opened a separate account (*dakhil*).' *Guide and Glossary.*

CHAPTER 3

Ordinary Rituals of the Jogadya Temple

In this chapter, we propose to highlight three main aspects of the ritual organization in the Jogadya temple: combination of caste occupations and ritual roles; the periodical shift of roles amongst the lineages and the status hierarchy in the ritual posts. These ritual data examined in this chapter are mainly classified into the ordinary rituals of the Jogadya temple, which shows the basic forms of the temple organization. The periodical rituals of the village held within and outside the temple will be considered later.

First, let us discuss the daily ritual service in the temple with examples of the ritual process of a day. We broadly presume that the various caste groups of the village are indispensable and perform the daily service. Second, the daily shift of the Brahman-sebait (temple priest) for daily ritual service (*nityaseba*) in the temple has been examined. It is noteworthy that the rotation system of the temple priests, being a kind of daily shift assigned to each lineage of the Brahman-sebait, is sufficiently effective to maintain their stable organization. Third, we examine the rituals on the last day of each month (*sankranti*) and the rituals of pulling up the image of the goddess (*ugalpuja*). Every *sankranti*, they perform the speical ritual of the Vedic fire (*baidik-hom*) and the ritual convocation. The *ugalpuja* is the ritual of pulling out the image of the goddess Jogadya from the pond of Kshirdighi by the eligible members of the ritual organization. It is performed seven times a year. These rituals show how the posts associated with the caste groups are ranked in a ritual hierarchy in the different rituals, such as, the *phonta*-giving (sacred marks to put on foreheads) by the fire ritual and/or the restriction the access to the goddess. They also show how various status groups in the hierarchy form the background of the caste system of the village and that of the ritual organization at the same time.

Daily Services in the Temple

THE EVERYDAY RITUAL PROCESS

Table 3.1 shows the list of the posts and the roles of various caste groups. In the ordinary temple service, we can easily point out the ritual position of various castes of the village such as the Brahman, the Malakar, the Hari, the Baiti, and the Bagdi. The specific roles they perform are related with their caste occupations in the village society. The temple ritual in a day shows the basic ritual pattern in the village, and gives an example of the elementary compositoin in the ritual organization.

The Brahmans hold many posts in the village society. They perform household rituals on various occasions as the family priests (*kula-purohit*) of their patron families and periodical rituals as priest, as well as the Brahman-sebait in the Jogadya temple. In most cases, they normally hold more than two posts concurrently. At the same time, in the temple, their services are subdivided and specialized. In the case of the priests in *nityaseba*, they have two divisions of the posts at the time of the ritual, namely, the priests and the reciter of the Candi (Candi-*pathak*). The work of priest is ritual service for the deity (*thakur-seba*) at the altar of the Jogadya temple. They have the title of 'Chakrabartti', and

TABLE 3.1: ROLE ASSIGNMENT IN THE JOGADYA TEMPLE

Time	Post	Role
Before dawn (*Bhore*)	Hari	Sweeping the temple ground
Morning (*Sakal*)	Malakar	Cleaning the temple inside, Preparation of flowers for ritual, Arrangement of the ritual utensils
9.00 am	Storekeeper	Arrangement of offerings
	Brahman-sebait	Daily ritual service in Jogadya temple and Kshideshwari temple
	Reciter	Recitation of the Candi (at Jogadya temple)
	Malakar	Striking a gong (*kashial*)
Noon (*Dupure*)	Brahman-sebait	Offering boiled rice (*annabhog*)
	Maid servant	Assistance for Brahman
Evening (*Sandhya*)	Brahman-sebait	Evening ritual service (*sandhyarati*)
		Offering flour puff (*luci*), sweets and milk (*sital-bhog*)
	Baiti	Playing the drum (*dhak-bajana*)
	Malakar	Striking a gong (*kashial*)
		Cleaning after the daily service

are constituted of nine lineages of the village. The reciters of the Candi have two lineages now, whose title is 'Bhattacaryya'. Their role in the ritual is to recite the sacred sutras and the verses as an assistant to the priests. One of the lineages takes charge of the daily service in company with the priests, and the others in charge of the annual rituals. In this way, each caste group and even the lineages of the castes have specialized roles. As for other Brahmans, their duty is to prepare daily offerings for the goddess as an assistant of the Brahman-sebait in the daily shift. This offering at noontime is called *annabhog.* Another Brahman family is the *bhandari,* keeping the ritual utensils in the temple storehouse.

In the dim light before daybreak, a woman of the Hari caste sweeps the temple ground with a broom. Three lineages of the village Haris have responsibility for this in rotation. Inside the temple, a Malakar cleans up before the daily ritual service. Around 9 o'clock, the Malakar prepares flowers from gardens and brings the ritual plate of brass, sacred water, and offerings to the altar. The Brahman-sebait in the shift comes to the altar after ablutions and performs the sixteen steps (*sora-shopacar-puja*) with various offerings. The Malakar waits behind the priest, and rings a gong following his ritual steps. Sometimes, the priest performs the ritual as required by some devotees at their private petitions. It takes about thirty minutes to finish the daily service at the altar. Soon after, he goes to the Kshideshwari temple and performs the daily service again, for Siva, the spouse god. After that he remains at the Bhogmandir in company with an assistant of a Brahman woman in order to prepare the daily rice offering (*annabhog*). At the Bhogmandir, they prepare the food for the goddess, to be offered by the villagers, with the water of the sacred pond of Khsirdighi.

In the evening, the Baiti in the shift tells the time of the *sandhyarati* by beating his drum in a specified rhythm. Inside and outside the temple the village people gather to dedicate and receive offerings. The Brahman-sebait performs his service to the goddess in the same way as in the morning. At the end of a series of offerings, he begins to dedicate a votive light (five wicks in a brass stand) in his hand. He stands up and holds it up to the altar. During the time of the dedication by the priest, every villager inside the temple stand up and pays respect to the goddess. The Malakar beats the gong very loudly and the women inside the temple perform *ulu* (sound by moving their tongue) to pay homage. The Baiti plays his drum at the Natmandir. In the end, people rush to receive the offerings from the Brahman-sebait. The Baiti returns to his house playing his drum, signifying the end of the evening service. The

Malakar cleans up the altar and locks up the door of the main temple. In this manner, the ritual process of the daily service of temple is based on distinctive roles assigned to each caste group and lineage.

OFFERINGS

There are three occasions for dedicating offerings to the goddess in the daily services, namely; daily service in the morning (*nityaseba*), rice offering at noon (*annabhog*), and offering at evening service (*sitalbhog*). In the days of the Maharaja the Brahman-sebaits, the storekeeper (*bhandari*), the servants of Bagdi, the maid servant of the temple (*jhi*), and the Malakar prepared the offerings under the superintendent of the temple (*rajkachari*) in his office. The debseba-office, the court of the Raj, in the town of Bardhaman, appointed a Brahman family in the village to be the superintendent, and paid the wages for this duty.

In addition to the monthly allowances the debseba-office would send a yearly buget sufficient for meeting the daily expenditures of these temple services. They offered, moreover, contributions for specified ritual occasions such as Jogadyapuja and Durgapuja and many goats and buffaloes for the sacrifices. Table 3.2 is a list of the items to be offered in daily ritual service, the expenses of which used to be carried by the Maharaja in those days.

2.5 seer is approximately 2.4 kg which means enough cooked rice for more than twenty persons. Now the quantity of rice for *annabhog* depends on the irregular donations by the villagers, and most of the donations are not sun-dried but ordinary rice. Fish is an essential item

TABLE 3.2: LIST OF OFFERINGS DONATED BY THE MAHARAJA OF BARDHAMAN

Offerings of daily service in the morning	
Grain soaked in water (*bhije-chola*)	5 catak[1]
Sweets	5 catak
Offerings in noon time	
Sun-dried rice (*atop-caul*)	2.5 seer
Milk	1.25 seer
Sweets (*mishthi*)	10 catak
Refined butter	5 catak
Fish	5 catak
Service for visitors	
Rice	8 catak

for the offering. Everyday of the year they use fish for her offerings except during the four days in the lunar month of Baishakh when the goddess is supposed to observe her fast.

The Brahman-sebait who is on the daily shift remains in the Bhogmandir, and prepares the offerings. The *bhanadari* arranges the cooking utensils. The servants of Bagdi manage the fish and vegetables, if they do not receive enough donations. The maid servant in the Bhogmandir makes preparatoin for the offerings, and washes the pots and pans after the sevice. Only the Brahman-sebait, however, has the duty to light a fire in the hearth of the Bhogmandir to cook, and to make offerings to the goddess. During cooking, nobody is allowed to look inside the cooking room without the Brahmans. When the Brahman-sebait finishes the preparations, he closes the door of the cooking room. Inside, he makes a ritual with a small vessel (*kosakusi*), the paste of sandalwood, and flowers, and serves the offerings to the goddess with a specified sacred verse, and sprinkles sacred water over the plates. Thereafter, he opens the door. He stands on the veranda of the Bhogmandir and tolls a bell anouncing the time of the offering; and for the devotees gathered there to receive the goddess's offerings from his hand. At this hour, those who are incharge of the daily service can receive the offerings regularly. These are the Brahman-sebait, the maid servant, the storekeeper, the Malakar, the Baiti, the Hari, and the servants of Bagdi. Besides, the temple has special times for visiting ascetics (*sadhus*) who come on pilgrimage: they may receive the service of food three times a day (*nityaseba*, *annabhog*, *sital-bhog*) for three days, for the temple.

At the time of the *sandhyarati*, the Brahman-sebait serves the offering (*sital-bhog*) to the goddess, which consists of flour-puff (*luci*), sweets, and milk. It is now donated regularly by a president of the rice mill in Kaicar town near the village. In former days, they used to put a small table beside the bed of the goddess inside the temple. After the evening service, the Malakar offered a glass of water, a *pan* on a plate, and a votive light on the table. Although he closed the door of the temple and locked it up every night, it is said that people found sometime the water and betel had been left half eaten in the next morning.

Role Assignment of the Brahman-Sebaits

The organization of the Jogadya temple routine by the Brahman-sebaits has a unique rotation system. Owing to this ritual system, there seems to be no competition among the lineages of the temple priests. At the same time, there is a sense of stability due to the sharing and succession of the service lands within the lineages jointly. We will examine here four points of view so as to make clear the outstanding functions of the *sola-ana* system for the management of the temple. First we will discuss the daily shift for each day of the year.

ROLE ASSIGNMENT

All priests of the temple hold the title Chakrabartti, and they all belong to one of the nine lineages. They have an oral tradition that they once shared a common ancestor, and then divided from him over the generations. The name of the legendary lineage founder is Krishna Sharma and at one time, it is said, the priests got their title of Chakrabartti from the Maharaja of Bardhaman. This story assures legitimacy and the nine lineages comprise an exclusive group of servants of the village goddess.

Table 3.3 is a list of the yearly shift allotted to each lineage for each day of the month. The heads of the lineages listed in the days of each month must send the temple priest of their family to perform the ritual. Only the person who is on the shift (*pala*) can perform the ritual for the day. If there is no a distinctive shift assigned to each lineage of the temple priest, they may compete among the nine lineages, and even within the family, over the right to perform the ritual. It is more attractive for the priests of the temple to perform the ritual service on specified days. On days such as *Bipattarinibrata* and *Laskshmipuja*, the priest on duty could get more worshippers and offerings than usual. In addition, the priests might leave the ritual on ordinary days, since they could not get as many offerings as on the days of the special rituals. The most important responsibility for the temple priest is to continue the daily service for the goddess and never miss a day. This rotation system is secure enough to maintain the daily ritual of the temple without interruption or competition.

THE RULE OF INHERITANCE

The organization of the temple priests debars priests from outside from participating in the ritual of the temple, as it would lead to disorder. Here, each head of the lineage is given the assignment of daily service to the temple, and the quota is fixed. It is the rotation rule called *sola-ana-puja* in Bengali that assures the legitimacy of the nine lineages to perform the temple ritual.

TABLE 3.3: ANNUAL SHIFT OF THE DAILY SERVICE FOR THE JOGADYA TEMPLE

Lunar month	Heads of each lineage (the name of priests)
Baishakh	
1–8	Bholanath (Bhaktaprakash/Kshirodmahan)
9–12	Shripati (Sanjib/Ciranjib)
13	Kailash (Ramnarayan Kalo/Naren)
14–19	Bholanath (Krishnadulal/Rajkumar/Pramkumar/Haradan)
20–5	Heranbanath (Nanugopal/Nimaicand/Paramasukh)
26–*Sank.*	Amiyanath (Dhanugopal/Nabakumar)
Jaishta	
1–2	Bholanath (Krishnadulal/Rajkumar/Pramkumar/Haradan)
3–5	Heranbanath (Nanugopal/Nimaicand/Paramasukh)
6–8	Amiyanath (Dhanugopal/Nabakumar)
9–12	Kalachand Chakrabartty
13–19	Abhayapad Chakrabartty
20–1	Kalachand Chakrabartty
22–7	Amalapati Bh. (Pranabkumar/Pankoj)
28–*Sank.*	Shripati (Sanjib/Ciranjib)
Asar	
1–7	Bholanath (Bhaktaprakash/Kshirodmahan)
8–11	Shripati (Sanjib/Ciranjib)
12	Kailash (Ramnarayan Kalo/Naren)
13–18	Bholanath (Krishnadulal/Rajkumar/Pramkumar/Haradan)
19–24	Heranbanath (Nanugopal/Nimaicand/Paramasukh)
25–*Sank.*	Amiyanath (Dhanugopal/Nabakumar)
Shraban	same as Jaishta
Bhadra	same as Baishakh
Aswin	same as Jaishta
13–16	Sureshwar (Kalidas/Taradas)
17–19	Abhayapad Chakrabartty
Karttik	same as Asar
Agrahayan	same as Jaishta
13–17	Sureshwar (Kalidas/Taradas)
18–19	Abhayapad Chakrabartty
Pous	same as Baishakh
Magh	same as Jaishta
Phalgun	same as Asar
Chaitra	same as Jaishta

Sola-ana-puja is a lineage organization of the succession and rotation according to the rule of sixteen system of traditional Bengali calculation. *Sola-ana* means sixteen *anas* or one rupee. In the ritual context, sixteen *anas* symbolize the unity of the ritual community, and at the same time, correspond to the total amount of the daily services of a whole year. In the culture of Bengali Hindus, the number sixteen is generally regarded as a symbol of totality, in particular in the ritual discourse. For example, the ritual of *sorashopacar-puja* is the most common ritual of offering performed by the Brahman-sebait, and it consists of sixteen steps for the ritual reception to deities. The offering of *adhibas* is an essential item in the marriage ceremony of Bengal, and it consists of sixteen ritual goods.[2] One *ana* was formerly equivalent to four *paisas*, and one *paisa* equal to three *pai*, or five *ganda*. On the other hand, one *ganda* is equal to four *kara*, and one *kara* is equal to three *kranti*. These calculations can be seen in Table 3.4.

The villagers state that the original founder was the holder of sixteen *anas*. This means that the right of the daily services of the temple over a whole year was inclusive. Every lineage of temple priests is supposed to have branched out from him. If a priest has two sons, they share the right of the ritual in halves and count both as holding eight *anas*. If these sons then have two sons each, the four grandsons will become the holders of four *anas* each and share one-fourth of the right over the temple ritual simultaneously. This means the duty to perform the ritual for three months out of a year. The total *anas* the temple priests hold respectively for the yearly ritual duties in the temple is always sixteen, or one rupee. The holders of the quota must be the heads of the lineages. After his death, the quota is divided again among his sons. The holder of this ritual quota is called *angshidar* in Bengali, literally, the holder of the quota (*angshadar*). For instance, the holders of the one-fourth right of the ritual, are called *char-ana-angshidar*.

As is shown in Table 3.3, each day in the calendar year is assigned to one of the priests of the nine lineages of the temple priest. This priest is naturally in possession of a certain quota corresponding to both his duty

TABLE 3.4: TRADITIONAL CALCULATION UNIT OF BENGAL

1 *rupee* = 16 *ana* = 64 *paisa*			
	1 *ana* = 4 *paisa* = 12 *pai*		
		= 20 *ganda* = 80 *kara* = 240 *kranti*	
			1 *kara* = 3 *kranti*

and right to the ritual of the temple on the specified days. The right and duty of every holder of the quota is always considered in connection with the total amount of temple service. This is the reason why the priests never miss their daily duty, in spite of the subdivision of the lineages of the priests for generations. In other words, it is an effective system to clarify who is in charge of the daily ritual on any specific day, and consequently to avoid conflict over the right of the service.

THE RIGHT AND THE OBLIGATION

The last unique point of this system is that the duty of the ritual is closely connected to the right of inheritance of the service lands according to this calculation system. The succession of right-over the ritual occurs at the same time as the inheritance of the service lands of the temple. It is the inheritance of the service lands that paradoxically ensures each temple priest a right to perform the ritual.

The service land is shared among nine lineages at present and the owner of the total area of service lands was the original priest of the temple ritual. He is accordingly called the holder of the *sola-ana-angshidar* (holder of the entire), and it is not only because he holds the right over the temple service, but because he is supposed to be the owner of the total service lands of the temple property. Consequently, if he handed over the service lands to his two sons, the sons would then become equal owners of half of the lands evenly, and share the rights in the ritual for everyday for half a year as well. Then, they are known as the holder of eight *ana*, as they both share equal ownership to the service lands and the rights over the ritual. In this way, if a son has inherited a certain quota of the ritual from his father, he in turn successes his father's right to a guaranteed number of fixed days to perform the ritual service, as well as the inheritance of the service lands within his father's possession. As a result, the descendants of the original priest share the service lands of the temple jointly, and this, as always, is tied up with the allocated right and duty to perform the temple daily service. It is, therefore, two sides of the same coin, the duty to perform the ritual of the temple and the rights over the inheritance are determined through the same calculation system. More detailed examinations of this succession rule will be given in Chapter 6 through an example of an Ugra-Kshatriya lineage regarding the rotation of their performance of Durgapuja.

The Rituals on the Days of *Sankranti*

Sankranti is the last day of the month. On the days of *sankranti*, a priest performs the ritual of the *baidik-hom* in the interior room of the main temple and goes around each household of the Ugra-Kshatriyas so as to give a *phonta* of the ash of the fire on their foreheads. In the evening of the *sankranti*, a ritual called *guya-dak* is performed at the altar (*guyabedi*) in the temple ground after the regular evening service for the goddess Jogadya.

VEDIC FIRE RITUAL

A member of the Bhattacaryya lineage living in the adjoining village of Nigan, who was endowed with the cakran land by the Maharaja for his duty, comes to the temple every *sankranti* day to perform the ritual of the *baidik-hom.* Besides these periodical performances of the fire ritual in the temple, the priest for the Vedic fire performs it twice at the a Jagyakund (the ritual stage for the Vedic fire at the pond Kshirdighi) during Jogadyapuja of Baishakh, although it is included in the ritual of every *sankranti* in the lunar month of Chaitra. This is an exclusive duty for the preist, who has special knowledge and experience of sacred verses (*mantras*) of the Vedic ritual in particular. The lineage of the priest in the Nigan village has succeeded to this duty of the temple for generations. The other priests in the Kshiragram village can perform the ordinary fire ritual on various occasions such as marriage ceremony and annual rituals. But, it is said that they follow the way of the tantric ritual (*tantra-hom*) using the tantric mantras, and never follow the way of the Vedic ritual.

In the early morning of every *sankranti*, a Baiti plays his drum announcing the day of the *sankranti.* After the daily service by the Brahman-sebait of the village on the day shift, the priest begins the fire ritual in the interior room of the temple. At first, he blows the conch-shell and purifies the central portion of the floor of the temple by the water of the river Ganga. He sets up a small altar with a few chips of the stone-apple tree on the floor, and pours *ghi* on it, and he lights a fire while chanting some mantras. Into the blazing fire, he throws 108 *bel* (stone apple) leaves dipped in butter one by one. In former times, the sacrifice of a goat used to be made. This sacrifice is recently done only on the day of the *sankranti* of Baishakh. After burning up the chips and the leaves, the priest gathers the black ashes into a vessel, and adds some butter again in order to make paste for the *phontas.* At first, he dedicates the *phonta* of the ashes to the goddess Jogadya putting it on the front wall of the interior room of the temple by his hand, next he puts ash on the foreheads of the Brahmans sitting around there, and then on the rest of the audience.

The priest then goes around each locality of the Ugra-Kshatriyas with the vessel in his hand. At first, he visits the locality of the Dattas and then the locality of the Samants. Next he visits the locality of the Chaudhuris which is composed of four lineages. Then, he visits further the localities of the Mallas, Joshs, Sanis, and the other localities where other Ugra-Kshatriyas of the village live in. In each house, the members of the family stand in a row at the courtyard or the veranda of their house to receive the (*phonta*) from the priest, making a deep *pranam* to the priest. The housewives also pay offerings to him. The contents of the offerings are usually rice, sweets, milk, and some vegetables, which they keep ready in their house shrines in the early morning. On his round in the village, the priest soon gathers too much to carry. Besides, he is treated cordially to tea and lunch by some families.

The prescribed duty of the priest for the fire ritual by the Bardhaman Maharaja includes this *phonta*-giving, to go around every family of the Ugra-Kshatriyas, and the fire ritual at the Jagyakund in the annual ritual. In the village, it is the verses of the *Yajurveda*, which the family priests of the Ugra-Kshatriyas follow for the rites of passages such as marriage and funerals for their patron families. The fire ritual held by the priest for the Vedic fire follows the *Yajurveda* too. On the other hand, the Brahmans in the village perform their rites of passage according to the verses of the *Samaveda*. This indiates that the monthly fire ritual is primarily practised for the village Ugra-Kshatriyas. The order in the *phonta*-giving for every lineage of the Ugra-Kshatriya has some defined pattern, which will be elaborated in the next chapter.

RITUAL CALLING

Ritual calling (*guya-dak*) is performed after the evening service on every *sankranti* at the courtyard of the temple. Immediately after the daily ritual, a Baiti walks back and forth seven times between the Natmandir (dance hall) and the *guyabedi*, a stone protuberant plinth at the south-western corner of the temple ground. He also plays on his drum with a specified rhythm of *danspahari*. A boy of the Malakar caste puts the goddess's copper pot filled with Ganga water on the altar. The Datta's representative brings the betel leaves and the tamarind nuts in his hand and stands in front of the altar. Many villagers also gather around.

The Malakar holds a betel leaf and a nut in his hand and raises his hands over the head. In the light rhythm of the drum, he turns around uttering loudly the following phrases:

Phopal mashaier guyo
Bharat Datta shas mallaber guyo
Eroyer aguri ke acho
Nasigramer aguri keu acho
Kusungramer aguri keu acho
Kurmuner aguri keu acho
Kolganyer acho
Majhi

After this calling, they return together to the temple with the drum playing, and then make a bow to the altar. The ritual of *guya-dak* is finished here. It is said that *Phopal mashai* is the chief of the Dom, and *Bharat Datta* is the chief of the Datta in Kshiragram. This belief is accepted by the villagers including the Brahman, and it is connected with the ritual fight called *domacoyarikhela* in the Jogadyapuja (discussed in the next chapter). All the following names referred in the ritual, viz., Eroya, Nasigram, Kusungram, Kurumun, and Kolgan, are the names of the villages which existed in the present Mangalkote block and the Bhatar block, in which the Ugra-Kshatriyas have been dominant for ages. As for the word of *Majhi*, someone think it is a calling to show the end of the ritual. Another think it means the name of the village of Majhigram in the Mangalkote block, where the Ugra-Kshatriya is dominated, and it is famous for the tmeple of the goddess Sakambhari (the goddess of crops).

The villagers suppose that the calling ritual of *guya-dak* is a vestige of the former local reign of the Datta Raj (Bharat Datta) who had a conference in the Kshiragram village every month summoning the chiefs from the different villages.

Ritual of Pulling up The Image from Pond (*ugalpuja*)

The only occasion for ordinary people to see the image of the goddess Jogadya in the whole year is during the Jogadyapuja at the Utthanmandir. Besides, the stone image of the goddess Jogadya is pulled out from the bottom of the pond of Kshirdighi to the bank for a little while six times in a year. These occasions are at midnight of the the ninth of the

TABLE 3.5: ROLE ASSIGNMENT IN *UGALPUJA*

Post	Role
Access to the image allowed	
Sabha-pandit	Director of the ritual organization
Brahman-sebait	Assistant priest, sacrificer of goat
Datta	Dedication of votive light and incense
	Preparation of offerings
Samant	Assistant for Datta, offerings
Chief servant	Setting of puja, guardian of the sacrifice
Dom	Dedication of flaming torch
Access to the image not allowed	
Patakadhari	Putting up the Maharaja's flags
Bara Ray (Chaudhuri)	Preparation for a rope
Other Ugra-Kshatriyas	Offering of goats
Mandal	Offering of straw for torch

month of Asar (*asar-nabami*), in the final day of Durgapuja (*bijaya-dasami*), the fifteenth of Paus (*paus-panera*), the seventh of Magh (*makari-saptami*), the twenty-ninth of Baishakh (*pathnaran*), and the fourth of Jaisshta (*abhishek*). It takes about an hour to install the temporary altar on the bank, and soon after the image is sent back to the bottom of the pond. Only a few members of each lineage can participate in the ritual.

The eligible lineages for this ritual are the Datta, Samant, Brahman-sebait, the chief servants of Bagdi (*mula-paik*), and the Dom. Although the lineages of the flag holder belongs to the Bagdi, the Chaudhuri, Mandal, and Malakar have sepcific roles. However, they are not allowed to stand in front of the image on the bank. They must wait behind the bank until the ritual is over. Among the Datta and the Samant, even unmarried men cannot approach the image, to say nothing of women. After their marriage, they must dedicate a goat to be sacrificed to the goddess at the altar at the time of their first participation in the ritual. Many of the Dattas and Samants put on the sacred thread to get on the altar on the bank. At ordinary times, the image of the goddess lies at the bottom of the pond. A red flag is set up to indicate the place where the image has sunk. Except for the days of the *ugalpuja* and the Jogadyapuja, nobody is allowed to approach the image under the water.

Table 3.5 gives the list of posts and roles in the *ugalpuja*. This system has basically the same pattern among the six rituals.

During nights of the ritual, a servant of Bagdi calls aloud (*ahban*) at the platform of the temple ground addressing the three titles three times as follows: *Datta masayra go, Samant masayra go, Domera go.* This mens 'Here goes, Sir Datta! Here goes, Sir Samant! Here goes, Dom!' At this, every member assembles on the banks of the pond, Dattas and the Samants bringing offerings for the goddess on plates in their hands. The contents of the offerings are mainly sun-dried rice (*atop-caul*), sweets, vegetables, and fruits. According to the season they also prepare particular items for the goddess, such as milk condensed by boiling, and jack-fruit (*kshir-kanthal*) in the month of Asar, dry sweetmeat of coconut (*narikel-naru*) in the final day of Durgapuja, and son on.

The servants of Bagdi lead the many goats to the altar on the bank for the sacrificial ritual to the goddess. The flag holders of the Bagdi stand by the Kshirdighi bank putting up the Maharaja's red flags. The particular lineages of the village and the Maharaja dedicate these goats for the sacrifice following the specified quota on each day of the *ugalpujas.* Private dedications are added to them.

The regular quota of each lineage in each *ugalpuja* are shown in Table 3.6. The total number of goats to be dedicated by each lineage and the Maharaja comes to forty-three in a year. The Maharaja is the biggest donor but three-fourths of the total is donated by the nine Ugra-Kshatriyas lineages. Although the Doms dedicate only once in the Jogadyapuja, they have the important role of sacrificing the goat for the goddess on the last day of the ritual.

Let us examine briefly the ritual process of the *ugalpuja* taking up an example in the day of *pathnaran.* First, the Dom illuminates the dark surface of the pond with flaming torches made of straw dedicated by the Mandals in the village the day before. That is called *mahagni* (great flame) in Bengali. At the sign of a flag put in the pond, the Brahman-sebait knows the place where the image of the goddess lies. They draw ropes tied to a small cart on which the stone image rests. The lineage of Bara Ray (Chaudhuri) dedicated the straw ropes for the *ugalpuja* before the day of *pathnaran* of Baishakh. The image is pulled out on the bank along with the cart. The Brahman-sebaits enshrine the image on the platform of the altar on the bank. They remove stains from the image, dedicate a floral wreath, votive lights, and incense. In front of the image, the *sabha-pandit* sits alone and performs a ritual for receiving the goddess without being accompanied by the reciter of sutras. After the ritual, they sacrifice the goats dedicated by the Maharaja, the Brahman, and the Ugra-Kshatriyas in turn. The chief servants of Bagdi hold down the goats in front of the altar. The Brahman-sebait has a sword in his hand

TABLE 3.6: ALLOTMENT OF SACRIFICES FOR *UGALPUJAS*

	Pa.N.	M.P.	J.4	A.9	B.10	P.15	M.7	Total
Maharaja		1		2	2	1	2	8
Brạhman							2	2
Datta				1	1		1	3
Samant				1	1		1	3
Malla				1	1		1	3
Sani				1	1		1	3
Ray				1	1		1	3
Bara Ray	1		1	1	1		1	5
Na Ray				1	1		1	3
Josh				1	1		1	3
Chota Samant				1	1		1	3
Chaudhuri				1	1		1	3
Dom		1						1
Total	1	2	1	12	12	1	14	43

Abbreviations:

	Date	Name
Pa.N.	29/Baishakh	*Pathnaran*
M.P.	31/Baishakh	*Mahapuja*
J.4	4/Jaishta	*Abhishek*
A.9	9/Asar	*Ugalpuja*
B.10	10/Durgapuja	*Bijaydasami*
P.15	15/Paus	*Ugalpuja*
M.7	7/Magh	*Makari-saptami*

and decapitates them. After the sacrifice, they send the image back to the bottom of the pond. The ordinary process of the *ugalpujas* ends here. The servants of Bagdi bring the sacrificed goats back and cut them up into pieces, which every member shares according to the custom. For example, the Brahman-sebait receive the heads of the goats, the person who sacrificed the goat gets the front legs, the meat of the bodies is for those who have dedicated the goats. Those dedicated in the name of the Maharaja are for the Brahman-sebait, and the rest are for the servants.

NOTES

1. Catak is about 60g, and 1 seer is about 16 catak.
2. J. Gonda discussed the dominance of the number 16 in Indian culture through the examination of various classical texts [Gonda 1985: 115–30].

CHAPTER 4

The Ritual of the Goddess Jogadya of the Maharaja

Jogadyapuja is the biggest of the village rituals, and a series of the rites associated with it are observed for more than a month. It is not only important as an annual ritual of the village, but an essential occasion to organize village society as caste groups and lineages. As a sacred centre of the sakta-pitha in this region, many people visit on the days of the ritual from the neighbouring villages. On the final day of the lunar month of Baishakh, the people's excitement reaches its peak at the sacrifice of buffalo dedicated by the Maharaja. Let us look into the ritual process of Jogadyapuja over one month, as it reveals the structure of the castes and lineages in the village through the ritual positions and roles.

THE THIRTY-FIRST OF CHAITRA: *KSHIRKALASI*

Kshirkalasi is the first step of the ritual of Jogadyapuja observed on the last day of Chaitra. This is a ritual of invocation of the goddess through a copper pot (in the narrow sense *kshirkalasi* means the pot itself) to the altar.[1] It involves all rituals observed on this day generally, though the pot is used continuously in the Jogadya temple over the whole month from this day till the 30th of the lunar month of Baishakh. The entire process of Jogadyapuja begins with it. In addition to it, the rituals at the end of every month, called the Vedic fire ritual (*baidik-hom*) and *guya-daks* as mentioned in Chapter 3, are held on this day. Chaitra is the last month of the year. Thus, the Jogadyapuja of Baishakh is the first occasion of the Bengali New Year in the village life as well as the biggest function.

RITUAL SETTING

The ritual starts on the Jagyakund (the ritual stage for the Vedic fire) at the fair ground to the east of the pond. On this occasion, the members who assemble around the altar are shown in Table 4.1. The *sabha-*

TABLE 4.1: ROLE ASSIGNMENT IN *KSHIRKALASI*

Post	Name	Role
Director of the ritual organization	*Sabha-pandit*	Assistant to the priest
Vedic priest	*Baidik-purohit*	Priest of the Vedic fire ritual
Chief priest	*Pradhan-purohit*	Chief priest of the rituals of the pot
Brahman-sebait	Brahman-sebait	Priests
Malakar	Malakar	Preparing for the goddess's pot and basket
Ugra-Kshatriya	Kshatriya	Representatives of the nine lineages of the Ugra-Kshatriyas
Flag holder	*Patakadhari*	Holding of the Maharaja's flags
Drummer	*Badyakar*	Drummers for the sacrifice
Bagdi Servant	*Paik*	Guardians of the sacrifice
Karmakar	Karmakar	Sacrificer

pandit functions as the assistant to the priest who supervizes all the temple priests and other personnel. The *pradhan-purohit* performs the *puja* for the pot. A Malakar brings the goddess's pot and a basket with materials of the ritual in it. The positions assigned to caste groups are ranked and collectively organized for the sacrifice. The table gives the mutual relationships.

All members must observe a regular fast (*upos*) from the morning and come after ablution. It is the period of strict abstinence and discipline for priests, the Malakar, and representatives of the Dattas and Samants. Only they are allowed to ascend the Jagyakund. The relationship of the *pradhan-purohit* and the *sabha-pandit* can be understood as the same relationship between a priest (*pujari*) who invokes deities through a ritual pot by the various steps of ritual procedure (*upacara-puja*) and an assistant priest (*tantradharak*) who supports him by chanting *mantras*. Only the *bradhan-purohit* can approach the goddess's *kshirkalasi* during the Jogadyapuja, just as only the priest *pujari* can approach the pot on the altar directly during the steps of *upacara-puja*.

The priest who belongs to Bhattacharyya lineage in the village Nigan can light the Vedic fire on the Jagyakund. None of the priests in Kshiragram can perform this fire ritual, only the tantric fire ritual (*tantra-hom*). For that reason, the Bardhaman Maharaja endowed cakran lands to the Bhattacaryya lineage in Nigan, specifically for this duty. On the last day of every lunar month (*sankranti*), a priest of the lineage comes to the Jogadya temple in Kshiragram to perform the Vedic fire and then gives *phonta* to all the Ugra-Kshatriyas. The fire ritual of Chaitra on the platform of Jagyakund is also considered a part of the monthly rites on the days of *sankranti*.

On the platform of the Jagyakund, representatives of the Dattas and Samants have to put on the sacred thread, usually considered exclusive to the Brahmans. This thread is a little smaller in diameter than those used by ordinary Brahmans. However, just as with the Brahmans, while they wear it they may not plough their fields and must observe regular abstinence. It used to be customary for the Ugra-Kshatriya in the village to put on the sacred thread even in their daily life, but few do so now. Nevertheless, they still wear it on the specified occasions such as marriage ceremonies or funerals. This sacred thread is also worn during all days of Jogadyapuja of Baishakh in particular by the representatives of the Ugra-Kshatriyas.

The Malakar is in charge of preparation of the utensils for the ritual and is the only rather low caste permitted to ascend the platform among the various service castes such as the Bagdi and the Dom. The Bagdi (*mulapaik*) prepares animals for sacrifice and they are admitted to stand in front of the image of the goddess at the bank of the pond during every *ugalpuja*. The Bagdi flag holder (*patakadhari*) holds the red flags of the Maharaja around the platform during the sacrifice. The villagers regard these flags as a symbol of the sovereignty of the Bardhaman Raj.

RITUAL PROCESS

At the beginning of the ritual, a Malakar brings the goddess's copper water pot to the altar. All the members who are assigned duties of the ritual receive a garland from him and wear it around their neck. These garlands are made of special flowers (*togal-phul*) and mango leaves. The chief priest puts the goddess's pot on a base of earth and unhulled rice. After a ritual purification of himself, the priest utters the name of the patron, the Maharaja of Bardhaman, and his *gotra*. The present patron is Pranay Chand Mahatab Tratri Barman, and his *gotra* is Kashyap. Then, the priest starts to perform a ritual invitation to the deity to the pot as the same context in ordinary *puja*.[2]

After that, the servants of Bagdi (*paiks*) drag a male goat to the platform after taking it for ablution to a pond. The priest purifies the goat and the sword for sacrifice with sacred water on the platform. Then, the *paiks* bring it again in front of the platform, and hold the head and the feet of the goat firmly. The Baiti beats a drum hard. The Karmakar holds the sword up, and, with the deep sound of a drum, decapitates the goat. The servants of Bagdi bring the body of the goat to the altar immediately. Spouting blood from the beheaded body is poured on to a peeled banana on an earthen plate. A blooded banana means that the goddess has accepted the animal. In a moment, the Vedic priest prepares a fire ritual (*hom*) on the fireplace of the platform, and lights a fire. He throws *ghi* and mango leaves repeatedly into the fire with sacred verses. The ash is then gathered and mixed with *ghi.* In the end, the priest gives *phonta* of the ash on foreheads of all present.

A ritual procession of *kshirkalasi* sets out from the Jagyakund to the Jogadya temple. The first day of Jogadyapuja, as already stated, is in the last day of the lunar month of Chaitra. This day is also the final day of Gajan (i.e. *carakpuja*, a folk ritual of rural Bengal observed at the end of Chaitra). Then, the ritual ascetics (*sanyasins*) of the Gajan ritual lead this procession, dancing in step. The servants of Bagdi hoist their flags and follow them. The Baiti plays his drum in the procession. The Karmakar lifts his bloody sword up in the line. The priest puts the goddess's pot on the head of the Dattas' representative. The goddess's pot on the head of the Datta occupies the central position of the procession. The chief priest, the director of the ritual organization, and the other Brahman-sebaits follow. The representatives of the Ugra-Kshatriyas, the other service castes and all other participants accompany them.

The procession proceeds along the southern side of the temple and enters through the eastern gate. The Datta lays the pot on a stone plinth (*ganes-mund*), which is at the foot of the eastern wall of the temple. The goddess's pot on the plinth is surrounded by the participants and the director proclaims to the assemblage the commencement of the Jogadyapuja of Baishakh; 'The goddess's great ritual has come. Perform all rituals according to the custom, and accomplish the ritual of Devi Jogadya!' Then the Datta enshrines the pot on the goddess's throne.

In the evening, a Brahman-sebait performs the usual evening ritual service (*sandhyarati*) and then pours water from the pot into another copper pot used in the temple. The representative of the Datta puts the empty pot on his head and brings it again to the Jagyakund with a Brahman-sebait and a Baiti beating a drum. On the platform of the Jagyakund, the Brahman-sebait performs his ritual service to the pot. They return to the temple again soon. Then they start a ritual at a stone protuberant plinth (*guyabedi*) on the ground of the temple, with ritual *guya-dak.* Finally, the pot filled with the water of Kshirdighi is left on the throne inside the temple for a whole month of Baishakh. The

Brahman-sebaits perform the ritual service to the pot twice a day (*nityaseba* and *sandhyarati*). Except in the month of Baishakh, there is nothing else to symbolize the goddess on the altar inside the temple.

RITUAL ORDER

At the end of the fire ritual, the priest calls each title by turn for the *phonta*. The first title is the Brahman-sebait and the other Brahmans. Next comes the Ugra-Kshatriya. The priest calls nine titles of the Ugra-Kshatriyas in the village, in a specific order. The order of the nine titles is Datta, Samant, Malla, Sani, Ray, Josh, Chota-Ray, Chota-Samant, and Chaudhuri. This order repeats in the various rituals in which the nine lineages of the Ugra-Kshatriya participate. He offers the *phontas* to the Datta and the Samant who are sitting on the platform. Then, addressing each title in this order, the priest gives the *phontas* to the representatives of the other lineages who are fasting for this ritual and waiting around the Jagyakund.

The other service castes such as the Malakar, *paiks* and *batakadhari*, the Baiti, and the Karmakar also receive the *phontas*. As no Brahman priest can offer the sacred marks directly by his hand to the foreheads of Untouchables (that is called usually *chota-lok* in Bengali), he gives the vessel to the Malakar on the platform to do so. The Malakar is not included among *chota-lok*, but is like a Shudra in the village. Strictly speaking he belongs to one of the nine craftsman castes (*naba-shakh*) of Bengal, and its ritual position in the caste ranking is usually regarded as a medium status between the Shudra and the Kshatriya in the ideal *varna* system.

The status groups in the *phonta* giving ritual are, therefore, first divided into two categories, namely *phonta*-giver and *phonta*-receiver, and secondly the order among the *phonta*-receiver. The village priest performs the dedication to the goddess (*upacara-puja*) and the fire ritual. But, the Vedic fire is monopolized by the *baidik-purohit* of Nigan. They give *phontas* to the Ugra-Kshatriyas exclusively. The Malakar gives it to the other service castes.

THE FOURTEENTH OF BAISHAKH: *JAL-ANA*

On the day before *lagna-utsab* (the fifteenth of Baishakh), people go to the Hugli at the town of Katwa to draw the sacred water of the Ganga. It is 22 km distant from the village to Katwa. People start from the village at midnight. In former days, they would go to Katwa by foot, draw water, and return early the next morning. Nowadays, they go only one way on foot. However, it takes still a whole night to return from Katwa. Accordingly, they think it still a hard penance not suitable for anyone but the young.

People carry a pole on their shoulder suspending small pots at both ends. During the course of their walking, they are forbidden to put the pots with the sacred Ganga water down on the ground. They must walk all the way by foot and never take rest anywhere. If they need to urinate, they must put the pole on the branches of a tree. During the whole night, they abstain from food and water. Because of the severity of this practice, it is the younger generation at present that participates in it for the most part. Recently, the participants count around twenty. People say that women and the elderly generation, used to do this practice and the number of such devotees counted more than one hundred from the village.

THE FIFTEENTH OF BAISHAKH: *LAGNA-UTSAB*

The word *lagna* means 'auspicious moment' or 'time', and astrologically it means the time of the sun's transition to a zodiacal sign. The ritual called *lagna-utsab*, therefore, means the 'ritual of time' in brief. An almanac of the Bengal lunar calendar for the new year (*panjika*) plays an important role in the ritual. After the *lagna-utsab*, people start to read new calendars in their houses. In this manner, 'time' is a main theme of the ritual. On the day of *lagna-utsab*, the Baitis play a pair of drums (*madal*), in the place of the ordinary drum of the evening ritual (*sandhyarati*) in everyday use. The special artisans who belong to the Muci caste in the village Baici and the village Gobardhanpur make the pair of drums for this ritual once a year. The Maharaja of Bardhaman granted them cakran lands for this duty. A few days before *lagna-utsab*, they come and stay at the small cottage situated at the square in front of the Jogadya temple and sit on seats of date palm leaves.

This continues for two weeks from the day of *lagna-utsab* to the thirtieth day of Baishakh to use the drums in the temple. After the sacrifice of buffalo of the Mahapuja on the final day of Baishakh, the Baitis bring the *madal* to the special place in the north-west fringe of the village and break the drums into pieces. For two weeks, the Baitis play them on particular occasions such as *sandhyarati*, *guya-dak*, and the *mayurnac* at the temple, and they have specified rhythms to play on them. In the early morning of *lagna-utsab*, a Baiti walks slowly from his residence to the temple playing a drum to announce the beginning of the ritual for all the villagers. That is called *tengai.* A Baiti performs it five times during the day between the residence and the temple, and the last *tengai* in the afternoon means the beginning of *lagna-utsab*. The Dom caste of the village makes a bamboo basket (*jhuri*) and dedicates it to the altar of the temple in the morning. Basket making once a year by the Dom caste is one of their duties. For this duty, they are also granted cakran lands by the Maharaja. The Brahman-sebaits put sweets (*manda*) and parched rice (*murki*) in the basket, which are donated by the Maharaja. Bangles of conch-shell and vermilion (*sindur*) donated by the lineage of Sureswar Chakrabartti are also placed therein. They also offer a mango and its leaf, red pigment a floral wreath, turmeric, and a piece of silk with the basket on the altar. A cloth coated with turmeric covers them.

In the ground of the temple the representative of the Datta lineage puts a bamboo basket on his head. The other participants form a procession before and behind him. The composition of the procession is seen in Table 4.2.

The head of the line is the representative of the Samant's lineage, who sprinkles sacred water for purification with a mango twig from a small vessel. The second is the scattering of sun-dried rice by the Brahman-sebait of the Sureswar Chakrabartti lineage. The third is the Datta representative with the basket. Then, a Malakar moves blowing a conch-shell and Baitis play their drums. In the last of the line, seven servants of the Bagdi caste holding seven red flags follow them. The procession goes round the main temple anti-clockwise seven times, is called *pradakshin.* Next, all members sit inside the temple and there the new calendar is proclaimed by the Grahacarya (astrologer).

In the interior of the main temple, the director of the ritual organization, the Grahacarya, and the Malakar take a seat on the left of the altar.

TABLE 4.2: ROLE ASSIGNMENT IN *LAGNA-UTSAB*

Post	Role
Samant	Sprinkling water for purification
Brahman-sebait (Sureswar Chakrabartti)	Scattering sun-dried rice
Datta	Carrying the bamboo basket
Malakar	Blowing conch-shell
Baiti	Playing drum
Bagdi (*Patakadhari*)	Holding seven Maharaja's flags

The Brahman-sebait belonging to the lineage of Sureswar Chakrabartti, the Datta's representative, and the Samant's representative sit on the right. Both sides face one another. Baitis and drum makers wait outside the Natmandir. The servants of Bagdis holding the raja's flags remain standing in the ground of the temple.

The Brahman-sebait performs the ritual in an ordinary way to the goddess's pot on the altar. Then, the Grahacarya starts to chant *mantras* holding an almanac of the new year calendar. Grahacarya comes from a Brahman family in Jobagram and Nigan in order to proclaim the new calendar at the Jogadya temple once a year. For this duty, the Maharaja granted cakran lands for them. After announcement of the calendar by the Grahacarya, all members present bow down to the almanac in his hand three times. Then the Grahacarya announces auspicious times written in the new calendar before the members inside the temple. He gives blessings by holding the almanac up to the foreheads of each member. The Brahman-sebait then, puts *phontas* on each forehead with yellow paste of turmeric. The Datta's representative puts the basket again on his head and comes out, accompanying the other members. With the sound of drums playing, all members assemble at the small stone altar (*guyabedi*) at the south-western corner of the temple ground. Many villagers awaiting there surround them. The Grahacarya stands in front of the *guyabedi* and proclaims again the auspicious time prescribed in the new year calendar twice in front of the villagers. This is the first occasion in a year to show the new calendar to the public. Formerly, the calendar was written on many pages of palm leaves, which was sent from the deb-seba-office of the court of Raj of Bardhaman every year. At the end of the ritual, the Grahacarya used to distribute this palm-leaf-almanac to the villagers. Every villager around him rushed to get the palm leaves.

Nowadays, the Grahacarya merely reads a new calendar at the altar. The Datta carries the basket on his head and the Brahman-sebait stands beside him. Then, the seven *paiks,* who are standing in a line opposite the Datta, dedicate their flags to the basket on the head of the Datta with the particular rhythm of the drum. The new calendar which the Grahacarya proclaims before people is still sent from the deb-seba-office of the court of Raj in a printed almanac (the *Gupta Press Dairektari Panjika*). Every social function of the village was performed according to the times as being auspicious or inauspicious in the almanac. After the popularization of the printed almanacs from Kolkata, anyone can refer to their ritual times. People in the village, however, keep to the old custom even now and they never open the almanacs of the new year before the day of *lagna-utsab*. Although a new year actually begins on the first day of the lunar month of Baishakh (*bangla-san*), people can read their new almanac only after the proclamation of the new year by the Grahacarya.

The Twenty-seventh of Baishakh: *Jagyakund*

After the fire ritual (*hom*) of the first day of Jogadyapuja on the last day of Chaitra, the Vaidik priest (*baidik-purohit*) performs the fire ritual for the second time on the twenty-seventh of Baishakh at the Jagyakund. The participants at the altar are the same as before. The chief priest invites the deity to the pot and burns fire on the altar. The representatives of the nine Kshatriya lineages and the other participants receive the *phontas* of the ash on their foreheads in the same order. The difference from the previous fire ritual at the end of Chaitra is that the bamboo-basket, which the Dom made and dedicated on the day of *lagna-utsab*, is offered in front of the altar. Besides, the Baitis play the drums in the place of the ordinary drum, and ritual calling by drum (*tengai*) from the Baiti's house to the Jagyakund occurs seven times on this day. Previously, the Karmakar used to slay a goat on this day also, which has gone into disuse since 1954.

In the procession from the Jagyakund to the temple, the Datta puts the basket on his head which is covered with a cloth (*gamcha*). The representative of the Samant puts the pot this time on his head. The priests, the Baitis, and the Bagdis are the same as before. But in place of the *sanyasins* dance of the Gajan, the holders of the Maharaja's flags of the Bagdi pay respect to the Maharaja with their flags by means of dedication to the basket on the Datta's head on their way. This is the same gesture with the dedication of the flags on the day of *lagna-utsab*. The procession stops to dedicate the flags seven times at the specified places on the passage to the temple. The Baitis play drums to the dedication of the flags by the Bagdis. Thus, we see that the ritual of the first day and of the twenty-seventh have a common pattern in the procession, *pradakshin*, sacrifice, and fire ritual. The course of the processions from the Jagyakund to the temple is the same as on the first day. In the procession on this day, they perform the dance of the peacock at the same place of the dedication of the flags on the first day.

When the procession arrives at the southern wall of the temple, the reciter of the *Ramayana* (*Ramayanapathak*) comes out from the temple and dedicates his small brush (*camar*) to the basket. At the foot of the southern wall, a small hole was made to look into the altar of the temple from outside. The Datta's representative and priests stand here at the back of the hole in the wall. Towards the basket on the Datta's head the Bagdis dedicate the flags again, and the reciter of the *Ramayana* chants a stanza. At night, he begins the recitation of the *Ramayana* at the Natmandir of the temple. The *Ramayana* which he sings with his performances and drum playing is a famous version translated by Krittibas Ojha into Bengali. During the four evenings from the twenty-seventh to the thirtieth of Baishakh, he recites the part of killing of Mohiraban. After this the procession enters the eastern gate of the temple and proceeds to the foot of the eastern wall of the temple. The Samant lays the pot down. It is the second assembly (*paramarsa*) by the members of the fire ritual at the Jagyakund. The director of the organization proclaims, 'The time of the great festival has come. Let's prepare carefully and receive visitors warmly!' The Datta pours the water of the pot into another copper pot on the throne inside the temple.

After the evening ritual, the reciter of the *Ramayana* reads the *Jogadya-bandana* and then the *Ramayana* of Krittibas. Incense, lights, and the sword for animal sacrifice are offered before him. He recites the *Ramayana* here with gestures and the accompaniment of a drum. It takes approximately three hours every night. After the recitation, every member of the fire ritual gather again in front of the Jagyakund. They make a procession again and perform the peacock dance on the way to the temple. Many villagers think it as a part of entertainment for the goddess. This performance, however, has no relation with on appearance of the peacock, and is really not so entertaining. Rather its gestures are a little odd and eccentric.

The Datta puts on a crown made of *shola* grass (sponge wood) and stands in front of the flag holders of the Bagdis. According to the drums playing by Baitis and the dedication of the flags by the Bagdis, he raises his right hand and foot sideways, and shakes them in a strange way. Then, he makes an upright position again, and then raises the left hand and foot in the same manner. He repeats this movement three times, and finally jumps up straight. In this strange dance, some villagers find vestiges of an ancient custom of human sacrifice. They think the movements of Datta indicate the manners of a man struggling against a sacrificial stake. Datta performs the dance of peacock to the last day of the Mahapuja four times on various occasions. They accordingly suppose that a man to be sacrificed was captured and detained on the stake for four days and was taken about on the street of the village every night in the same course of *mayurnac*. On the last day of Baishakh, the sacrifice used to take place, which is substituted by a buffalo now.

The Twenty-eighth of Baishakh: *Ramayanpath*

On the twenty-eighth of Baishakh, the recitation of the *Ramayana* is about the killing of Ravan and return of Rama. From the twenty-eighth to the thirtieth the offering of boiled rice (*annabhog*) to the goddess at noon is stopped and flour-puff (*luci*) is offered instead. People think that the goddess observes her fast during the three days. As the killing of Ravan is in recitation for these days, out of the grief of the goddess from the death of the demon Ravan, she abstains from eating rice for three days. After the recitation the dance of the peacock is again performed.

The Twenty-ninth of Baishakh: *Pat-naran*

The ritual of *pat-naran* is one of the rituals for pulling up the image of Jogadya from the Kshirdighi and a preliminary ritual for the Mahapuja on the day after as well. The Mahapuja is the only occasion for ordinary people of the village to see the image of the goddess. In this *pat-naran*, the Brahman-sebaits cleanse the image, dedicate offerings, and sink it again to the bottom of the pond to a near by place to facilitate pulling out of it easily on the day of the Mahapuja.

In the morning of the *pat-naran*, a member of the Chakrabartti lineage from Narashana brings offerings to the temple (rice, mango, fish, etc.). At noon, a lineage member of Ray dedicates a male goat for sacrifice and straw rope for the ritual. They receive the offering (*anna-bhog*) at noon at the Bhogmandir but never attend the ritual in the night. In the same way as previously a recitation of the *Ramayana* is performed after the evening service at the Natmandir. The villagers offer huge piles of rice and vegetables on the floor of the Natmandir. These offerings are dedicated for Lakshman, because the recitation of the *Ramayanapath* falls on the chapter of Lakshman's banquet on this night.

After the recitation, a servant of the Bagdi call the names of the main three lineages in a loud voice from the eastern stage of the temple. He calls: *Datta mahasayera go, Samant mahasayera go, Domera go*. This ritual calling is performed over again in the other rituals of pulling up the image (*ugal-pujas*). The member for the *pat-naran* is the representative of the Datta, Samant, and other lineages of the Ugra-Kshatriyas, the lineage of the Dom, the Bagdi flag holders (*patakadhari*), the chief servants of the Bagdi (*mulapaik*), the director of the ritual organization *sabha-pandit*, and the other Brahman-sebaits. The Brahman-sebaits pull the ropes of the image. The flag holders of Bagdi hold the Raja's flags, but after the installation of the image, they leave the place of worship. Only *mulapaik* can remain to guard the sacrifice. The Brahman-sebaits cleanse it and purify it with turmeric and *ghi* and dedicate a floral garland. The *sabha-pandit* himself worships it. The Datta and the Samant keep incense and votive lights ready. The Dom burns the straw torch during the ritual. It takes nearly an hour to finish all the ritual. In the end, the goats dedicated by the Ray and the Maharaja are sacrificed in front of the image and then they sink the image again to the bottom of the pond attached with ropes. The Datta subsequently performs the dance of peacock for the third time from the Jagyakund to the temple.

THE THIRTIETH OF BAISHAKH: *HAL-NAGAL*

On the day before the Mahapuja on the last day of Baishakh, the fire ritual was performed for the third time and a pair of bulls plough the fields of the village. This ritual ploughing makes a round of the village. A Baiti plays his drum to inform the beginning the ritual (*tengai*), and this ritual notification for villagers is repeated nine times from the early morning to the afternoon. Then, the members of the fire ritual assemble around the Jagyakund and practice the ritual in the same manner as before. They sacrifice a male goat in the name of the Maharaja, and the priests give ashes of the fire to the foreheads of all the members in order. On this day, a *paik* belonging to the Khara lineage newly joins the members, and gets a garland around his neck. He has the duty to drive the bulls with a traction plough. There is a pot of the goddess on the altar instead of the Dom's basket.

After the fire ritual, they form a procession to the temple again. The Datta carries the pot on his head and puts it down at the foot of the wall of the temple. Here, the *sabha-pandit* proclaims the Mahapuja on the next day for the third time. Then the Datta brings the pot into the temple, and pours water into it. The foregoing is nearly the same procedure as the previous two, but this time the ritual ploughing is performed after that. The Datta returns once to his house to take rest for a while. At this time, a *paik* carries him on his shoulders and two other *paiks* flying Maharaja's flags lead him to the house. A Baiti playing his drum also follows them. In the courtyard of the Datta's house, many villagers are already gathered. While he takes rest, his family serves chickpea beans (*chola*) soaked in water, fruits, and vegetables to everyone gathered there. He puts on a piece of cloth coated with turmeric, and returns to the temple on the servant's shoulder again. On the temple ground, a crowd waits. A Brahman-sebait belonging to the lineage of Kailas Chakrabartti brings the pot enshrined in the temple to the veranda of the Bhogmandir. He stands on the veranda and sprinkles water from the pot with a mango twig over the crowd. Then he hands over the pot to the Datta when he returns to the temple. The Datta himself starts to sprinkle water over the villagers. It causes an excitement among the people. Soon, a pair of bulls arrive at the temple led by a few servants of Bagdi belonging to the Khara lineage. Most of the Bagdi boys are intoxicated and begin to go around the building of the temple seven times. The drummers beat their drums vigorously, and follow them. Finally, they set out from the temple through the eastern gate.

The Datta sprinkling water from the pot takes the lead of the procession. The Bagdis holding the flags and the Baitis with drums follow him. A few Bagdi boys drag a pair of bulls. The head of the Bagdi lineage Khara brings a plough on his shoulders. This plough is made of a *bel* tree. In the morning, the Karmakar from Jabagram has made it in the ground of the temple from a specified *bel* tree. The procession marches along the main street of the village to the Utthan-mandir. In front of the house of the Ugra-Kshatriya belonging to the lineage of Josh, the pair of bulls stand and wait on the street. The Brahman-sebait puts garlands around the bulls' necks, and vermilion on their foreheads. The Bagdi head of the Khara lineage joins the plough to the bulls. Then, the ritual tillage starts from this place. They go round the exterior of the village tracing the old road of which some parts are now turned into agricultural fields. (Map 4.6 shows the route of the procession of *hal-nagal.*) The procession goes ahead to the Utthanmandir and passes by it to the locality of Mallapukur-para, and Das-para. On both sides of the street, village women dressed in fine saris make a deep bow on the ground to the procession. The Datta sprinkles the sacred water from the goddess's pot over them. The *paiks* come later with the bulls and the plough. It is believed that even barren women could become pregnant by blessing of the sacred water.

In each locality of the village people rush to the plough and the bulls to touch them. The route is a round of the village perimeter. Therefore, it includes many localities of the lower castes such as the Bagdi, the Muci, and the Dom as shown in Map 4.1. From the house of Josh-para, they pass by Utthanmandir, and Mallapukur-para, and then, the

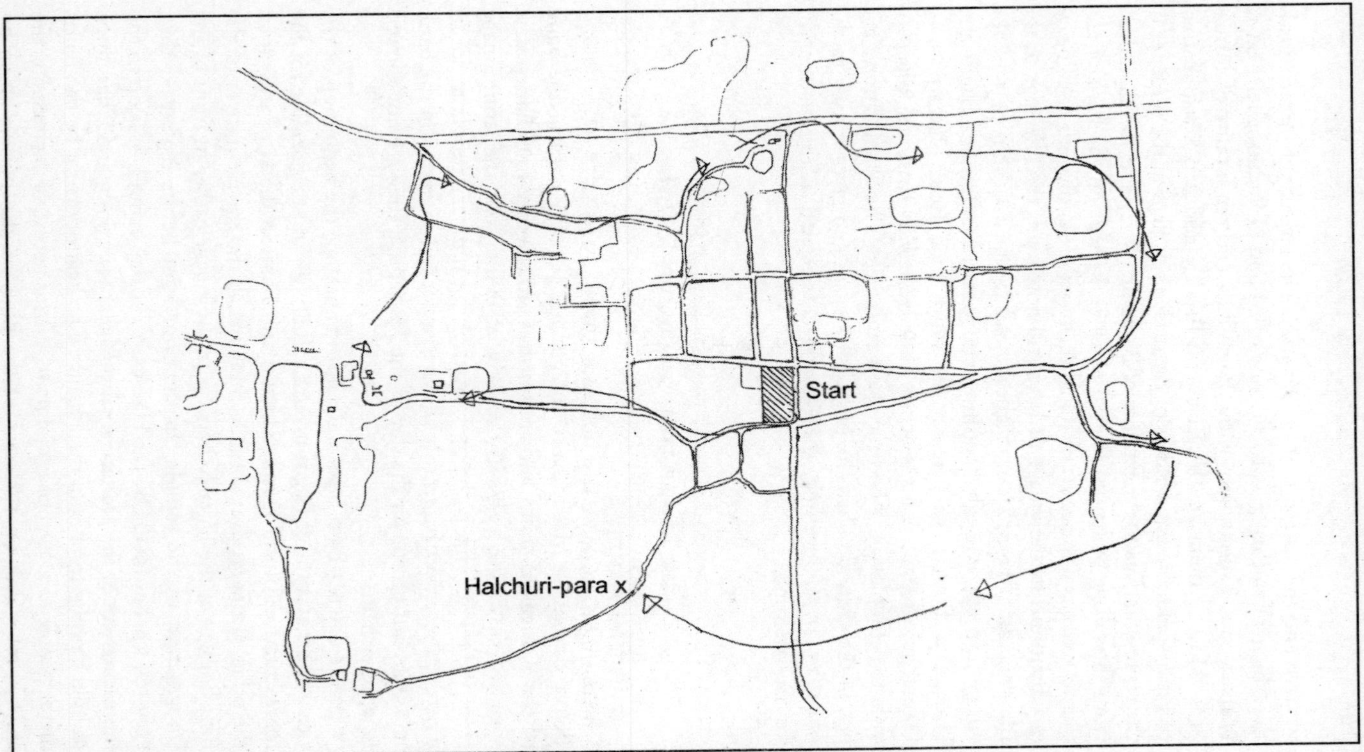

Map 4.1: The Procession Course of *Hal-nagal*

western and the eastern part of Das-para. The residents here are mostly the Muci. Then they pass by the side of a pond of Pudipshaher next to Manasa-para, Durgodighi of the Bagal-para and the locality of Purba-para. Most of them are the Kusmethi Bagdi's residence. On the street of Purba-para, the flag holders of Bagdi fly their flags in the presence of the representatives of the families of Bandyopadhyay and Raychaudhuri from the village of Ittya. (They used to be present on the back of elephants sent from the court of Raj at the town of Bardhaman.) A lineage of Chaudhuri in the village of Ittya still now sends the offerings to the Bhogmandir. The procession goes ahead to the southern part of the village and cut through Dakshin-para, where the Tetuliya Bagdi and Dom live. Finally, they reach the south road from Datta-para to Damacpukur-para. This place is called *halchuti-para*, the place to unfasten the plough. The procession ends here. The Datta throws the pot to the ground. Then, he picks it up again and gives it back to the *bhandari*. In the evening, the *Ramayana* is recited at the Natmandir for the last time.

THE THIRTY-FIRST OF BAISHAKH: THE MAHAPUJA OF THE GODDESS JOGADYA

THE UTTHANMANDIR

Before dawn, the Mahapuja of the goddess Jogadya starts at the bank of the Kshirdighi pond and it continues for twenty-four hours. The specified castes are assigned the duty of pulling out the stone image from the pond. This is the only occasion for ordinary people to see it. There are seven occasions to pull out the image (*ugalpuja*) on the bank in a year, but except on the day of the Mahapuja, they are not allowed to approach it.

Before dawn a Baiti beats a drum to announce the beginning of the ritual and a servant of Bagdi make a calling (*ahban*) to assemble for the representatives of the Datta, Samant, and Dom in the same way as in the other *ugalpujas*. But actually this time all the representatives of the nine lineages of the Ugra-Kshatriyas in the village gather in front of the Bhogmandir of the temple. In the poor light before daybreak, they light ten torches (made by the Hari caste the day before). It is up to the representatives of the Datta, Samant, Malla, Sani, Josh, and Chaudhuri to hold flaming torches in their hands. The beat of drums by the Baitis drives people to a level of excitement. In this course of excitement, the chief priest stands on the stage of the Bhogmandir, purifies them by sacred water, and refers to the titles of each Ugra-Kshatriya. The order of calling the titles is the same as on the occasion of the fire ritual (*hom*) at the Jagyakund. Then, he gives *phontas* of red marks of vermilion to their foreheads after calling each of the titles in this order. Everyone sets out for the bank of Kshirdighi where the image of the goddess is pulled out. The Karmakar holds the sword, the servants of Bagdi fly the flags and drag goats, and the Dom carries torches of straw. They follow the Ugra-Kshatriya and the Brahman-sebaits in a procession. The spectacle filled with excitement is like a scene of soldiers marching to battle through the fields.

Those who haul the ropes of the cart on, which the image of the goddess is placed, are the Datta, the Samant, the Malla, the Sani, the Josh, and the Chaudhuri. At the bank of the Kshirdighi pond, the image on the cart rests for a while. During this time, a Brahman-sebait sacrifices the goats by his hand, which the Datta and the Chaudhuri dedicated to the goddess. The Datta brings the decapitated bodies of the goats and pours the blood onto the image with sugar, sweets, and a little wine. The Brahman-sebaits sit on the cart with the image. The cart is pulled by the people until it reaches the Utthanmandir. The image is then enshrined on the altar of the Utthanmandir and unveiled to everyone. The villagers rush to the altar of the Utthanmandir to worship the goddess and women in particular dedicate bangles of iron, conch-shell, and vermilion. The Utthanmandir is situated at a little higher place, and someone brings water of the pond and pours it onto a slope of earth in front of the Utthanmandir. Those who are deeply touched throw themselves on the slippery, muddy slope. This way of showing devotion to the goddess is called *satyarangada*. In the meantime, the Brahman-sebaits, the Datta, and the *paiks* perform the dance of the peacock. Then, they perform *domacoyarikhela* in the temple.

THE RITUAL FIGHT BETWEEN DOM AND BRAHMAN: *DOMACOYARIKHELA*

Domacoyarikhela is a ritual fight between the Brahman and the Dom and between the Brahman and the Ugra-Kshatriya. At daybreak the chief priest, the Datta, the Samant, and the Dom assemble in the ground of the temple. At first, the Dom's representative raises bamboo sticks in both hands over the chief priest's head at the door of the main temple. The priest receives them by iron swords crossed in both hands. In the playing of *madal*, the Dom raises his sticks again and again over the priest. They step back from the door to the eastern gate of the temple in the course of the fight and return to the front of the door again. Finally, the Dom puts down his sticks on the ground and makes a deep bow (*pranam*) to the foot of the chief priest standing in front of the door of the temple. It is supposed by villagers that the *pranam* means the surrender of the fighter Dom to the Brahman. Then, the Dom brings out a date palm leaf fan and uses it for the priest. In this way, they take rest for a while.

Next is the Datta and the chief priest. He holds bamboo sticks in both hands and gets ready to attack the priest. On the slow rhythm of the drum, he slashes over the priest's head, and the priest receives it by his iron sword. Finally, the priest defeats the Datta. He puts down the sticks and makes a deep bow to his foot. The third is the Samant and the priest. He performs a mock fight and surrenders to the priest in the same way. In the end, the Dom serves his fans for the Datta and the Samant also.

THE MAHAPUJA

There is an old temple at the bank of Kshirdighi near the place where the image of the goddess is placed under water. The building is very old, and the roof and parts of the wall are already destroyed. The altar of this temple is the place of the initial rituals of the Mahapuja to the goddess in the morning, at the end of Baishakh. The people prepare the ritual putting vermilion on the altar and spread a canopy over it. A procession comes from the Jogadya temple. The flag holders enclose the altar, and the Malakar draws water of Kshirdighi with a pot and dedicates it to the altar. A number of priests sit in front of the altar: five priests and five reciters (*tantradharak*). Other villagers surround them, carrying the plates of offerings. After they enshrine the pot at the altar, the priests dedicate special offerings for the goddess such as bangles of iron and conch shell, and vermilion. The chief priest starts a ritual of sixteen steps, and the other five reciters chant the sacred verses of the Candi. After the ritual, the *paiks* prepare a block of sacrifice in front of the temple, and bring a goat to the altar, which was dedicated by the Maharaja.

The Maharaja goat is guarded by the *paiks* for a few days. They put the goat into the pond initially to make it an ablution and bring to the altar. The chief priest scatters the sacred water over it and chants a sacred verse. The sword for sacrifice is also dedicated to the altar and receives a blessing from the priest. The *paiks* bring the goat to the block and fix its head and hold the legs. The Baitis start to beat the drums and the chief priest chants a sacred verse into the ear of the goat. After sprinkling water over the goat, the Karmakar swings the sword downward. The decapitated head is brought to the altar quickly and poured the blood on to peeled bananas on a plate. The body of the goat is taken to the pond for washing. The flesh of the goat is shared among the Brahman-sebait. After the sacrifice to the Maharaja's goat, the *paiks* prepare another block for sacrifice by the side. Next is the sacrifice to the goats offered by the Ugra-Kshatriya. The seven goats are brought to the block in turn. The chief priest puts *phonta* of the blood of the sacrifice at the altar on each forehead of the attendance.

After the ritual of Mahapuja, the Karmakar hold the bloody sword and makes a procession with the Baiti playing the adrums. They go a round the pond in clock-wise. The villagers of every stratum of the village society assemble on the bank of Kshirdighi along with their goats to be dedicated. The blocks for sacrifice are set up in everywhere on the bank of Kshirdighi, and people are crowded around each altar of the block, to which a number of plates of offering are dedicated. The priests make rituals to goats at each altar, and give a marks of blood to each forehead after sacrifice. In the case of the lower caste the priest, called *deyasin*, of each locality performs the role of the priest and the sacrifice is done by themselves. But each sacrifice has basically a same procedure with the sacrifice of the Maharaja's goat. On this day, almost every household of the village offers a goat. Moreover, the other people from the neighbouring villages and relatives from a distance participate the ritual, because it is also the biggest occasion for the people in the area to visit the sacred place of sakta-pitha in a year. As a result, the number of the sacrifice to goats at the bank of Kshirdighi counts more than one thousand, and the surrounding of the pond covered with blood. The fresh of the goats are brought back to their houses and are cooked as the finest offering of the goddess (*mahaprasad*).

THE SACRIFICE TO THE BUFFALO: *MOSHBOLI*

The climax of a the Jogadyapuja is the sacrifice of a buffalo dedicated by the Maharaja. It is on this day that the excitement of the people reaches its peak. In the temple of Jogadya, the *baidik-purohit* practices the Vedic fire ritual in the morning. Immediately after this the Brahman-sebait and the Karmakar begin the sacrifice of goats. This time, the goats are offered by a family of the superintendent of the temple, a family of the director of the ritual organization, a former landowner of the village and a lineage of the Baiti.

The *mulapaiks* and many other Bagdi youth lead a buffalo to the temple. They enter the temple precinct with the buffalo, where crowds of people are waiting. The Baitis begin playing their drums furiously and the Bagdi youth start to jump up and down and into a dance with the beat of drums. At the same time, a servant of Bagdi brings a basket of ritual utensils on his head. He goes ahead to the Utthanmandir attended by the flags of the Maharaja with the drums playing. In the meantime, other servants of Bagdi use their sticks on the buffalo to lead it around the main temple. The head of this procession is the Maharaja's buffalo, followed by other buffaloes of personal offerings. The third is the goddess pot on a servant's head. The fourth is the Maharaja's sword for the buffalo sacrifice held up by the Karmakar who executes the sacrifice. The fifth is the Baitis playing their drums. Finally, the Maharaja's flags are waved by the Bagdi. This procession goes around the main temple seven times.

After the procession, they assemble in front of the Bhogmandir. The chief priest stands on the stage, and gives red marks of vermilion on their foreheads one by one. At one time, the chief priest gives vermilion on the foreheads of the member of the Ugra-Kshatriya. The lower castes receive vermilion from the hand of the Malakar. After that, the buffalo is made to enter the temple and receives a mark of vermilion on its forehead. Then they start for the Utthanmandir. In the place around the Utthanmandir, crowds are waiting for the arrival of the buffalo. On the muddy ground in front of the Utthanmandir, the uproarious youth are gathering. Most of them are of the lower castes. They are half-naked and put on merely a *gamcha*, and shove and push one another. From the morning, many devotees bring and sprinkle a pot of water from Kshirdighi over the muddy slope.

With the arrival of the buffalo at the Utthanmandir, devotees reach the peak of their enthusiasm. The half-naked youths jump up and down, grapple with one another, and pull each other down onto the ground. Rows of spectators surround the muddy square. Into the tumultuous crowd, the Maharaja's buffalo enters the place of sacrifice. A thick wall of youths close around the buffalo. They jostle and scuffle with each other and drag the animal to the block of sacrifice. A crowd of people is waiting for the moment with breathless interest. Among the throng of the naked youths, a small circle of men forms around the buffalo. At the centre of the circle, the Karmakar holds high up a sword of the Maharaja and swings it downward at one stretch. Instantly, the youth shout out, shake their hands, and begin to dance boisterously. The crowd of people also chants and cries out the name of the goddess

Jogadya in an uproarious atmosphere. It throws the whole square into a state of feverish excitement.

The youths compete for the carcass of the buffalo and scramble. The man getting the freshly severed head begins to dance putting it on his own head. The body is dragged around the muddy ground. Everyone struggles for the genital organs of the buffalo especially, tear off a little piece, and eat it immediately. Youths of the lineage of the *mulapaik* take away the head and the carcass finally to their residences. At one time, the Dom used to receive the carcass at the end and dispose it off. Nowadays, the Santals receive it. After the sacrifice, devout spectators begin to throw themselves onto the muddy road, stretching out their hands and legs. Even a woman wearing a fine sari for formal occasions expresses her deep faith to the goddess by throwing herself on a veritable sea of mud. On this occasion, they follow the long route from Kshirdighi or the Jogadya temple to the image of the goddess at the Utthanmandir. The way of the most pious is to advance every step by throwing their body on the ground. So that it is necessary to guide the steps by an attendant who has a stick to mark the ground. The devotee must throw themselves from the position where their heads were laid down. We can see a long queue of devotees on the muddy road leading to the Utthanmandir on this day.

All through the twenty-four hours when the image is enshrined on the Utthanmandir for all the people, the Brahman-sebaits and the servants of Bagdi guard the image in rotation. The Brahman-sebaits stand in front of the image and receive dedications from the villagers. The priests give the vermilion on the image and onto their foreheads. Then they return a part of the offerings to the villagers as *prasad* of the goddess. The *paiks* watch and regulate the thronging people. They stand at the gate of the Utthanmandir both at the entrance and the exit.

MERYA-KATHA

People's worship and their dedications of flowers, sweets, iron bangles, and vermilion in particular by women continue all day long until after midnight. They form a long queue to the image of the goddess at the Utthanmandir. A little while before dawn, the image is sent to the bottom of the pond again. At first, in front of the image they light two torches of straw, about three meters long.[3] In the light of the torches, they load the image very slowly onto the wooden cart. People gather around the Utthanmandir, and drag the ropes connected to the cart of the goddess.

At the bank of Kshirdighi, the Brahman-sebaits prepare for the altar of the sacrifice. In front of them, the head of a lineage of the Dom caste is waiting for the arrival of the goddess holding a sword in his hand. He brings a goat to dedicate. In the light of torches, many villagers bring the cart to the bank, and set up the image of the goddess in the altar of the sacrifice. At this time, the sacrifice is performed without purification by sacred water or mantra. They use also no sacrificial block but only a rope. The head of the Dom executes the sacrifice by his hand. The blood spouting out from the decapitated body is poured onto the image of the goddess at the altar. At that moment, the Dom shouts: *Ma! nara rakta khao!*—'Goddess! drink the blood of the human!' This is the ritual called *merya-khata*, in which the Dom used to cut the own finger of his own right hand and dedicate the blood to the goddess.

Watched by a crowd of people around the bank, the Brahman-sebaits slowly sink the image of the goddess in to the water. The servants of Bagdi stand around the slope of the bank holding the raja's flags in their hands. During this time, people used to sing a song in praise of the goddess in the rhythm of the drum by the Baiti as follows: 'The Goddess, the figure of the goddess Shyama, dance in the field of battle! (*shyama digambari ranamajhe naco go ma*!)' Having sunk the image under the water, the water of the pond is splashed over the surrounding people on the bank. The Brahman-sebaits and other servants then return to the temple.

Three days after the *merya-katha*, that means the fourth of Jaishta, the image of the goddess is pulling up onto the bank for about one hour for one of the *ugalpujas* again. The image is cleaned and worshipped, then, sent back to the deep place at the bottom of the pond until the next year.

NOTES

1. It corresponds to the initiatory rite of *ghatastapan* in the ordinary Hindu ritual, which is installation of ritual pot to the altar.
2. In Bengal, the basic system of *upacara-puja* is composed of the five steps to receive the deity, which is called *pancopacara-puja* [see, e.g. Bhattacaryya 1986]. In the formal procedure the priest takes sixteen steps for the reception, which is called *sorashopacara-puja*. In the *upacara-puja* for Jogadya, the chief priest follows the latter formality.
3. The torches are dedicated by the lineages of the Josh and Ray, but used to be the donation by the Maharaja Krishnacandra from the court of Krishnanagar of the Nadia district. Hence, it is called *nadermashal* (torch from Nadia).

CHAPTER 5

Rituals Around the Village

The number of animal sacrifices in a year at the Jogadya temple was 52 during the British period, and it was reduced to 48 after Independence. Among them, there are ten animal sacrifices still dedicated by the deb-seba-office in the name of the Maharaja, but most of the sacrifices are now supported by the localities and the lineages in the village. This means the financial patronage to the temple rituals shifted away from the Maharaja to the village middle class, but at the same time, the Maharaja still plays an important role in the temple. The annual rituals in the village can be divided into three categories; (1) the rituals solely performed in the temple, (2) the rituals performed in both the temple and the localities, and (3) the rituals performed mainly in the localities. According to the annual ritual list given below, we shall examine each annual ritual following the three categories. This shows the relationship between the temple and the localities, and its transition after Independence. At first, we shall examine the annual calendar of the rituals in the temple as the official schedule for the rituals of the village goddess.

Before Estate Acquisition

In the days of the Maharaja, the deb-seba-office, the court of the Raj in Bardhaman, sent every year for the expenditures of all the sacrifices of the Jogadya temple. There were 41 occasions in a year to perform the sacrifices amounting to 52 animals. These are two buffalos (*mahisbali*), one sheep (*mes-bali*), and 49 uncastrated goats (*pantha-bali*). The largest number was in the month of Baishakh and the second largest was in Aswin. Sacrifice in the Vedic fire ritual were performed on the last day of each month. The budget of the court of the Raj covered all the occasional expenditures for the sacrifices as well as for the daily service in the temple. After Independence, most of the budget were reduced to 10 sacrifices sponsored by the Maharaja spread over 8 occasions. That included two buffalos and eight goats. Some of these have now been taken over by the villagers, such as the lineages of Chaudhuri. The right column on Table 5.1 shows the number and the donors of the sacrifices after 1954.

The analysis of Table 5.1 indicates following three features. First, the sacrifices conducted by the Maharaja are reduced drastically, but the leading castes in the temple organization such as the Ugra-Kshatriyas took over the role. Second, the number of animal sacrifices is reduced from 52 to 48, but the annual system of the temple ritual is almost preserved as before. Third, while the villagers maintain the system of the temple ritual, there are many other rituals which are now taken up in the localities and households of the village. These trends are the

TABLE 5.1: ANNUAL RITUAL BEFORE 1953

Bengali calendar		Name of Ritual	Sacrifice by the Maharaja	After 1954
Chaitra, *Sank.*		Jogadyapuja		
Jaishta,	4			
Chaitra, *Sank.*		*Kshirkalasi*		
		Jagyakund	*Pathabali* (1)	Raja-1
		Ritual calling	*Pathabali* (1)	
Baishakh	1	Offerings to the goddess	*Pathabali* (1)	
	15	*Lagna-utsab*		
	27	Jagyakund	*Pathabali* (1)	
		The recitation of the *Ramayana*		
		Mayurnac		
	28	*Ramayanpath*		
		Mayurnac		
	29	*Ramayanpath*		
		Pathnaran	*Pathabali* (1)	Raja, Ray-1
		Mayurnac		
	30	Jagyakund	*Pathabali* (1)	Raja-1
		Hal-nagal		
		Ramayanpath		
Sank.		*Ugalpuaja*	*Pathabali* (1)	Datta, Caudh.-1
		Mayurnac		
		Domacoyarikhela		
		Mahapuja	*Pathabali* (7)	Raja-1, UKY-7
		Offerings to the goddess	*Pathabali* (1)	
		Mahisbali	*Mahisbali* (1)	Raja-M1
		Masi-Pisi-Jhuri		
		Shankha-Para		
		Ritual calling	*Pathabali* (1)	UKY, Baiti, BHM

Contd.

Table 5.1 (Contd.)

Bengali calendar		Name of Ritual	Sacrifice by the Maharaja	After 1954
Jaishta	1	*Merya Katha*	*Pathabali* (1)	(Dom-1)
	4	*Abhisheka*	*Pathabali* (1)	(Ray-1)
		Ugalpuja	*Pathabali* (1)	
Sank.		Ritual calling	*Pathabali* (1)	
Ashar,	S.9	*Ugalpuja*	*Pathabali* (2)	(Raja-2, UKY-10)
Sank.		Ritual calling	*Pathabali* (1)	
Shraban, *Sank.*		Ritual calling	*Pathabali* (1)	
Bhadra, *Sank.*		Ritual calling	*Pathabali* (1)	
Aswin	K.8	Durgapuja		
	S.10			
	K.9	*Nabami*	*Pathabali* (1)	
	S.4	*Catrutipatrika*	*Pathabali* (1)	
	S.7	*Saptamipuja*	*Pathabali* (1)	(Caudh.-1)
	S.8	*Asthamaipuja*	*Pathabali* (1)	
		Offerings to the goddess	*Pathabali* (1)	
	S.9	*Nabamipuja*	*Mahisbali* (1)	(Raja-M1)
			Mesbali (1)	
			Pathabali (1)	
	S.10	*Bijaydashami*		
		Ugalpuja	*Pathabali* (2)	(Caudh.-1)
	S.15	Kojagari Lakshmipuja		
Sank.		Ritual calling (*guya-dak*)	*Pathabali* (1)	
Kartik	K.14	Shyamapuja	*Pathabali* (1)	
	S.9	Jagadwatripuja	*Pathabali* (1)	
Sank.		Ritual calling (*guya-dak*)	*Pathabali* (1)	
Agrahayan		*Nabanna-utsab*	*Pathabali* (1)	
		Offerings to the goddess		
Agrahayan, *Sank.*		Ritual calling (*guya-dak*)	*Pathabali* (1)	
Poush		*Pousalla*		*Pathabali* (1)
		Offerings to the goddess		
	15	*Ugalpuja*	*Pathabali* (1)	
	28	*Grahapuja*	*Pathabali* (1)	
Sank.		*Pisthakotsab*		
		Offerings to the goddess	*Pathabali* (1)	
		Ritual calling (*guya-dak*)	*Pathabali* (1)	
Magh	S.7	*Makari-saptami*	*Pathabali* (2)	(Raja-2, UKY-10, BHM-1)
Sank.		Ritual calling (*guya-dak*)	*Pathabali* (1)	
Magh, *Sank.* -Phalgun, *Sank.*		*Nishidhambal*		
Phalgun, *Sank.*		Ritual calling (*guya-dak*)	*Pathabali* (1)	
Chaitra		Nilpuja (Kshireshwar)	*Pathabali* (1)	

Abbreviation: Sank. = Sankranti; last day of lunar months.

result of the historical changes around the village like the abolition of the zamindari system after Independence, the decline of the local kingship, and the emergence of the rural middle classes. However, it is interesting that in the village these transitions do not necessarily lead to simple decay of the village rituals, but rather enable the people of the localities and households to engage in the rituals actively and voluntarily than ever before. It is in striking contrast to many ruins of the Hindu temples which lost their patronage by the former zamindars. As discussed in Chapter 1 the situation in Bangladesh gives a clear example.

The Temple Rituals

Regarding the temple rituals, the eight occasions which are important to understand the annual cycle of the village temple are, namely (a) the rituals of *Sankranti* at the end of each Bengali month, (b) *ugalpujas* (the rituals of pulling up the image of the goddess from the pond of Kshirdighi, (c) *nishidhambal* (the ritual of drum playing), (d) *makari-saptami* (the marriage ritual of the goddess), (e) *grahapuja* (the worship of the planets), (f) the ritual of rice harvest (*nabanna-utsab*), (g) *pousalla* (the rice offering in the field), (h) the last day of Pous (*pistaka-utsab*). In Chapter 3, the rituals of (a) and (b) are already discussed, and Chapter 4 deals with Jogadyapuja, which is the biggest occasion as one of *ugalpujas* in the month of Baishakh. Among the other rituals, (c), (d) and (e) are solely performed at the temple, and (f), (g) and (h) are connected with both the temple and the localities. Now, we will discuss each of these ritual occasions in turn.

Nishidhambal (The Ritual of Drum Playing)

During the entire month of Magh, a Baiti gives a special performance of his drum called *nishidhambal* in the Jogadya temple every night. This drum playing consists of eight kinds of strokes and it takes place for about thirty minutes after midnight. The Baiti who performs this *nishidhambal* must keep to a special vegetarian diet, which contains parched rice and refined butter. He observes it for a whole month and sleeps on the floor in a separate room as an ascetic.

At the beginning of *nishidhambal*, the Baiti plays the drum on the way to Jogadya temple to announce the ritual time to the village. At the gate of the main temple, he puts a sevenfold bandage over his eyes, and steps into the temple with his right foot. His left foot is outside. Keeping this stance, he performs the tunes of *nishidhambal*. He is forbidden to see or talk to anyone. The villagers are also prohibited from walking on the streets of the village while the drum is playing. They never see the playing in the temple and just sit indoors to hear it. If the playing has started on their walking, they must rush into a nearby house and stay there till the performance ends.

In the village, the people believe that during the playing of *nishidhambal* the goddess Jogadya dances to the rhythm of the drum inside the temple. The heavenly maidens attend to the goddess and evil spirits appear in the courtyard of the temple. Because of this belief, no one enters the temple except the Baiti. The Baiti claims to feel the presence of the goddess inside the temple while he plays his drum. He can even hear the faint sounds of the foot rings (anklet) trembling according to her dance and sense a sweet aroma of the goddess. Much folklore passed down by the villagers tells of bad luck befalling those who break a taboo during *nishidhambal*.

The tunes of *nishidhambal* are prohibited from playing except on this ritual occasion. The Baiti explains that all these tunes are compiled from the basic patterns of every ritual tune performed on various occasions such as Durgapuja, Kalipuja, and so on. The Baiti plays it usually following the rhythm of seven beats (*sat-tal*) of the Bengali drum, but if he is highly skilled, he plays according to the rhythm of twelve or eighteen beats. The tunes of *nishidhambal* handed down to the lineage of the Baiti are of eight kinds at present:

(1) *Tengai* and its *Danshpahari*
(2) Drum playing for the dance of peacock
(3) Drum playing for the dance of peacock of Malakar after Durgapuja
(4) Drum for forming a line with hands up in the ritual of Gajan
(5) Drum for the dance imitating the gestures of frogs in Gajan
(6) Drum for dancing of *kalikapata*
(7) Drum playing to fill up the pot in the ritual of awakening of the goddess (*badhan*)
(8) Drum playing in the rhythm of dancing the Sani.

MAKARI-SAPTAMI THE MARRIAGE RITUAL OF THE GODDESS

On the seventh of Magh, the Brahman-sebaits perform a ritual called *makari-saptami* at the Jagyasthan, which is a square basin designed for the fire ritual (*hom*) located at the northeastern corner of the Natmandir of the Jogadya temple. At first, the servants of the Bagdi (*paiks*) make a square flat pedestal from a large quantity of ashes on the ground of the south side of the Jagyasthan as is shown in Map 5.1. They also bring a pot, put inside it frogs and *cyen* fish caught the previous day in the fields. Meanwhile, a Malakar prepares a copper pot and puts it down in the northwestern corner of the Jagyasthan. He also prepares many offerings, which include seven nuts of the *kul* (*Zizyphus jujuba*), seven leaves of *akand*, milk, unthreshed rice, sesame seed, *durba* grass, parched rice, and sandalwood paste. In front of the Jagyasthan, a Baiti and two flag holders of Bagdi holding the flags of the Maharaja in their hands remain standing. Before the ritual to the pot on the Jagyasthan, the Brahman-sebait performs a ritual called the offering to the sun (*surjarga*). After that, they perform another ritual called '*cyen-beng*' (*cyen* fish and frogs) at the pedestal of ashes. At the beginning, a Brahman-sebait purifies the pedestal with flowers and water. Then, the Malakar performs a ritual cultivation on the pedestal with a hand holder of Indian black ink (*kajalata*) in his hand. He simulates it for cultivation by scratching the surface of the pedestal. First, he puts it on the outer portion of the surface, then he pushes it to the centre likewise drawing an eddy which encircles the middle point of the pedestal. Reaching to the middle point he turns it towards south and then cuts straight through it. The direction of the circle on the pedestal of ashes is the same with the way of the procession around the temple and around the outer fringe of the village.

The Malakar sprinkles the unthreshed rice over the surface of the pedestal. The Brahman-sebait stands and dedicates an offering over it which consists of a nut of the *kul*, a sesame seed, milk, and *durba* grass on a leaf of *akand* with sandalwood paste. He dedicates it over the pedestal seven times with sacred verses. After that, the Malakar releases the fish and frogs from the pot over the pedestal. At that moment, people surrounding there rush to catch then with their hands. They also take a little ash home, to sprinkle over their agricultural fields, or mix with manure for cultivation. This is believed to bring about a good harvest.

After that, the Malakar goes out of the temple, attended by the flag holders of Bagdi and a Baiti playing the drum and gong. The procession moves through the eastern gate of the temple and goes towards the northern side of the village to the streets of the locality of Uttar-para and then turns to the Manasa-para. They pass by the pond Natunpukur and reach the agricultural field to the north of the Karuapukur pond. The Malakar stands at the northeastern corner of the field and digs a small hole again and puts a little bit of *cire* (flattened rice) and *murki* (parched rice) in the hole. The procession then returns to the temple accompanied by the sounds of drum and gong. Arriving at the temple they have a ritual to prepare for the marriage ceremony of the goddess. A daughter of the Malakar dressed up with the wedding sari enters the temple. The lineage of Babataran Bhattacaryya has the duty to help her get dressed. She has a pot of the goddess under her arm and stands beside a Malakar boy in front of the temple. Just as in an ordinary marriage ceremony, the ends of their clothes are tied and a priest gives them a blessing with sacred verses. They go out of the temple through the eastern gate and proceed to the cow shed owned by the lineage of Bhattacaryya, located on the north-eastern side of the temple. They stand on a low stand (*pire*) at the door of the cow shed. The head of the lineage gives them a reception with *supari* and *pan* as in the ritual reception at the entry of the bride in the second day of the marriage ceremony. The women surrounding them receive the couple with the sounds of *ulu* and sprinkle over them *cire* and *murki*.

This ritual is supposed by the villager as the ceremony of marriage of Jogadya and Kshirkantak (another name of Siva). The villagers solemnize their own marriage rituals in the village only after *Makari-saptami*. All through the month of Magh, it is thought to be suitable time for an ordinary Hindu to marry but in the village, they are prohibited from performing any marriage ceremony before the ritual of *Makari-saptami*. The villagers were also used to tilling their fields after *Makari-saptami*.

GRAHAPUJA THE WORSHIP OF THE PLANETS

The word of *graha* means planet, planets constituting nine houses in the Hindu astrology, *grahapuja* signifies the worship of the planets to propitiate them. On the penultimate day of Pous, *grahapuja* is performed at the foot of an old tree located in the rear garden in the locality of a Bagdi entitled Sinha. They belong to the sub-caste of Kusmethi-Bagdi. Many pieces of broken images of stone gods and goddesses are gathered at the foot of the tree and installed into a small altar. The people of the locality practice their daily service to the stone pieces everyday.

The priest for the ritual is from the lineage of Sat-bhai of the temple Brahman-sebait. The high ranking Brahman priests (*uccasreni-brahman*) are prohibited from engaging in this ritual. The lower rank of Brahman (*nimnasreni-brahman*) may practise it exclusively, as also the rituals of death (*shyama-santi*), and the expiatory rite (*dosh-katano*). In this case, a lineage of Bhattacharyyas who used to live in the village performed it in the past. They belong to a section called *kathal-brahman* in Bengal, lower ranking Brahmans engaged exclusively in family rituals for their *jajmans* of the lower castes such as the Bagdi and the Muci. At around 3 o'clock in the afternoon, a Baiti goes around the village playing the drum to mark the time of *grahapuja* and then arrives at the altar. He prepares for the ritual at the altar, and people gather, with offerings on plates. People dedicate the offerings, and daub the sacred stones with paste of turmeric, mustard oil, and vermilion one after another. The priest purifies first his body, the seat, and the surrounding by sacred water, and then starts the ritual in the name of the Maharaja of Bardhaman.

After the ritual, they sacrifice an uncastrated goat. The priest sprinkles sacred water over the goat and a sword of the Maharaja. A Karmakar has the sword in readiness. People gather around there. With the sound of the drum, he brings it down on the neck of the goat. The fresh blood from the sacrificed goat is poured onto the stones at the altar. People make a deep bow to the poured blood on the altar. They receive a part of the offerings on each plate which they take home as *prasad*. Formerly, the budget of the court of the Raj covered the expenses of this sacrifice, but now it is the people in the locality who dedicate the goat. The meat is, therefore, shared among them.

The Rituals of the Temple and the Localities

THE RITUAL OF NEW RICE HARVEST (*NABANNA-UTSAB*)

The ritual of *nabanna-utsab* is performed in the lunar month of Agrahayan when the winter rice (*aman*) is in the fields. The date of the ritual is, however, not prescribed in the Bengali ritual almanac as the other rituals are, and every village has its own harvest ritual date in Agrahayan, determined by themselves. In Kshiragram, the *sabha-pandit* decides the date every year and proclaims this to the village. In this decision, he takes it into consideration that the harvest time of the *aman* rice in each year, and the auspicious days in the month of Agrahayan. In this way, most of the villages have their own persons such as *pandit* (a learned man in religion) or *moral* (an influential person in village) to decide their date of the ritual. It is one of the most important rituals of the agricultural affairs in rural Bengal, and this ritual shows how it is connected deeply to the village life and society.

The Ritual in the Temple

People instal altars of the rice harvest ritual in both their homes and the Jogadya temple. In the Jogadya temple, the villagers participate in the ritual jointly. In the morning, the village women wash, and then bring dishes of offerings to the temple. They stand in the interior room of the temple and place them on the floor. After the drum beating of the Baiti, the Brahman-sebait belonging to the lineage of Sat-bhai, the *sabha-pandit* and the *rajkachari* perform the ritual. Every representative of the Ugra-Kshatriyas is present. The priest sprinkles sacred water over the dishes on the floor and dedicates them with flowers. During the dedication of fire (*arati*), every member stands up with the sounds of gong and *ulu* and makes a deep bow to the floor. The women who dedicated offerings in plates bring them back it to their respective houses and cook the offered rice of the new harvest. After the ritual, the *rajkachari* distributes the offerings from a big plate to everyone around. The Brahman-sebait addresses each title of the Ugra-Kshatriya standing at the threshold of the temple and offers the wreath of *shola* grass (sponge wood) to every representative by turn. The order of the nine titles is the same as in the ritual of *phonta*-giving in Jogadyapuja. They bring the offerings in the bowls to their localities and share them among the households.

The storehouse of the temple is filled with huge piles of offerings which the village people dedicate on the occasion. In particular, the lineages of Bara-ray, Chota-ray and Chaudhuri offer sun-dried rice (*atop-caul*) and vegetables respectively. The Brahman-sebaits prepare the rice offering in large quantity after the noon at the Bhogmandir. This is a special offering and to cook it the Brahman sebaits use an earthenware pot in place of the ordinary brass utensils. They boil the rice in the pot on the hearth of the Bhogmandir. Closing the door of the cooking room, the priest performs his ritual with a special verse (*bhogmantra*) for the goddess, and sprinkles sacred water over the boiled rice, soup, stewed vegetables, and fish. Then he opens the door and strikes a gong from the veranda, announcing end of the ritual. The priest serves the food to the many people sitting in the courtyard. In front of the people, the priest breaks the pot with an iron scoop into nine pieces, and dishes out the boiled rice, vegetables, and fish on these nine sherds, which are called *tikla-biri*. Standing on the veranda, the Brahman-sebait addresses again each title of the Ugra-Kshatriya by turn, and puts down the nine pieces one by one. Every representative of the lineages takes his share home.

The Ritual at the Shrines of the Village Localities

The *nabanna-utsab* in rural areas is now generally known as the ritual of the goddess Annapurna (*annapurnapuja*), one of the popular festivals in Bengal, is observed at temporary shrines by the local communities. In this ritual, they enshrine the image of the goddess Annapurna and invite priests to the altars. The sequence of the ritual is nearly the same with the other rituals. Six such shrines for the goddess Annapurna were constructed in the village in 1994 as shown in Table 5.2.

The ritual organizations on this list are mostly based on voluntary associations, called *baroyaripuja* in the village, which are mainly organized by the village youth in each locality. The oldest organization for this ritual can be traced back to almost a hundred years ago. The others are formed in each locality one after another. Now the rituals have festivity with decoration and music. Only the lineage of the Sani of the Ugra-Kshatriyas in the village maintains this ritual as its lineage ritual since early times. They have their own shrine for this ritual at the corner of their residence. In this year, a shrine has been newly built in the locality of the Hari, which began as the lineage ritual. Altogether six such ritual organizations exist in the village.

The ritual starts with the installation to a ritual pot by priests and the ritual steps on proclamation (*sankalpa*), purification (*shuddhi*), invocation (*baran*), and reception to the image of the goddess (*arati*) in that order. On the next day, they perform a ritual for the goddess and the fire ritual (*hom*) in the morning and evening. This continues for three days and the farewell rite (*bisarjan*) to the image is done on the fourth day. These procedures are almost the same as in rituals for Kali and Kartik. But, rather the people enjoy their decorations and the magnificence of the image in the temporary shrines, modelled on the myth of the *Ramayana*, from which motifs enable them to produce

TABLE 5.2: THE RITUALS OF THE GODDESS ANNAPURNA

Locality	Patron	Priest	Establish
Josh-para	Josh-para	Satbhai	about100 years ago
Badyagachtala	Samant-para		about 50 years ago
Chaudhuri-para	Chaudhuri/Brahman	Adhikary	unidentified
Kshireshwaritala	Brahman	Bhattacharyya	about 20 years ago
Sani-para	Sani (Suta-sguri)	Kalidas	unidentified
Purba-para	Hajra (Hari)	Mantu	in 1994

imaginative sceneries of various deities, besides the basic orientation of Siva and Annapurna. In particular, the days of the ritual in Agrahayan is a yearly occasion of amusement for the youth in the village along with the ritual occasion to Saraswati in Magh. The music over loud speakers, various kinds of stalls on the streets, and dramas (*jatra*) of youth clubs give delight to the villager.

On the same days, at the square of the temple of the goddess Manasa, the priests of the lineages of the Bagdi (*deyasin*) put ritual pots pots in front of the Manasa temple and the shrine of the god Panchanan. The people in the locality dedicate the offerings of new rice and other harvests. This is mainly performed by the people of the Bagdi caste. Offerings in the pots are shared among the lineages of the Bagdi priests. One part is for the priest of the Manasa temple. The other part is divided into two for the flag holder (*patakadhari*) and the chief servant (*mulapaik*) of the Jogadya temple in the same way as on other occasions. Every family of the village prepares meat of castrated goats (*khasi*) for dinner. Only at the shrine of the god Panchanan, do they sacrifice an uncastrated goat (*pathabali*) on the second day of the ritual. Many people of the locality go to the local town of Katwa to make ablutions in the Ganga.

The Ritual in the Village Households

From early in the morning, every household of the village prepares for the ritual. The most important offering of the day is made from the new rice of the year. This rice is categorized as *raghu-caul* (japonica rice), and it is usually called *nabanna-dhan*. It is not a common type of rice in south Asia. Many people plant only a small amount of it for the ritual. *Nabanna-dhan* has less production than the other winter varieties. But for the ritual, the people cultivate this rice and dry it in the sun. From *nabanna-dhans* people make various kinds of food for the ritual. The most popular item is the raw rice offering (*caul-nabanna*), in a dish of condensed milk (*kshir*), banana, and other fruits and vegetables along with the new rice. After the dedication to the goddess, people mix them and eat them raw. Some villagers grind the rice with a pestle and mortar, and serve it on a banana leaf with fruit and sweets. The second is the boiled rice offering (*bhat-nabanna*), made by boiling (*siddha-caul*) new rice. The third is the rice cake (*caul-pithe*) made of boiled rice mixed with wheat flour and molasses (*gur*), then fried deep in mustard oil.

They have many other dishes in the day such as fried bean cake (*fuluri*) and fried aubergine (*begun-bhaja*). Usually, they have vegetable diet until afternoon. Fish is served at dinner. The day after the new rice ritual, they eat the meat of castrated goats and celebrate their harvest with their relatives. In the village, the occasion of the ritual is the biggest function in a year when relatives assemble.

POUSALLA

A few days before of the last day of the month of Pous, the rice offering to Jogadya is prepared on the west bank of Kshirdighi, which is usually dedicated at the Bhogmandir in the temple. That is called *pousalla.* In general, *pousalla* means a popular event in the winter season by villager to go on a picnic on a vacant land at the outskirts of villages. They have some recreation for a day, cook outside, and lunch together in the open air. In the *pousalla* at the bank of Kshirdighi, however, this consists of a part of the temple ritual of Jogadya.

The date of the *pousalla* is decided at the time of the rituals of pulling up the image of the goddess (*ugalpuja*) on the fifteenth of Pous by the *sabha-pandit.* According to the other events of the village and the almanac of the year, he usually fixes the date a few days before *pous-sankranti.* On the day before *pousalla*, the *paiks* dig hearths at the slope of the bank in the western side of Kshirdighi, on the opposite shore where the image of the goddess is sunk. On this day, the *mulapaiks* and the Doms are in charge of preparation for them. On the day of the *pousalla*, a Brahman-sebait practises his duty for the daily service at the altar of the Jogadya temple. At the same time, other Brahman-sebaits prepare the rice offering for *pousalla* at the Kshirdighi bank. Many villager bring sun-dried (*atop-caul*) and vegetables to the bank as offerings. Only on the day of *pousalla* in a year, they have an rice offering (*anna-bhog*) at the bank outside the temple. A few big brass pots are used for cooking food for many villagers. As it takes much time to prepare the food, the ritual of offerings starts in the late afternoon. At that time, the Brahman-sebait in charge of the day, the maid servant of the Bhogmandir, every one of the nine lineages of the Brahman-sebait of the temple, and the *paiks* help in preparation of the offering. They use water of Kshirdighi for cooking the offering. Formerly, a goat dedicated by the Maharaja was sacrificed here and served in the dishes of the *pousalla.*

In the beginning, the rice offering is served to the goddess. A Brahman-sebait strikes a gong telling the time and performs the ritual in front of the hearths on the bank in the same manner as in the Bhogmandir. He picks up a small earthenware pot for the ritual of the goddess, and puts cooked food in the pot such as boiled rice and vegetables. After his ritual, with a mantra, he breaks the pot into nine pieces, and serves the offering on them. It is called *tikla-biri*, and the procedure to serve them is almost the same way as in the (*nabanna-utsab*). The priest addresses each title of the nine lineages of the Ugra-Kshatriya and their representatives receive the offering on nine pieces of the broken pot by turn. Many other people of the village sit down on the bank and receive the offerings on banana leaves from the Brahman-sebaits. All participants sit and eat together. After serving, them the Brahman-sebaits begin to eat them-selves. The leftovers in the pots are shared among those who take part in the preparation for the *pousalla*, according to a specified quota, which is one portion for the lineage of the Dom, two for the chief servant, eight for the lineage of Sat-bhai of the Brahman-sebait, eight for the other Brahman-sebaits, and one for the priest in charge.

THE LAST DAY OF POUS (*PISTAKA-UTSAB*)

On the last day of Pous, the Brahman-sebaits make a rice cake offering to the goddess Jogadya in the Bhogmandir. Every household in the village makes them, but those made at the Bhogmandir are very large, about of 20 cm each, and in large quantities. There is the special rice field, of about 0.25 acre (15 *katha*) called the 'rice cake field' (*pithe-bhumi*), which belongs to the temple. Cakes are made from the new rice of the field, along with other dishes, for the goddess. At the time of the daily ritual in the temple, the ritual of *tikla-biri* is performed again at the platform of the Bhogmandir. Rice cakes are placed on nine pot sherds and there is an offering of boiled rice, vegetables and fish. This is the fourth time that *tikla-biri* is observed in the year. Formerly, a goat donated by the Maharaja for the goddess was also sacrificed.

THE RITUALS OF THE LOCALITIES

The following discussions are regarding the rituals mainly organized in the localities in the village, namely the Kalipuja, Jogdatripuja Kartikpuja, and Saraswatipuja. All the rituals are popular in rural Bengal, and the analysis on the ritual organizations would make clear the transformation of the popular rituals since Independence. It could be summarized that the disintegration of the Hindu kingship, which used to strengthen the vertical solidarity in the local society, and the increasing participations by the people in these rituals extend the horizontal linkages beyond the boundaries of kin and locality in the rural society.

THE RITUAL OF THE GODDESS KALI (KALIPUJA)

The ritual for Kali, Kalipuja, in the month of Kartik is the most popular occasion in the village locality, although there are various other rituals also for the goddess. In the month of Kartik in 1994, 31 Kalipujas were performed in the village localities. Table 5.3 lists these Kalipujas against the type of ritual organization and caste group concerned. It is clear that 18 were held by the village households, and most of the Brahmans tend to perform this ritual style. Five rituals are the *sola-ana*, organized by a corporate lineage organization (as discussed in Chapter 3). The ritual of *baroyari* is a community ritual organization, nowadays very popular in the urban setting. In this village, four such managements were held. The ritual of *deyasin* is held of a personal altar, at which the non-Brahman priests perform. In general the *deyasins* are ascetics and enshrine the goddess personally. They mediate the people's prayers to the goddess, and are occasionally possessed by the goddess and give oracles to the villagers on request. One case listed in Table 5.3 is practically an altar of such a *deyasin* of the Bagdi caste, and it has developed as a permanent temple. Another case of the temple is the ritual to the goddess Kali at the Jogadya temple, which is performed in the month of Kartik by every villager in the name of the Maharaja. In this case, Kali is regarded as an

TABLE 5.3: DISTRIBUTION OF THE RITUALS OF THE GODDESS KALI

Caste of Ritual of the Locality	Household	*Sola-ana*	*Baroyari*	*Deyasin*	Temple	Total
Brahaman	12	1				13
Ugra-Kshatriya (*Suta-Aguri*)	2	2				4
Bagdi (Tetuliya)	1	1	3	1	1	7
Bagdi (Kusmethi)	1	1	1	1		4
Hari	2					2
Maharaja					1	1
Total	18	5	4	2	2	31

incarnation of Jogadya. In all, there were 31 Kalipujas held in 1994 in the village.

Distributions of the Kalipujas in the Village

The distribution pattern of the Kalipujas among various caste groups of the village indicates following three features. First, the sub-caste of the Ugra-Kshatriyas (*jana-aguri*), the Gaela and the Muci never organize Kalipuja as a locality ritual, but the Bagdi and the Hari are actively engaged in it. Second, it is in the month of Kartik when the Kalipujas are held by the localities of the Brahman, the Bagdi, the Hari, and the sub-caste of the Ugra-Kshatiryas (suta-aguri). In the meantime, for the Bauri caste in the southern outskirts of the village, the Kalipuja of the month of Magh is the main festival of all, and they have no Kalipuja in the month of Kartik. Third, in the Bagdi locality, the organizations of the Kalipuja are mainly the rituals of *baroyari* (community ritual) to mobilize the residents, and an occasion for healing and oracle telling by the non-Brahman priests (*deyasins*) at the goddess's altar. However, among the Brahmans and Kshatriyas all the Kalipujas are either rituals of *sola-ana* (corporate lineage rituals), or rituals of the household (*parivarpuja*), in which each head of the household becomes the priest of the altar.

In this way, the village upper castes participate in the ritual at the level of the household or lineage. The rituals of *sola-ana* and household are fundamentally based on the kinship relations. On the other hand, among the Bagdis it is a personal ritual by the *deyasin*, or the corporate ritual of the entire locality, which mostly relies on the personal intentions and donations. The contrast is clear: the former strengthen solidarity amongst kin, the latter unite the people of the locality beyond their blood relations.

The Sequence of Kalipuja

During a couple of days before Kalipuja, people of the village visit the local town of Katwa to take ablutions in the Ganga (the Hugli River). Many of village women, especially of the lower castes, go together to Katwa on the day before Kalipuja, observing a fast. In case they are not able to visit Katwa, they take an ablution in their house. They go to a cow shed and sprinkle Ganga water on their body. They keep abstinence until the end of the ritual and take the offerings of the Kalipuja after the sacrifice.

The Fourteenth of Kartik

Kalipuja starts on the night of the fourteenth of Kartik, which is a day before the new moon. The people of every locality in the village enshrine clay images of the goddess Kali at temporary altars and prepare offerings for them. At first the Baiti in the Jogadya temple beats the drum announce the starting time of the ritual, in all the localities in the village. The Brahman-sebait begins his ritual for the goddess in the temple, and every priest starts to perform the rituals at their altars. The priests purify seats on the altar and themselves, and proclaim the name of their patron (*sankalpa*). Then they perform the installation of the ritual pot (*ghatasthapan*), the ritual reception to the goddess (*baran*), and the sacrifice (*balidan*), which is usually of goats. After that, the priests please the goddess by the votive lights (*arati*) and lit the ritual fire (*hom*). On each altar, people receive the offerings from the priest. At the time of the sacrifice in the Jogadya temple, the Brahman-sebait specially addresses the titles of the Ugra-Kshatriyas in order and gives them a necklace made of *shola* tree.

Women mostly belonging to the lower castes receive the ritual fire of the goddess Kali on her heads, if she has some personal prayers to make (*mansik*). They sit in front of the altar and put an earthenware bowl on their head. Incense keeps burning in the bowl. The priests sprinkle the incense powder (*dunu*) into the bowl. The powder flares up the flame on their head. The area around her thus gets filled up with white smoke and sweet fragrance. Most of the special prayers are for recovering from diseases on getting children.

The New Moon (Amabasya) *of Kartik*

The day after the ritual, the priests extend services to the deity in the morning and perform the ritual of farewell (*bisarjan*) to the pot at the altar. The villagers invite their relatives for a meal of the sacrifices. The image of the goddess is retained until night. At night the villagers from each locality move out in procession around the village. At the altar, people rush to touch the feet of the image and make a deep bow. They get the vermilion as a *phonta* on their foreheads. The men carry the image of their locality on a palanquin of bamboo. With the sound of *ulu* performed by the women, they swing the image a little in the beginning in front of the altar and then start the procession. At first, they go to the Jogadya temple and in front of the gate of the temple, they bring down the palanquin of the image to the ground once. Soon they shoulder it again in order to join a parade around the village. The processions of the lower castes also visit the residences of their landlords or the masters. They bring down the images once to the ground just the same manner as at the Jogadya temple. Then, they receive the bow of the masters to their image of the goddess and get some donations. The labourers carry the image of their landlords or the masters, with whom they are engaged as agricultural labourers.

THE RITUAL TO THE GODDESS JAGADATRI (*JAGADATRIPUJA*)

Except in the Jogadya temple, none in the village performed rituals for Jagadatri (*jagadatripuja*) in 1994. Even in the temple, the priests perform the ritual only to the copper pot on the altar. Formerly, two lineages of the village namely, the *sabha-pandit*, and the lineage of Mukhopadhyaya used to observe the ritual at their residences every year. But, they had no image in their altar, and adopted only a small icon of the goddess with a small pot.

As one of the 51 sakta-pithas, people in the village observe especial customs. The sakta-pitha means the abode of Sati (Durga), and Jogadya is one of the incarnations of Durga. Hence, people think the goddess in the village is not a temporary visitor on particular ritual occasions as is Durga in the Durgapuja and Kali in the Kalipuja, but rather stays in the temple all through the year. As people have already the goddess in the village, they cannot bring the other one inside the village. There is no restriction on the image of the god Kartik in the Kartikpuja, or the god and his spouse goddess of Radha-Krishna, but people never brought the images of Durga and her incarnations such as the goddess Jagadatri into the village.

THE RITUAL FOR KARTIK (*KARTIKPUJA*)

Kartikpuja is famous and elaborate in the towns of Cuncura and Katwa in West Bengal, but in the village, no one performs it periodically. Only those who have a personal prayer (*mansik*) for the god, set up an altar and invite their family priests to perform worship. Most of their prayers are for getting children by barren women, Kartikeya is considered as the guardian of children. One can begin the ritual at the end of the month of Kartik in any year. But, once started, it must continue for another two years at least. Most of the patrons of this ritual are the upper castes (*bara-lok*). In 1994, four families of the Ugra-Kshatriya (*suta-aguri*) and one Gaela family performed this ritual.

On the night of the end of Kartik, people set up the altar of Kartik and invite their priests. The patron, the prayer, the priest, and one who has prayers observe a fast from morning until the end of the ritual. At first, the patron of the ritual put a small pot on his head and goes to draw water in company with a Baiti playing his drum. He puts the pot on the altar and the priest starts the ritual. The patron sits beside the priest and follows his instructions. The ritual includes a number of acts in the same way as the other annual rituals. They perform this ritual cycle for four times until very late at night. The basic procedure is almost same with other rituals, but one must add a sweet of *naru* as offering for the god, which is made of parched rice (*muri*) and molasses (*gur*) rounded into a ball. This is a favourite sweet for children and the image of Kartik always has a *naru* in his right hand. The day after the ritual, the patron gives donations to the priest. Then he puts the pot on his head and goes to the pond to pour out the water. The offerings served after the ritual immersion is called *dadikarma*, which is a another kind of sweet. At night, the farewell ritual to the image takes place. The procession of the image accompanying drums parades round the village. An empty pot and a coconut on top of it are left at the altar for other eight days.

THE RITUAL TO SARASWATI

The *Saraswatipuja* in the village is organized by youth clubs of the locality as a community ritual (*baroyaripuja*). The origins of these rituals are of recent years as compared with the others. The oldest ritual in the village is in the building of the Kshiragram high school, adjacent to Kshirdighi. The students and the teachers of the high school manage it. The sequence is almost the same as the other annual rituals in the village. The images of the goddess Saraswati go generally to the farewell rite two days after the ritual. Table 5.4 gives the list of the rituals to the goddess Saraswati organized in 1994.

Twenty-four rituals were held in the village. Most of them are in the style of *baroyaripuja*, and are voluntarily organized by youth clubs or the people of locality. This means that these rituals are basically formed following the division of the localities or caste groups in the village. Therefore, it is clear that most of the youths in the rituals belong to the

TABLE 5.4: THE RITUALS OF THE GODDESS SARASWATI

Patron	Youth Club	Locality	Household	Total
School	2			2
Brahaman	2		3	5
Brahman & Ugra-Kshatriya	2			2
Ugra-Kshatriya	2	3	6	11
Bagdi		2		2
Muci		1		1
Bazar	1			1
Total	9	6	9	24

village upper castes. It seems to be easy to explain the reason: Saraswati is the goddess of arts and learning; and higher education in the village is mostly the prerogative of the youth of the upper castes. The rituals are similar to the other annual rituals, but are regarded as a major event and the young people plan various cultural programmes such as drama and chorus in front of the altar. In Kolkata, it is very popular to organize the rituals of Durgapuja or Kalipuja in the form of community ritual; however, these rituals are fundamentally based on the kinship relations such as lineage ritual (*sola-ana-puja*) in the village, and very rarely in the style of community ritual. In other words, the intrroduction of the modern education to the village enables them to newly form the voluntary association for their rituals.

CHAPTER 6

The Rituals of the Goddess Durga by the Dominant Caste

In this chapter we shall focus on the rituals of Durgapuja in the localities of the Ugra-Kshatriya as well as in the Jogadya temple. The analysis will be particularly on two topics, the relationship between the Jogadya temple and the locality in the course of the rituals, and the ritual organization within the localities. In the village, Durgapuja is one of the biggest annual functions; five Durgapujas are performed in the localities of the Ugra-Kshatriya, dominant caste of the village today. The temple Durgapuja is regarded as a model for the other Durgapujas of the localities, and each Durgapuja in the locality is closely connected in and integrated into the Durgapuja of the temple. In the meantime, there is a rotation system of the ritual organization in the locality, the *sola-ana-puja,* which has been discussed in Chapter 3. In the ritual of *sola-ana-puja,* every household of the priests jointly shares the responsibility for the daily temple service based on the rule of *sola-ana.* The case to be examined here is the ritual of *sola-ana* in the lineage locality in the northern part of the village.

The Durgapuja in Bengal

Durgapuja is an annual autumn festival in Bengal. The magnificent urban festival in Kolkata (Calcutta) is specially famous. Akos Ostor, a pioneering anthropologist who surveyed the Durgapuja in the historical town of Bishnupur in West Bengal (1978, 1980, 1982, etc.), pointed out that it is generally community puja that is performed in Bishnupur town, in contrast to the king's ritual at the court of Bishnupur.[1] Ostor indicates that there are different kinds of community pujas: *para-sola-ana* (the ritual of a locality), *jati-sola-ana* (the ritual of a particular caste), and *sarbajanin-puja* (the ritual of a community people), but ultimately takes notice of a common characteristic among these community pujas through the comparison with the king's ritual. He emphasizes the contrast of the ritual composition between them.

It is indeed certain that *sola-ana-puja* and the *sarbajanin-puja* stimulate the local people to integrate into the ritual community, which is shaped by its ritual organization. Members of a community stand together as a whole in front of the altar of the goddess. However, it is only in recent years that the ritual style of *sarbajanin-puja* has emerged, especially in urban communities such as Kolkata and Siliguri.[2] The ritual organization of *sola-ana-puja* seems to have been passed down chiefly in the rural society of Bengal for generations, and the succession and rotation system in this ritual is deeply embedded in the Bengali kinship system.

Let us first examine in detail the sequence of Durgapuja in the temple, which is closely connected with the rituals of the locality. Then we shall examine minutely the Durgapujas of *sola-ana* organized by the lineages of the Ugra-Kshatriyas, taking into account the genealogical data on lineages among them.

The Sequence of the Durgapuja

Table 6.1 presents the elements of the Durgapuja at the Jogadya temple in their ritual sequence. Durgapuja is famous as a popular urban festival in Kolkata. In this case, the Durgapuja is held for four days from the seventh to the tenth bright fortnight in the month of Aswin. In the village, the Durgapuja in each locality is held as per the ordinary schedule. But in its traditional style in the old temple such as the Mrinmaymandir in Bishnupur of Bankura district, it takes sixteen days from the ninth of the dark fortnight in Bhadra to the tenth bright fortnight of Aswin. The Durgapuja in Kshiragram has, however, a schedule of seventeen days from the eighth dark fortnight in Bhadra to the tenth bright fortnight of Aswin (from *ashtami* to *bijaydasami*) in the temple. The first column of Table 6.1 gives the date of the Durgapuja according to the lunar calendar, beginnings with the ritual of *bel-baran* in the eighth of the dark fortnight to the *bijaydasami* in the tenth of the bright fortnight. The next is the date in the Bengali almanac in 1994, which begins on the tenth of the lunar month of Aswin and ends on the twenty-seventh of Aswin.

The Durgapuja in the Jogadya Temple

The Tenth of the Lunar Month of Aswin: *Bel-Baran*

Bel-baran is the first ritual step to invoke Durga through worship of the *bel* or stone apple tree on the bank of Khelopukur pond. Formerly, there were 108 *bel* trees here. The Durgapuja in the temple begins with

TABLE 6.1: SEQUENCE OF THE DURGAPUJA AT THE TEMPLE

Dark fortnight	Lunar month of Ashwin	Ritual names
8th	10th	Bel-baran
9th	11th	*Nabami*/ *Puja* (*belphal*)/evening service/ *tarpan*/ *durgaghat*
10th	12th	*Puja* (*ghat*)/evening service/*tarpan*/*durgaghat*
11th	13th	*Puja* (*ghat*)/evening service/*tarpan*/*durgaghat*
12th	14th	*Puja* (*ghat*)/evening service/*tarpan*/*durgaghat*
13th	15th	*Puja* (*ghat*)/evening service/*tarpan*/*durgaghat*
14th	16th	*Puja* (*ghat*)/evening service/*tarpan*/*durgaghat*
New moon	17th	*Mahalay*/*tarpan-sraddha*/*puja* (*ghat*)/evening service/ *durgaghat*
The bright fortnight		
1st	18th	*Puja* (*ghat*)/evening service/*durgaghat*
2nd	19th	*Puja* (*ghat*)/evening service/*durgaghat*
3rd	20th	*Puja* (*ghat*)/evening service/*durgaghat*
4th	21st	*Caturthi-patrika-puja* (*C.P.*) *Puja* (*C.P.*)/evening service/*durgaghat*
5th	22nd	*Puja* (*C.P.*)/evening service/*durgaghat*
6th	23rd	*Sasthipuja* *Puja* (*C.P.*)/evening service/*durgaghat*/ *Naba-patrikapuja*
7th	24th	*Saptamipuja* (to *Naba-patrika, N.P.*) *Naba-patrikasnan*/*pathabali*/evening service/*durgaghat*
8th	25th	*Mahastamipuja* (*N.P.*) Evening service/*durgaghat* *Sandhipuja*/ *pathabali*
9th	26th	*Nabamipuja* (*N.P.*) *Mahisbali*/fire ritual (*hom*)/*candipath*/ evening service/*durgaghat*
10th	27th	*Dasamipuja* (*N.P.*) Farewell rite (*bisarjan*)/*bijaypranam* *Ugalpuja*

the ritual invocation to the *bel* tree on the seventh of the dark fortnight every year. After the regular evening service at the temple, a Brahman-sebait of the Sat-bhai lineage (temple priest on duty) marches through the street of the village from the temple to the Khelopukur with a Baiti playing his drum. At the base of the *bel* tree at the bank of Khelopukur, he sits in front of the tree and performs *bodhan*. This is a ritual invocation to the goddess Durga inside the tree. People think that the *bel* tree symbolizes the abode of the goddess Durga as a wife of Siva, and she usually stays with him. The ritual to the *bel* tree, therefore, is the invocation to the goddess living in the tree to the altar on the earth once a year.

The priest offers to the goddess sugar, sweets (*manda*), vegetables, incense, vermilion, *durba* flowers (Cynodon dactylon), and hibiscus (*jaba*) in particular, and leaves of *bel*. He uses the ritual utensils such as a small vessel (*kasakusi*), conch-shell, and bell, but without using the pot as in the *bodhan* in the other ordinary rituals. After the purification of himself, his seat, and the utensils, he starts the proclamation of the beginning of the ritual (*sankalpa*) in the name of the Bardhaman Maharaja. Then he performs the *bodhan* to the *bel* tree. At the end of the ritual, the priest cuts down a pair of *bel* fruits on the tree to which he performs the ritual. He carries them in his hand and marches back to the temple accompanied by the Baiti playing his drum. He enshrines the pair of *bel* fruits on the altar of the temple. In every ritual occasion during the Durgapuja, the priests perform to the fruits at the altar until the *bisarjan* on the final day.

THE ELEVENTH OF ASWIN: *NABAMI*

The ninth of the dark fortnight is traditionally regarded as the first day of Durgapuja, although the village priests start their ritual two days before the ninth in the temple. In 1994, the ninth of the dark fortnight (*krishnapaksha-nabami*) fell on the eleventh of Aswin, which means the twenty-eighth of September 1994. The ritual starts at the temple, where the Brahman-sebait, the Baiti, the servants of Bagdi, and the Malakar assemble. They make a procession from the temple to the Khelopukur again. The front position of the procession is occupied by the paik beating the gong in his hand. The Brahman-sebait holding the ritual utensils follows him. The Malakar with the copper pot on his head and the Baiti playing his drum follow them. On both sides of the street of the village, many villagers are waiting for the arrival of the procession. The housewives (*ginni*) receive them with incense, votive lights and small ritual pots (*durgaghat*). They make a deep vow to the street for the procession passing through them. After that, they draw water by the pots, and enshrine them at their household altars. This will be discussed later.

At the bank of the Khelopukur, the Malakar takes an ablution in the pond, and draws water with the pot. Soon, the procession returns to the temple. Many villagers receive them again on the street. Inside the temple, the *sabha-pandit* and the Candi-*pathak* are waiting. The pot is enshrined at the left side on the altar of the temple. They begin the ritual to the pot, and recite the Candi. After the ritual, the director of the ritual organization receives the goddess with a lamp with five wicks (*pancha-pradip*), a conch-shell and flowers, accompanied by the sound of the gong by the Malakar. Then the Brahman-sebait stands at the threshold of the main temple and gives the garlands made of *shola* grass (sponge wood) to every lineage of the Ugra-Kshatriya. At first, he calls the name of *Daraga babu*, and then *Pala-dhar. Daraga babu* means the superintendent of the Jogadya temple (*rajkachari*). *Pala-dhar* means the person in charge of holding the head of the buffallo in sacrifice on the ninth bright fortnight (*nabamipuja*). The lineage which is in charge must offer the special offerings to the temple. Then, he calls the names of nine lineages of the Ugra-Kshatriya two directorial posts in the same order as in the Jogdyapuja of Baishakh. (*Daraga babu*, *Pala-dhar*, Datta, Samant, Malla, Sani, Ray, Josh, Chota-Ray, Chota-Samant, and Chaudhuri.) Every representative of the lineage receives the garland in front of the door of the main temple from the hand of the Brahman-sebait. He puts, then, the mark of vermilion on their foreheads. From this day, the pot is enshrined until the farewell ritual at the end of Durgapuja, and the Brahman-sebait performs the daily service to it twice a day.

THE SEVENTEENTH OF ASWIN: *MAHALAY*

On this day, many villagers go to the bank of the Ganga at Katwa for ablution, at a specified moment described in the almanac. This is still a very popular custom all over Bengal. Those detained by work can take an ablution in the Kshirdighi or sprinkle water of the Ganga over their body entering into the cow-shed. Some villagers make a group to visit Katwa accompanying their *kula-purohit* and perform the ritual called *tarpan-sradha*. Some others invite the priest to their houses in the village and perform the ritual. At first, the priest performs the ritual of *tarpan-sradha* for the spirits of the ancestors of his clients. This is followed by the ritual of *pitri-bhoj*. Villagers pay the priest with lunch or sweets. It is actually the first day of the ritual of *tarpan*. The priest continues to perform the ritual of *tarpan* every morning from this day until the *bisarjan* at the end of the Durgapuja.

THE TWENTY-FIRST OF ASWIN: *CATURTHI-PATRIKA*

Before the daily service in the morning, a Brahman-sebait of the Sat-bhai lineage prepares a bundle of plants (*patrika*) inside the temple. This *patrika*, the *caturthi-patrika*, is made of four kinds of plants, banana, arum (*man*), taro (*kacu*), and rice (*dhan*). The bunches of arum, taro, and rice are put around a branch of banana tree with wide opened leaves. The people think that these plants together constitute a symbol of the goddess Durga. All altars in the village do not have images of the goddess Durga as is generally found in the festivals in Kolkata. They enshrine only a bunch of the plants of the *caturthi-patrika* on the day of the fourth bright fortnight (*caturthi*) and the *naba-patrika* on the ninth fortnight (*nabami*) at the altars as symbols of the goddess Durga. Kshiragram being one of the fifty-one sakta-pithas, the people have usually restrained from bringing any anthropomorphic figures connected with the ritual. They think that the temple Jogadya is the abode of the goddess for all the year round and the goddess Jogadya is an incarnation of Durga. As they have already the goddess in their village, they cannot bring other goddesses into the village.

The Brahman-sebait carries the *caturthi-patrika* in his arms and goes to the bank of Kshirdighi with the *mula-paiks* striking a gong and a Baiti playing the drums. At the stairs of the ablution bank of Kshirdighi, they perform ablution of the *caturthi-patrika* to the beat of drums and the gong. The Brahman-sebait returns to the temple carrying the *caturthi-patrika* and enshrines it on the altar of the temple. He performs the daily service in the morning at the temple altar. After the ritual, the *sabha-pandit* and the Brahman-sebait of the Sat-bhai lineage take seats in front of the altar. The Brahman-sebait performs the ritual to the *caturthi-patrika* (*caturthi-patrika-puja*), and the *sabha-pandit* assists him, chanting sacred verses. They put a simple cover with the face of the goddess on the *caturthi-patrika* and dedicate a wreath to the neck of the *patrika* and put paste of vermilion on her forehead. After that, they stand up and perform the reception ritual with a lamp, conch-shell, flowers, and ritual brush (*camar*) to the playing of drum and gong. Finally, they make a deep bow to the altar. From this day, they enshrine the *caturthi-patrika* on the altar and perform the rituals everyday until the day of *naba-patirka-puja* on the ninth bright fortnight. At the threshold of the main temple, the Brahman-sebait calls the titles of the nine Ugra-Kshatriya lineages again and gives garlands of *shola* grass to every representative of the Ugra-Kshatriyas in the same way as on the eleventh of Aswin. He also puts marks of vermilion on their foreheads. Meanwhile, the Malakar gives vermilion marks and sweets to the temple servants of the Bagdi and the Baiti.

THE TWENTY-THIRD OF ASWIN: *SASTHIPUJA*

After the evening service (*sandhyarati*) on the sixth of the bright fortnight, the Brahman-sebait bundles nine kinds of plants in the interior of the temple, the *naba-patrika.* The way of setting the *naba-patrika* is the same as in the *caturthi-patrika.* The nine plants are banana, taro (*kacu*), turmeric (*haridra*), stone apple (*bel*), egyptian sesban (*jayanti*), pomegranate (*dadima*), ashok tree (*ashok*), arum (*man*), and rice (*dhan*).[3] The *sabha-pandit* and the Brahman-sebait sit in front of the *naba-patrika* and place the offerings and start the ritual. At the directions of the Brahman-sebait inside the temple, the Baiti standing at the Natmandir plays the drum intermittently according to the course of the ritual steps. After that, they receive the *naba-patrika* with the gong beating by the Malakar standing inside the temple. The *naba-patrika* is left on the altar of the temple for the night. At every altar of Durgapuja in the localities, they prepare *naba-patrika* in the same way as in the Jogadya temple. The next morning, the priests of different altars of the village each bring *naba-patrika* out of the temple or the altar in the locality and set out for the bank of Kshirdighi for ritual ablution.

At night many Baitis visit the temple. They are employed from other villages for playing drums during Durgapuja in different localities of the village. They usually form a group of four members which consists of two drummers and gong players. They stand at the Natmandir and play their instruments in order to dedicate their performances to the goddess of the temple. In this way, they visit the temple at first and then go to each locality of the village to play their drums in each ritual.

THE TWENTY-FOURTH OF ASWIN: *SAPTAMIPUJA*

In the early morning of the seventh of bright fortnight, they perform the ritual for the *naba-patrika.* Before dawn, a Baiti plays the ritual calling by drums (*tengai*) signifying the beginning of the ritual. First, a Brahman-sebait brings out the *naba-patrika* enshrined on the altar of the temple to the front of the door of the main temple. The Brahman-sebait lays it down on a special palanquin made of bamboo and covers it with a fine sari. At the signal of the sound of the drum by the Baiti at the Natmandir, the priests bring out each *naba-patrika* from the altars of every locality in the same way. The priests carry them on their shoulders. The Baitis accompany them, playing drums and gongs. Boys from the localities carry the pots of the goddess Durga on their heads. The other followers hold the incense burners, brushes (*camar*), and large plates of offerings in their hands. All the *naba-patrikas* of the localities in the village go towards the Jogadya temple together. They enter the eastern gate and assemble at the Natmandir. The *naba-patrika* of the Jogadya temple is placed at the head of the line in front of the door of the main temple. The other *naba-patrikas* form a line sideways on the floor of the Natmandir. When all the *naba-patrikas* have lined up, they start the march simultaneously to the bank of Kshirdighi accompanied by priests and Baitis playing drums and gongs. Many attendants holding offerings and ritual utensils follow them. The other villagers follow. They go out through the western gate straight ahead to the stairs of the ablution bank of Kshirdighi.

At the bank of Kshirdighi, every priest holds the respective *naba-patrika* in hands, and stand in knee-deep water of the pond facing towards the bank where the *sabha-pandit* stands. At the side of every *naba-patrika,* assistants are waiting. They hold the plates of offerings for the purification of the *naba-patrika*s. At the signal of the director of the ritual organization, every priest performs the ritual of taking ablution of the *naba-patrika*s in the pond (*naba-patrika-snan*). According to the recitation of sacred verses the priests make ablutions ten times with a series of ten ritual items. Finally, they pour water thoroughly on the *naba-patrika.* Then, they bring them back to the bank again and cover them with sari. The attendants put the *naba-patrikas* on the palanquin to carry on their shoulders. The pots carried by the boys are filled with water of the pond, and a twig of mango leaves put onto the mouth of the pots. Boys carry them on their heads again. The procession of the *naba-patrikas* goes back towards the Jogadya temple again. They assemble once at the Natmandir in the same manner as in the beginning. After making a line in front of the main temple, each *naba-patrika* returns to the altars in the locality. At each altar, the priests perform the ritual ablution called *mahasnan* (great ablution) for the *naba-patrika* with the water of the pot and the other ritual materials. The *naba-patrikas* are enshrined at the altars and regular services to the goddess in the morning starts. The ritual order on this day in the morning (*saptami-puja*) is almost the same as the ordinary ritual, but the difference is a procession made for the sacrifice of goats to the localities. This procession for the sacrifices make clear the relationship between the temple ritual and the other rituals in every locality of the village as follows.

Soon after the ordinary rituals, the Karmakar of village Jabagram performs the sacrifice of the goat at the ground of the Jogadya temple. With the sound of the drums and gongs, the *paiks* hold the head and legs firmly on the block and the Karmakar brings down his sword. The decapitated head and the body are offered to the altar. The Brahman-sebait starts the ritual reception (*arati*) to the *naba-patrika* inside the temple. Thereafter a procession of the Karmakar, the servants of Bagdi, and the Baiti sets out from the temple to every altar in the Ugra-Kshatriya localities. At the head of the procession, the Karmakar is holding the bloody sword of the sacrifice up in his hand. The *paiks* beat the gongs and the Baiti plays the drum. At first, they visit the locality of Mallapukur-para in the north-western extremity of the village. Then, they go to the Malla-para, Ray-para, Kalibangra, and Samant-para in the end, which is on the eastern side of the village. When this procession moves, the participants virtually run.

At every altar of the localities, each priest performs the rituals according to the same ritual time described by the almanac. At every altar, they finish the rituals at almost the same hour and await arrival of the procession from the temple. They stand ready with the goats to perform the sacrifice. When the procession arrives, they put the goats on the block of the altars. The Karmakar of the temple has the bloody sword ready in his hand. The *paiks* and the Baiti play their instruments. In the same manner as in the temple, the goats are sacrificed by the Karmakar, and the fresh blood is poured on the altars. Then, the procession runs for the next altar without delay. The priests of the localities begin the *arati* to their *naba-patrikas.* In this way, the sacrifice of the Jogadya temple is performed first, and then other sacrifices are performed at various altars of the localities. After the ritual in the Jogadya temple, the Brahman-sebait calls the titles of the nine lineages again at the threshold of the main temple. Every representative receives garlands of *shola* grass from his hand. The order of calling the titles is the same as the rituals of the eleventh of Aswin, and the *caturthi-patrika.* The Malakar offers sweets to the *paiks* and the Baiti. In the evening, ritual services to the goddess is performed at every altar in the ordinary way.

THE TWENTY-FIFTH OF ASWIN: *MAHASPTAMIPUJA*

In the morning of the eighth of the bright fortnight, some villagers observe abstain from food for a day. Otherwise, many of villagers at least abstain from boiled rice and (parched rice) *muri* and eat only bread (*ruti*) made of flour at in the afternoon. People in the village dedicate many offerings to the altars of each Durgapuja on this day. The three lineages of the Chaudhuris (the Rays) in particular dedicate the fixed offering to the Jogadya temple every year. The contents are 20 kg of *atop-caul*, spices, and vegetables per lineage. They dedicate these offerings in return for the right to hold the head of the buffalo at the block of the temple for the sacrifice of the ninth (*nabami-puja*). Every three years, they select a representative from each lineage by turn for this role. They have the duty associated with this role to prepare a goat for the sacrifice in *pat-nalan* on the 29th of Baishakh as well as the offerings on this day.

In the afternoon, the Brahman-sebait prepares *annabhog* in a pot at the hearth of the Bhogmandir in the same way as in the *nabanna-utsab*. After boiling the rice, they break the earthen pot into nine pieces. They serve boiled rice, vegetables, bean soup (*dal*), and cooked fish on them. They strike the gong signifying the time of the offering, and call the titles of the nine lineages in the usual order. The rice offering with vegetables and fish on the plates is dedicated in front of the altar inside the temple. There is only one occasion to serve the rice inside the temple each year. Otherwise it is served at the Bhogmandir.

THE RITUAL OF BORDER: *SANDHIPUJA*

The liminal moment between the eighth and the ninth of the bright fortnight is called *sandhi*, meaning border, and occupies an important place in the ritual system of Durgapuja. The moment of *sandhi* is prescribed on the pages of the Bengali almanac every year, and a ritual is performed at the exact moment between the eighth and the ninth of the bright fortnight. In the village, the *rajkachari* gives the signal for the moment of *sandhi* in the Jogadya temple to all the altars in the village. Every altar follows the direction of the superintendent for each ritual procedure. This is another case to show the close relationship between the temple ritual and the rituals in every locality.

At the Jogadya temple, the Brahman-sebaits perform the *sandhipuja* inside the temple. In the centre the room they prepare a platform with a pile of sand, and dedicate the offerings on plates. They perform the sacrifice of a goat on this sand altar. The *rajkachari*, the *sabha-pandit*, the Candi-*pathak* and the Brahman-sebaits prepare for the sacrifice. The *sandhipuja* here starts twenty-four minutes (i.e. one *danda* in Bengali traditional calculation) before the moment of the *sandhi* as in the Bengali almanac. The Brahman-sebaits make many devotees come out from the interior room of the temple. Without the Brahman caste, the other people are prohibited to enter the temple during this ritual. The Brahman-sebaits close the door from inside, and cover the window with a cloth. A few minutes before the time of *sandhi*, the Brahman-sebaits light flaming torches of straw inside the room; they perform the sacrifice of the goat on the altar of sand, as the room fills with smoke.

A little while before the moment of *sandhi*, two of the Brahman-sebaits put the goat into position and tie the head and legs with ropes on the altar. A Brahman-sebait holds the sword of the goddess. The others surround the goat, holding torches in their hands. The superintendent stands beside them looking at a watch in his hand. At the signal of a shout by him; 'O! Ma!', the sword is brought down onto the goat at one stretch. The spouting blood is dedicated to the *naba-patrika* on the temple altar. Immediately after the sacrifice, they open the door of the temple and give the signal of the sacrifice to the Baitis waiting at the Natmandir. The Baitis begin to play at the Natmandir all together. At the sound of the drums from the temple, every priest on the altars in the localities knows the time to start their sacrifice to the goddess.

Messengers giving the time of *sandhi* used to be posted in the fields of the village in every direction. They relayed the signal of the time, shouting; 'Ma!' from the temple to all villages around. The people who stood in readiness for the sacrifice at every altar executed the sacrifice at the moment they heard the signal of the time from the village Kshiragram. It is also known at the temple that they formerly employed an earthenware pot and a small plate which has a very small hole at the bottom for their measurement of the time. The small plate is set to afloat on the surface of the water in the pot. They measured twenty-four minutes (one *danda*) by the time of a sinking of the plate, and grasped the exact time of *sandhi* with this measurement of a *danda* and the almanac sent from the royal court. Moreover, at the Sarbamangala temple of the Maharaja at the town of Bardhaman, they fire a cannon at the time of *sandhi* even now at the Kamantala in front of the temple. All the altars neighbouring the town of Bardhaman followed their time of the *sandhi* at the sound of the cannon from the temple of the

Maharaja. Even in Kshiragram, 64 km distant from Bardhaman, the people could hear the sound of the cannon, as the time of *sandhi* is the silent middle of the night.

After the sacrifices, the Baitis set out from the temple to go round the altars of the village playing their drums. Within the next twenty-four minutes every priest at the altars must finish the reception ritual (*arati*) with lamp, incense, brushes and flowers to Durga; finally the Baitis return to the Jogadya temple. Now the Brahman-sebait starts his reception ritual at the altar inside the temple. Hence, the reception ritual in the Jogadya temple is the last of all the rituals in the village. After that, the Brahman-sebait addresses the titles of the nine lineages of the Ugra-Kshatriya again and offers necklaces of *shola* grass to them. This is the end of the *sandhipuja*. After all rituals are over the people rush to receive remnants of sand, torches, and ropes used to hold the sacrifice inside the temple and take them home.

THE TWENTY-SIXTH OF ASWIN: *NABAMIPUJA*

The ritual in the morning of the day of the ninth bright fortnight (*nabamipuja*) is almost the same as on the other days; there is besides the sacrifice of a buffalo in the afternoon, at the temple. The servants of the Bagdi bring the buffalo to the temple. In front of the Natmandir, they set up a special block for the sacrifice of a buffalo. The people of the village surround the place. The Brahman-sebait purifies the block and the large-sized sword for the buffalo sacrifice. The *sabha-pandit* chants sacred verses, the Karmakar holds the sword in his hand beside the buffalo, a servant of the Bagdi holds a copper pot of the goddess on his head. Surrounding the buffalo, a crowd of youths gather and jostle each other. Most of them belong to the lower castes, the Bagdi, the Muci, and the Bauri. They are all half-naked, wearing a short piece of cloth on their waists. A large crowd of other villagers makes a wider circle around them. The courtyard of the temple overflows with people during the occasion.

After chanting to the buffalo, the priest makes a purification with sacred water. He throws a piece of fresh cloth over the body of the buffalo and puts vermilion paste on its forehead and its horns. He does the same for the sword with water and vermilion. The excited youths enclose and hold the buffalo. But the person who holds the head at the block is a representative of the Chaudhuri lineage. People swarm the roof of the Natmandir and the eastern gate of the temple to watch. At the centre point of the block, the Karmakar raises the sword and brings it down. At this moment, the half-naked youths cry and dance boisterously, lifting up their hands. Some rush to the block of the sacrifice and make a deep bow and tumble about on the ground soaked with the fresh blood of the buffalo. Others scramble for the freshly severed head of the buffalo, hold it on the head, and join the dancing. Others struggle for the beheaded body and bring it to the locality of the chief servant of the Bagdi.

After a little while, a dancing march sets out from the temple to the village with the wild striking of drums and gongs. The *paik*, with the head of the buffalo on his head, and the Karmakar lifting the sword in his hands lead the parade of excited people. They go round the streets in the village and visit altars in every locality. The route of the parade is the same with the procession for the sacrifice on the seventh bright fortnight: Mallapukur-para, Malla-para, Ray-para, Kalibangla, and then Samant-para. As the parade arrives at the altars, to the sacrifice of goats begins. The parade comes in the square of the locality with great excitement. The people of the locality treat the dancing youths with country liquor. The Karmakar proceeds in front of the block of goat sacrifice, and holds up the sword which was used for the sacrifice in the Jogadya temple. After the sacrifice in the locality, they go to the next altar. The decapitated heads are carried on the shoulders of the Bagdi servants, who join the dancing parade on the streets of the village.

Soon after the sacrifices, each priest of the altars performs a ritual to dedicate the fire to the goddess (*arati*), and the ritual to dedicate flowers to the goddess (*puspanjali*). At every altar in the village, the people of the localities participate in the ritual to dedicate flowers to the goddess in accordance with the recitation of the sacred verses by the priests. Then, another priest performs the fire ritual (*hom*). In the Jogadya temple, a Brahman-sebait performs it indoors in the tantric style. The reciter of the Candi then starts the ritual recitation of the passages of the *Mahisasura-mardini* in the *Devimahatmya* in front of the altar. The Brahman-sebait calls aloud the titles of the nine lineages of the Ugra-Kshatriya again and offers the necklaces of *shola* grass to them.

THE TWENTY-SEVENTH OF ASWIN: *DASAMIPUJA*

The final stage of Durgapuja is the *bisarjan* for Durga, which is performed after the ritual in the morning of the tenth bright fortnight (*dasamipuja*) at each altar. In the village, the farewell ritual for the *naba-*

patrikas is performed only after they complete a ritual for cows in cowsheds (*bhagabatipuja*), which is mostly performed by the Gaela caste in the village. After all the *bhagabatipujas* in the cowsheds are over, the Baiti of the temple plays a drum announcing the hour to perform the farewell ritual. At the altars in the localities, every priest completes the final ritual for the pot of the goddess, which is also called *bisarjan* according to the ritual texts for the Durgapuja in Bengal *paddhati*). People gather at the altars and bid farewell to the *naba-patrika*, the symbol of the goddess.

At the signal of the drum of the Baiti, people move the *naba-patrikas* carefully from the altars to palanquins of bamboo with the sound of conch-shell and *ulu* by the women. Persons carrying the palanquins on their shoulders at both ends swing the *naba-patrikas* back and forth several times. People think that this gesture means the farewell to the goddess at the altar, which is her temporary abode on the earth. They dress a fine sari over the *naba-patrika* on the palanquin. With the white smoke of incense burners (*dhunuci*) and using fans for the palanquin, the *naba-patrika* set out to the temple Jogadya. Already many *naba-patrikas* have assembled at the temple. The priests and followers attend to each palanquin holding the plates of offerings, incense burners, and *camar* in their hands. Some carry pots and flowers of the altars. From the locality of the Brahman of the village, many people bring trees of Manasa from their garden and join the parade of the *naba-patrika*. These were planted on the day of Manasapuja in the lunar month of Bhadra. The family who enshrines a Durga-pot (*durgaghat*) in their household altar brings out the pot putting a twig of mango in it and participate in the procession. In the same manner as in the *naba-patrika-snan* of the day of the seventh fortnight, each *naba-patrika* form a line in the Natmandir once and then the procession of the *naba-patrikas* set out to the bank of Kshirdighi.

At the stairs of the ablution bank of Kshirdighi, all priests hold the *naba-patrika* in their hands and stand in a line in the water of the pond. All the priests look toward the *sabha-pandit*, standing on raised ground. According to his recitation of the sacred verses, they perform the farewell ritual to the *naba-patrika*. At the same time, the other utensils used in the ritual such as for carrying flowers, incense, and pots of water are thrown into the pond. The trees of the goddess Manasa and the *durgaghat* are thrown too. From the bank of Kshirdighi to the Jogadya temple, they used to perform the *mayurnac* in the same manner as in the ritual of Jogadyapuja. The people return to the temple to make a bow once and then go back to the altars of their localities. At the altars, people accept offerings of *dadikarma* (parched rice, flattened rice, roasted rice, and sweets). After all the rituals finish, the villagers cele-brate the triumph of the goddess over the demon Mahisasura. The priests give a vine of butterfly pea (*aparajita*) to the people, and put it around their left hands. Some receive a mark of vermilion on their foreheads from the priests in exchange of a deep bow made to them. Some others drink a kind of juice mixed with water, sugar, lime, salt, and hemp (*siddhi*).

In the evening of that day the people pay a ritual visit (*bijay-pranam*) to each other. The younger generation visits the older persons of their locality, relatives, and the house of the family priest (*kula-purohita*). They celebrate the day of Durga's triumph over Mahisasura, and make a deep bow to the elders and embrace each other three times. The people belonging to the lower castes of the village visit the house of their masters belonging to upper castes. They dedicate a pair of small fish in a sieve of bamboo to the master. The master puts paste of vermilion on the fish and offers it to the household altar. Afterwards they cook and eat them. In exchange for the fish, they give the offering (*dadikarma*) to the lower castes who visit them. The custom to visit the house of the upper caste or the master by the tenants or agricultural labours continues till the day before the ritual of Kalipuja for one month in the village. It is custmary that within this period the people of the lower castes visit many houses of the upper castes, simply to receive foods and old clothes.

The Durgapuja in the Village

In this section, we shall concentrate on the ritual system of *sola-ana-puja*, which is a lineage organization based on the succession and rotation of rule in the Bengali kinship system. In the ritual context, the sixteen *ana* symbolizes the unity of the ritual community. The ritual of *sola-ana-puja* is usually managed by a particular lineage of a caste group in the rural area, or by a landholding family. As a patron of the ritual, every member of the lineage shares a quota of the privilege over the ritual in accordance with the calculation system of *sola-ana*. The holders of the quota are simultaneously assigned responsibility for the ritual perfor-mance on behalf of all the members of the lineage. Every member of the lineage is, therefore, jointly responsible for the lineage ritual accor-ding to their shares, and these shares are passed to the members of the lineage through the calculation of *sola-ana.* Here we examine the genealogy of the Ugra-Kshatriya lineages, because the *sola-ana* Durgapujas in the village are mainly organized by the Ugra-Kshatriya.

THE DURGAPUJAS IN THE LOCALITIES OF THE UGRA-KSHATRIYA

There were five Durgapujas held in 1994 in the village beside the Durgapuja in the village temple. Table 6.2 is the list of the Durgapujas in different localities held in 1994. As is shown in Table 6.2, these rituals are organized by the five Ugra-Kshatriya lineages of the village. Each lineage forms a small local community within the village society. In other words, each locality roughly corresponds to the lineages of Ugra-Kshatriyas, distinguished from each other by nine titles. For example, the Dattas reside in the locality of Datta, and the villagers call it Datta-para. The Samant dwells in the locality of Samant (Samant-para). The Malla in Malla-para, the Josh in Josh-para. But the Ray, the Bara-Ray, and the Chaudhuri inhabit the northern part of the village side by side. Their residential area occupies a large portion of the northern village and is generally called Uttar-para (the locality of the northern part). They are considered to be originally derived from a lineage of the Chaudhuris and are now recognized as sub-lineage to each other.

The Ugra-Kshatriya organizes all Durgapujas in the village, except for that in the temple. Certainly, some of the Brahman caste is hired in this ritual as priests. But members of the other castes in the village never organize this ritual as patrons. They only participate as worshippers or onlookers. Meanwhile, each caste has its own ritual in their locality, and the social importance of each ritual depends on the caste, and its locality in the village. For example, the ritual for Manasa is the most important ritual for the Bagdi caste in the village. Kalipuja (the ritual of

TABLE 6.2: THE DURGAPUJAS OF THE UGRA-KSHATRIYA IN THE VILLAGE

Locality	Person lineage	Place
(1) Uttar-para	Bara-Ray	Durgabangla
(2) Uttar-para	Na-Ray	Ray-para-mandir
(3) Mallapukur-para	Chaudhuri	Mallapukur-para
(4) Malla-para	Malla	Malla-para-mandir
(5) Samant-para	Chota-Samant	Samant-para-mandir

the goddess Kali) is important for the Bauri caste and the Muci caste, and so on. Although Durgapuja is often regarded as a typical and popular festival in Bengal today, this fact suggests that it was the dominant caste of rural Bengal who was the main supporter of this ritual. The other populations generally took a subordinate attitude towards this ritual.

Every Durgapuja in the village is thought to have original founders who belong to the particular lineages of the Ugra-Kshatriya. With regard to the Durgapujas in Table 6.2, it is possible to trace the lineages of the founders of the ritual five generations back in the rituals of (1), (2) and (3) in Uttar-para and Mallapukur-para. As for the Durgapujas of (4) and (5) at Malla-para and Samant-para, it is difficult now to trace the generations back from the original founder. Nonetheless, they regard it as their exclusive rituals to the other lineage members and restrict their memberships strictly. At first, we shall analyse the lineage structure of the Samant briefly.

THE LOCALITY OF SAMANT

The Samant-para is divided into the Bara-Samant-para (the locality of the big Samant), and the Chota-Samant-para (the locality of the small Samant). According to oral tradition, they share common ancestors among the members dwelling in the present two localities. Once they divided into two sub-lineages, they could not trace the name back to their common ancestor through their genealogy. But, they believe that it is obvious that all of them have the common title of Samant, and live in the neighbouring sub-localities in the eastern side of the village. They even have, now, marriage relations in a few families between the two sub-localities, but some villagers regard that the members within the seven generations of common lineage (*bangsha* in Bengali) should not be allowed to have marriage relations among them. If the couples are beyond the seven generations, however, they could marry, although many still believe they have common ancestors as an agnate (*gosthi* in Bengali).

It is said that the two sub-lineages of the Samant branched off earlier than seven generations ago, and at the same time, the originator of the sub-lineage of the Chota-Samant is the founder of the Durgapuja of their locality. This fact suggests that the membership of the ritual organization of Durgapuja in the locality always corresponds to the lineage group derived from the common ancestor of the lineage as well as the common founder of the ritual. The case of the Durgapuja by the Chaudhuri of the Uttar-para would be useful to examine as a further example.

ON THE GENEALOGY OF THE LINEAGES OF THE CHAUDHURI

The genealogical relationship of the lineages of the Chaudhuri is no longer remembered by anyone in detail. They consist of four sub-lineages and several dwell within the four localities in the northern part of the village. This is collectively called 'Uttar-para'. The three lineages are known as the lineages which participate in the temple ritual, namely the Bara-Ray (the first Ray), the Chota-Ray (the last Ray) and the Chaudhuri. The other is the lineage of the Na-Ray (the fourth Ray), which is one of the patronal lineages of the Durgapuja in Uttar-para. At present, each introduces themselves with the title of Chaudhuri, although the three lineages hold still the former title of 'Ray', i.e. Bara-Ray, Chota-Ray, and Na-Ray in the ritual discourse of the Jogadya temple.

Some elderly persons still remember the genealogy of a few of the generations of the Chaudhuri. Persons belonging to a branch of the Haradhan, for example, say that the founder, Haradhan had four sons. At present, most of the children of these four sons are the heads of each family of the branch. There are more than twenty households within this branch of Haradhan. They could recognize the kinship relations among them easily. Haradhan had a younger brother named Nahar. Nahar had two sons and the descendants from these two equal more than ten households today. It is also easy to acknowledge the kinship relations among the lineage members of Nahar, although only a few elderly persons in the locality can exactly recognize the kinship relations between the two branches, namely the Haradhan and the Nahar.

However, what is called the lineage of the Bara-Ray is regarded as descended from these two branches collectively, and can trace their ancestry back to the father of Haradhan and Nahar. According to one elderly person, Jaykali was the father of Haradhan and Nahar. Thus, it could be inferred that Jaykali is the original founder of the lineage Bara-Ray, which has now branched out into two sub-lineages. This lineage of 'Bara-Ray' is one of the titles, which consists of the nine lineages of the Ugra-Kshatriya of the village, and at the same time, one of the four lineages of the Chaudhuris in Uttar-para, as well. Table 6.3 helps to explain the detailed genealogy of the lineages of the Chaudhuris. The

TABLE 6.3: GENEALOGY OF THE LINEAGE OF BARA-RAY AND ITS *ANGSHIDAR*

The first is 'De' title
The Bardhaman Maharaja endowed with the titles of 'Chaudhuri' & 'Ray Chaudhuri'

Raja Udaychand Ray
Lakshan Candra Ray (migrated to the village Eruyar; 1746/7)
Badan Candra Ray (migrated to the village Kshiragram; 1774/5)
Bararam Raychaudhuri
Bara-Ray (the first Ray) → Jaykali
Meja-Ray (the second Ray) → migrated out
Seja-Ray (the third Ray) → migrated out
Na-Ray (the fourth Ray) → Dubraj
→ Bancharam
→ Bara, Meja, Seja, Na, and Chota
Chota Ray (the youngest Ray) → Gopal Chaudhuri

following discussion shall make clear the relations of the Chaudhuris according to this table.

HISTORICAL EVIDENCE

Let us now examine the historical evidence supporting the origin of the lineages of the Chaudhuri in the village. The family of Raychaudhuri is scattered across the Pargana Dhenya (*pargana* was a collection boundary for taxes in the Mughal period), which roughly corresponds to the Mangalkote Block at present. This has been handed down through the main family of Raychaudhuri in the village Caitannyapur near Kaicaur on the eastern part of the Mangalkot Block. According to the chart, the actual founder of the lineage of Chaudhuri in the village Kshiragram came from a lineage entitled 'De' in the village Eruyar situated in the present Bhatar Block, as shown in the following quotation:

> *The chart of the lineage of Raycaudhuri family . . .*
> *The original founder of this lineage (bangsha) is the Raja Udaycand Ray Deb Tatri Barman. His people were a family entitled 'De' in the pargana Dhenya, and their original gotra was 'Bishnu' . . .*
> *The original founder in the village Eruyar was Lakshan Candra, who migrated to the village in 1154 (Bengalisan B.S.) . . .*
> *The original founder in the village Kshiragram was Badan Candra (his wife's name is Parbbati), who migrated to the village in 1182 (B.S.) . . .*
> *Ram Candra (his wife is Harasundari) lived in the village Caitannyapur in 1202 (B.S.) . . .*

These descriptions indicate that the original family of Raychaudhuri migrated to the village Eruyar around AD 1746/7 and they migrated from the village Eruyar to the village Kshiragram around AD 1774/5, and then to the village Caitannyapur around AD 1794/5. These suggest that Badan Candra Ray De is the original founder of the lineages of the present Chaudhuris in the village Kshiragram. As we have seen, all those who are called Chaudhuri, used to be addressed as Ray in the other localities a few decades ago. Just after Independence, most of the members of the Ray in the village began to introduce themselves as the Chaudhuri. This is supported by the fact that in the ritual of the Jogadya temple, the temple priests still call aloud their old titles such as, Bara-Ray and Chota-Ray, referring to the present lineages of the Chaudhuri.

Furthermore, we have yet another clue to indicate the relationship between the lineages of the Chaudhuri (i.e. the former Ray). It is obvious that the lineages of the Chaudhuris originally had five names according to the manner of addressing by order of age in the ritual discourse as shown in Table 6.3. At the Jogadya temple today, the temple priests call aloud the three titles of the Chaudhuris; these are 'Bara-Ray', 'Chota-Ray', and 'Chaudhuri'. Besides, there is another lineage called 'Na-Ray', which is one of the lineages of the Chaudhuris. The old tradition in the village tells that the branches of 'Meja-Ray' (the second Ray) and 'Seja-Ray' (the third Ray) had migrated out of the village a long time ago. Due to these facts, we can presume that the lineage of Chaudhuri, which used to be called 'Ray', was composed of the five sub-lineages originating from the five brothers at one point on time. It is, therefore, probable to assume that all the four lineages of the Chaudhuri today had a common ancestor, although now it is difficult to recognize them as coming from the same lineage. This fact seems to coincide with the descriptions from the historical evidence, which will be discussed next.

As reported by an old man of the lineage Bara-Ray, their lineage began with Jaykali who had two sons, namely Haradhan and Nahar as already mentioned. The younger generations of the lineage today regard their ancestors as being four brothers, Kunjalal, Ramlal, Shamlal, and Matilal. It is clear that the father of the four brothers is Haradhan, although it is now difficult to identify who the father of Jaykali is. On the other hand, according to the historical evidence, the legendary ancestor of the Chaudhuri was a local chief in former times. The name of the chief was Bararam Raychaudhuri and his original title was De. He came from the village Eruyar and he had five sons. It is said that Bararam Raychaudhuri was the actual ancestor of the branch of Bara-

Ray in the village, and the eldest son of Bararam equals to the original founder of the Bara-Ray. This leads us to the assumption that the other lineages of the Na-Ray, Chota-Ray, and Chaudhuri in the village share the same traditions as their ancestors with the Bara-Ray. In the case of the Chota-Ray, it is said that they had an ancestor named Udaynarayan Raychaudhuri, and he is supposed to have been related by birth to Bararam Raychaudhuri. This is the same case with the lineage of the Chaudhuris in the village. According to a written document preserved by one family, their original ancestor is described as the Raja Bararam Raychaudhuri. Thus, it seems clear that the members of the lineages in the village holding the title Chaudhuri at present have a common ancestor, Bararam Raychaudhuri, as is shown in the reconstructed relationship in Table 6.3. The analysis regarding the rotation system of Durgapuja in the lineage of Bara-Ray shall support this assumption.

THE *SOLA-ANA-PUJA* IN THE LINEAGE OF THE BARA-RAY

The lineage of the Bara-Ray perform their own Durgapuja every autumn. In the case of the temple organization, it is the duty of the temple priest to perform the daily service, but in the Durgapuja of the Bara-Ray, it is the responsibility of each household head to carry on the annual ritual for all generations in his lineage. When the time to perform the Durga-puja comes, the household head is responsible for arrangements for the ritual, and performs it pompously on behalf of his lineage. He must arrange every necessary expense and a great deal of labour to perform the ritual by himself. The ritual of Durgapuja ordinarily lasts for more than four days. It is the most splendid ritual ceremony in Bengal, and requires a great amount of preparation, such as preparing altar and images, providing many offerings, hiring priests, and so forth. In this sense, *sola-ana-puja* has a reasonable system to share the burden by a lineage group, which is jointly responsible for the performance of the ritual.

THE HOLDER OF QUOTA IN THE LINEAGE OF BARA-RAY

Let us now look more carefully into the inner system of the organization of the ritual in the locality of Bara-Ray. Table 6.4 shows the families of the lineage of Bara-Ray. In the lineage Durgapuja, the shift assigned to each household head implies the duty to perform the annual Durgapuja

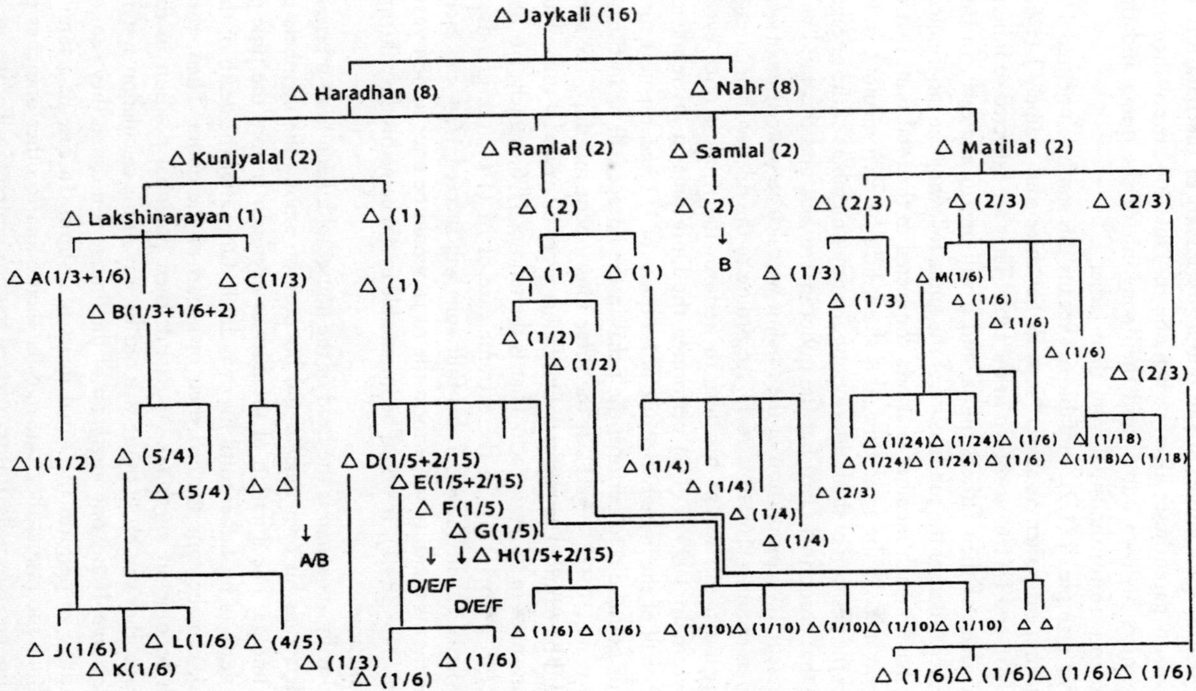

TABLE 6.4: FAMILY TREE OF THE LINEAGE OF BARA-RAY

in the allocated year according to the quota of each member. This quota (*angsha*) of each holder of the quota (*angshidar*) of the Bara-Ray is shown in parentheses after each name in Table 6.4. Every member recognizes his own quota, and their sons inherit the quota and the right to perform the ritual from their father.

For example, 'I (1/2)' in Table 6.4 means this son has inherited 1/2 *ana* from his father A's share. Now, he has three sons, namely J (1/6), K (1/6), and L (1/6) as shown in the table. They are expected to inherit their share of their father's quota, and it will be 1/6 *ana* each. In this way, regardless of the subdivision of the quota following the inheritance, the share of each member is always connected to the total sum, that is sixteen *ana*. At the same time, this share, held by each member, indicates the position of the holder among the other members of the lineage. On that account, J (1/6) has the quota in 1/6 *ana*, and this ratio will represent 1/96 proportion of the total, if we calculate sixteen *ana* (*sola-ana*) as the unit (16:1/6 = 96:1). According to the rules of their lineage Durgapuja, this means his duty to perform the ritual is once every 96 years. In 1993, I (1/2) performed the Durgapuja in his residence on behalf of the lineage. Because of his quota of 1/2 *ana*, the next turn of his household to perform the ritual in the lineage will be in thirty-two years (16:1/2 = 32:1). If the three sons inherit this duty, the sons would be required to perform Durgapuja every 32 years by turn. This means once in 96 years each. That is the ratio of 1/96, namely 1/6 *ana* (1:1/96 = 16:1:1/6). In the extreme case of M (1/6), the grandson of Matilal (2) in Table 6.4, his four sons will succeed 1/24 *ana* each. This means the duty to perform the ritual would be once in 384 years (16:1/24 = 384:1). It would be impossible to discharge his duty during his lifetime.

Usually, *angshidar* is the head of the house-hold. Each head precisely understands his own *angsha*, and his position among the members of the lineage. The duration of the duty as *angshidar* is from the time of the death of his father until his own death. Only after the death of the head, can the sons succeed their own part of the quota. Then, they each become an *angshidar*. As regards their potential position in the lineage, they can easily figure this out by way of the calculation system of *sola-ana*. If any one *angshidar* of the lineage is missing, they cannot continue to perform the ritual in its total form. In case of a family without successors, they can transfer their quota to other branches of the lineage. Normally, it is transferred to one's nearest kin. For instance, I (1/2) in Table 6.4 has a grandfather named Lakshinarayan. Lakshinarayan is the son of Kunjyalal, and held one *ana* as his quota of the ritual. Lakshinarayan had three sons, namely A, B, and C. They each inherited to 1/3 *ana* after his death. One of the sons, C (1/3), wanted to give up his duty and the quota for some unknown personal reason. Thus, he divided his quota into two portions, i.e. 1/6 *ana*, and gave it to his two elder brothers. As the result of this transfer, his two brothers, A and B, held 1/2 *ana* (i.e. 1/3 + 1/6). This is the reason that I (1/2) inherited 1/2 *ana* from his father A.

Regarding the quota of each *angshidar* of the lineage, each member can easily recognize the position of his ancestor, as well as other members in the lineage. If the father's quota is the sum of the quota among his brothers, the quota of the grandfather counts as the total sum of his brothers and cousins. In this manner, one can understand easily his position in the patrilineal relations of his lineage, as long as he knows the quota of each member. The upper generations always possess a relatively larger ratio. It naturally follows that the original founder of the ritual holds the total amount of the quota; that is *sola-ana*. In the case of the Bara-Ray, each *angshidar* recognizes precisely his own quota even today, though they do not know who is the actual founder of the ritual. Through the recording of the quota among the members, we can calculate the quota holding of past generations. As far as the villagers know, Lakshinarayan had one *ana*, and he had one younger brother. Because of that, we can easily estimate that the father of Lakshinarayan had two *ana*. Thus, Haradhan, the grandfather of Lakshinarayan, had eight *ana*, because he had four sons. In this way, we can see that the holder of the *sola-ana* of the lineage was the father of Haradhan and Nahar, whose name is Jaykali. These facts make it clear that the actual founder of the ritual is Jaykali, who is, at the same time, supposed to be the original founder of the Bara-Ray lineage which is one of the lineages of Chaudhuris in the village. This calculation of the ritual quota of the Bara-Ray supports the thesis that all the members of the Bara-Ray are descended from this original ritual founder as stated by the old man of the Bara-Ray. The Bara-Ray can recognize their lineage relationship by way of the calculation of their ritual quota.

On the occasion of Durgapuja, the *angshidar* represents all members of the lineage every year by turns. The *angshidar* bears all the expenses for the arrangement of the ritual, and performs it on behalf of the entire lineage. During the course of the ritual, he is required to prepare all the necessities of the ritual as is given in Table 6.5. If he fails to perform the ritual successfully, the members of the lineage would fear

TABLE 6.5: LIST OF THE OFFERINGS PREPARED BY THE *ANGSHIDAR*

Sacrifices:

Male goat not emasculated

1 goat	*Saptami* (Jogadya temple)
1 goat	*Dasami* (*Ugalpuja*)
3 goats	*Saptami/Sandhipuja/ Nabami* (Kalibangla)
	Shared in by the three persons: the hind legs by the reciter of the *Candi* and the priest for *hom.* The heads by the Karmakar.
1 sheep	*Nabami*
1 Wax gourd	*Nabami*

Offerings by the patron (*paladharer naibedya*):

Offering of boiled rice (*annabhog*) for the temple
Sundried rice (*atop-caul*: 20 kg, vegetables, and spices)

Offerings to the Brahman (*bhujhu*):

Boiled rice and vegetables (82 plates, for the all housholds of the Brahman in the village)

The other offerings:

Dedications by the patron to the priests and the reciter (*naibedya*)
Sundried rice (*atop-caul*, 2.5 kg per day), vegetables (8 plates for four days)
Dadibandya (boiled rice, offering plates, offering pots for four days)
Cloths for the priests and the reciters on the day of *sasthi* (*dhuti* 2 pieces)

Offerings (*utsarga*) in the rituals to the priests and the reciters for four days
sari (4 pieces), washcloth (*gamcha*; 4 pieces), *chador* (2 pieces),
Money offerings (*dakshina*: Rs. 5 each),

Offerings to the priests in the fire ritual
Offerings on the plate of banana (1 plate per day)

Offerings to the recitor of the *Candi* and the priest of the fire ritual
Washcloth in Nabami (*gamcha*: 2 pieces)

Offerings by the patron on the day of *Mahastami* (*Bara-naibedya*):

Sundried rice (*atop-caul*, 21 kg, 3 plates: 2 plates for the priest, 1 plate for the reciter)
Sweets and fruits for four days to the priest and the reciter
Banana 1 bunch (*kafun*) to the priest and the reciter
Sweets offerings (*dhadikarma*; *cire*, *murki*, molasses, yogurt, and hemp (*siddhi*) to the assemblage, the priest, and the reciter)

The others:

Baiti	Offerings (*naibedya*: 4 plates)	
(drums and gongs)	Money offering	Rs. 180
Priest	Money offering	Rs. 151
Reciter	Money offering	Rs. 151

that they will fall out of favour with the goddess. In this manner, the *angshidar* in his turn is regarded as the representative of the entire lineage and symbolizes the lineage as a whole. It is the *angshidar* who dedicates himself to the altar of the goddess as the patron (Skt. *yajamana*) in the ritual process of sacrifice as prescribed in the classical texts.[4]

Discussion: Ritual towards the Totality

As was mentioned before, the ritual of *sarbajanin-puja* bears some resemblance to the ritual of *sola-ana-puja* in terms of social integration of the people who participate in it. But, in spite of the seeming resemblance, there seems to be an essential difference between the two. The *sarbajanin* is a coöperative organization among the urban community in Bengal. The spread of this ritual style in the form of urban festivals is a relatively recent phenomenon. This ritual form is characterized as a cooperative organization, in which any member in the community is able to participate equally as a patron of the ritual.

On the other hand, the ritual of *sola-ana-puja* is a ritual organization based on the succession and rotation rule of *sola-ana*. Nowadays, it is rare in its traditional style, even in the remote villages. From the standpoint of structural-functionalism, both rituals of *sola-ana-puja* and *sarbajanin-puja* contribute to the integration of the members of their community. A symbolic way of dealing with the ritual structure can throw light on a symmetrical model, in which the ritual community as a whole faces the goddess in its ritual process, as if the king stands in front of the goddess. There is, nevertheless, a sharp contrast between both ritual forms if we look into the inner system of the membership and the partnership. It is the analysis of the rules of the role and rotation of the individuals that can explain the mechanism of the formation of the ritual organization in its changing state. As for the ritual of *sola-ana-puja*, it could be briefly described using the following three points to compare it with the ritual of the modern 'community puja'.

First is the membership of the patron of the ritual, in which the lineage is traced by their *angsha*, which precisely prescribes the participants of the ritual. It ensures the exclusive privilege of the member over the ritual, as well as the obligation to join in. Second is the rule of the succession and rotation regarding the ritual role of the lineage member, in which each member can recognize clearly his position in the lineage down the generations. In the temple ritual, we observe that this rotation system is secure enough to maintain the daily service in the temple without interruption or competition. The last is the strong orientation of the member towards the totality of the lineage. The quota of the individual is always considered in connection to the lineage as a whole. This calculation system shows clearly the role, and the position of the member within the lineage. Whether he is aware of it or not, the relationship of the *angshidar* is inherently united with the original founder of the lineage by means of their calculated quota of *sola-ana*.

In other words, the ritual of *sarbajanin-puja* is characterized as an open-ended system, in which a diverse membership is attracted and absorbed in it; while the ritual of *sola-ana-puja* is a closed system, in which a diverse membership is attracted and absorbed in to it; whereas the latter is a homogeneous group, in which the members, derived from the same origin, are always integrated toward uniformity through their shared quota.

The Durgapuja in the Households

During the period of the Durgapuja of the temple Jogadya, the village people have several ritual practices in their homes. These rituals are performed by the dominant caste groups such as the Brahman and the Ugra-Kshatriya, although some parts of the rituals are held by all the villagers.

THE RITUAL TO THE POT OF THE GODDESSS DURGA (*DURGAGHAT*)

The housewives of each household perform the ritual to a small pot, called *durgaghat* at their household altars every day during the Durgapuja. In the day of the ninth of the dark fortnight of Aswin, they bring out small copper pots in the houses at the signal of the sound of the drum by the Baiti in the temple Jogadya. Soon a procession of the pots starts from the Jogadya temple to the Khelapukur. They ordinarily draw water from the ponds neighbouring their houses. But ritual march of the pots from the temple to draw the water from Khelapukur has become a part of the tradition. The housewives at the northern locality of the village hold the pot in their hands and stand on both sides of the street from the Khelapukur to the temple. They burn incense and votive lights, and make a deep bow to the march of the pot on the street. Then, they bring back their pots to their houses to enshrine on the altar and put a twig of *bel* onto the pots. They perform the same ritual associated with the pots every morning and evening. Most of the households of the dominant castes of the village enshrine them in their houses except for the families belonging to the lineages which organize Durgapuja of the locality such as the Bara-Ray and the Na-Ray.

They bring out the pots to the neighbouring ponds again in the day of the fourth of the bright fortnight (the day of the ritual to the *caturthi-patrika*), and replace the water at the signal of the ablution to the *caturthi-patrika* by the Baiti at the temple. On the day of the ritual to the *naba-patrika*, which is on the seventh of the bright fortnight, they repeat the performance for the third time to the sound of the Baiti. They continue to perform the ritual to the pot twice a day until the final day of the tenth of the bright fortnight (*bijaydasami*). At the time of the *bisarjan* at the altars, they bring out the pots along with the procession of the *naba-patrika* and throw the water inside the pots into the ponds. Some households of the Brahman-sebait in the village perform this ritual in a little different way. They draw the water on the day of the seventh dark fortnight of Aswin (*badhan*), and throw the water in the early morning in the next day. They draw again on the day of the *caturthi-patrika*, and throw it in the next morning. They perform the ritual to the pots only during the four days from the day of the seventh bright fortnight (*saptamipuja*) to the tenth (*bijaydasami*). They throw the water at the time of farewell ritual in the end.

TARPAN

After the *nabami-bodhan* in the day of the dark fortnight, the households of the Brahman perform the ritual for the ancestors of the seven generations. That is called *tarpan* in the village. The Brahman-priests perform the ritual of *tarpan* every morning from the day of *nabami-bodhan* till the day of *mahalay* in their houses. Some devout families of the dominant castes perform it too, although they need the guidance of their family priest. The day of *mahalay* is in the new moon before Durgapuja. It is generally supposed in Bengal as the day of beginning to recite the sacred lore of the goddess Durga (the story of the *Mahishasuramardini*) and the final day of *tarpan* for ancestors as well. On this day, the family priests bring the heads of the *jajman* families to the ablution bank of the Ganga and perform the ritual service to the ancestors (*tarpan-sraddha*). These rituals consist roughly of three steps of reception;

namely, reception for the spirits of seven generations of ancestors, the various kinds of deities, and the reception for the family priests.

NOTES

1. Ostor argues; 'The more recent phenomenon of community puja includes all people, just as the king's puja includes all subjects. The collectivity is the offerer in *sola-ana* or *sarbajanin* pujas' (1980: 151). He puts it another way: 'The community is to the goddess as the king is to the goddess, the king ranking above the community because of his alliance with the goddess.'
2. The author has already discussed the historical development of this ritual in light of the structural changes of its ritual organization (Togawa 1992). The ritual style of *sarbajanin-puja* (everybody's ritual, or *barayaripuja*) has emerged in the modern history of Bengal along with the growth of popular nationalism, especially in the urban areas concentrated around Kolkata.
3. The botanical names of these plants and the the goddess associated with each plant are as follows: *kala* [musa sapientum; Brahmani], *kacu* [alocasia indica; Kalika], *haridra* [curcuma domestica; Durga], *bel* [aegle marmelos; Siva], *jayanti* [sebania sesban; Karttiki], *dadima* [punica granatum; Raktadantika], *ashok* [sarca indica; Sokarahita], *man* [colocasia esculenta; Camunda], and *dhan* [oryza sativa; Lakshmi].
4. In this respect refer, in particular, to H. Hubert, and M. Mauss, *Essai sur la nature et la function du sacrifice.* (*Sacrifice: its nature and function.* translated by W.D. Halls, 1899 [1964.])

CHAPTER 7

The Rituals of the Goddess Manasa Among the Lower Castes

In this chapter, we shall discuss the rituals of serpent worship, generally called *manasapuja*, which is one of the popular folk cults in rural Bengal. Especially in the country of Rarh (present day Birbhum, Bankra, Purulia, and Bardhaman), the cult of the goddess Manasa enjoys great popularity among the rural people. Manasapuja means the rituals for the serpent goddess Manasa, who is characterized by its ambiguous nature. She is regarded as an incarnation of the harmful serpents and at the same time is a guardian deity, protecting the people from the dangerous serpents. Manasapuja is usually observed on the last day of Bhadra. But the series of the rituals cover over five months, from 10th of the bright fortnight in Jaishta (*dashahara*), to the day of the farewell ritual in Durgapuja in Aswin. Manasapuja held in the Manasa temple at the Bagdi locality is the biggest ritual occasion in the village. The priest of the Bagdi (*deyasin*) performs the most important role in the ritual course. The analysis on this ritual will, therefore, bring us a perspective to see the village social structure from a standpoint of the lower castes. To use the phrase of Menchar (1974), we can see the caste structure from the bottom up.

THE CULT OF MANASA

THE RITUALS OF THE GODDESS MANASA IN THE VILLAGE

Although the Manasa temple is the most influential place of the cult of Manasa in the village, there are many other places to worship the goddess such as the small shrines (*manasa-tala*), the small altars in the gardens, and the wild trees of Manasa (*manasa-gach*; Euphorbia neriifolia). At the temples, small shrines (the altars of the goddess Manasa), there is always an association of Manasa plant. It is believed that the Manasa plant is the abode of the goddess and in many cases, the plant itself symbolizes the goddess. The total number of rituals regarding the goddess Manasa observed in 1994 is 79, and they are held among various localities and castes in the village.[1] Ten had sacrifices to animals and the others were without. These ritual forms of Manasapuja are diverse, ranging from the annual ritual at the Manasa temple, one of the biggest ritual occasions in the village, to the rituals at the small altar in each household. These too are spread over five months from the 10th bright fortnight of Jaishta (*dashahara*) to the 10th of Aswin (*bijaydasami*). In this regard, Tables 7.1 and 7.2 show places and occasions of the rituals in the village severally. These tables indicate the composition of the cult of the goddess Manasa in terms of the space and time in the annual ritual cycle.

The altars of the Manasa (*manasa-tala*) are small shrines under the Manasa tree. There are eight places for the goddess Manasa in the village, namely the locality of the Dom (*bagal-para*), the locality of the Muci (*das-para*), the Kusmethi-Bagdi in the eastern side of the village (*purba-para*), the Bauri in the south fringe of the village (*damacipukur-para*), the Tetuliya-Bagdi on the western side of the village (*kshirdighi-para*), the household of a Chaudhuri family (*uttar-para*), the household of Gyan Kundu, and the household of a Bauri family. The shrines belong to the lower castes in the village. Only two families, a Chaudhuri and Gyan Kundu, belong to the Ugra-Kshatriya. They founded the shrines privately. There are many small altars even in the courtyards of the Brahman, the Muci, and the Ugra-Kshatriya, which are temporary altars

TABLE 7.1: LIST OF THE PLACES OF RITUALS TO THE GODDESS MANASA

(1) The Manasa temple
(2) The altars of the goddess Manasa (*manasa-tala*; eight places)
(3) The courtyards of the Brahman
(4) The courtyards of the Muci
(5) The kitchens of the Ugra-Kshatriya

TABLE 7.2: LIST OF THE RITUAL OCCASIONS OF THE GODDESS MANASA

(1) *Dashahara*	The 10th bright fortnight of the lunar month of Jaishta
(2) *Panchami*	The 5th bright and dark fortnight in the months of Asar and Sraban
(3) *Sesi-panchami*	The last day of the 5th fortnights in the month of Sraban
(4) *Bhadra-sankranti*	The last day of the month of Bhadra
(5) *Bijaydasami*	The 10th bright fortnight of the month of Aswin (The farewell ritual in the ritual occasion of Durgapuja)

under small plants of Manasa. In the households of the Brahman and the Muci, they perform the rituals in their courtyards during the periods from the day of *dashahara* to the day of the farewell ritual in Durgapuja. Only the households of the Ugra-Kshatriya place their altars near the hearth in their kitchens on the day of *sesi-panchami.* The occasions of the rituals for the goddess are shown in Table 7.2.

The day of *dashahara* is on the 10th of the bright fortnight in Jaishta. The ritual of Manasa begins that day at every altar of the Manasa in the kitchens of the Ugra-Kshatriya. The days of *panchami* mean the 5th day of the bright and the dark fortnight in the month of Asar and Sraban after the day of *dashahara.* It is called *sesi-panchami* in particular that is the last day of the *panchami,* which means the last *panchami* in the bright or dark fortnight before the end of the month of Sraban (*sraban-sankranti*). But, the most important day for the Manasapuja is *bhadra-sankranti,* at the end of Bhadra, and the rituals in the temple of Manasa starts two days before *bhadra-sankranti.* At the time of Manasapuja in the Manasa temple, the people of Bagdi dedicate many offerings to the goddess. In cities like Kolkata *bhadra-sankranti* falls on the day of the ritual for the god Vishwakarma, while in the rural area of Bengal, it is still very popular as the day for the Manasapuja. The farewell ritual of Durgapuja means the 10th bright fortnight in the month of Aswin. On this day, twigs of the Manasa plants also join the procession to the pond of Kshirdighi along with the processions of the *naba-patrikas* to be thrown into the pond.

The Manasa Temple

TEMPLE ORGANIZATION

The Manasa temple is situated in the locality of Manasa-para at the north-eastern side of the village. It is the main centre of Manasa worship in the village. The majority of this locality is the Kusmethi-Bagdi, and the lower castes such as the Bagdi, the Bauri, and the Muci are the main donors for the daily service at the temple. The snake goddess has always an ambiguous meaning in the folk culture in Bengal. Manasa always makes her appearance as the highly poisonous snake and at the same time she would become the benevolent goddess protecting the people from its poison. It is the deadly poison of the snake that the people fear, when they move along the fields in the rainy season. Thus, the people pray to the goddess Manasa for protection and for cures from the poisoning.

The priest of the Manasa temple, the *deyasin,* belongs to a lineage of the Kusmethi-Bagdi. He performs the daily service at the temple, and leads the devotees of the other castes of the village for the special ritual occasions. He took initiation as a priest of Manasa from a spiritual master (*diksha-guru*) of another village and can recite the sacred verses of the goddess. The priest of Manasa is usually called *ojha* in the village, meaning one who has the special skill of handling snakes. *Ojha* is usually regarded as a medicine man in rural Bengal; on the other hand, it is referred as *saple* who is skilled in snake charmer. The priest of the Kusmethi-Bagdi has, however, not only the skill of handling snakes as an *ojha*, but the Maharaja of Bardhaman also gave him authority as a *deyasin* of the Manasa temple. The family of the priest is endowed with tax-exempt lands for daily service and annual rituals in the Manasapuja. Except for the priest of the family, nobody can perform the rituals at the temple. Even the Brahman priests has no right to receive the offerings of the villagers during the rituals. The Maharaja also endowed service lands to the Baiti and the Malakar for the ritual of Manasapuja. Thus, the ritual organization of the Manasa temple consists of the Bagdi priest (*deyasin*), a member of the Kusmethi-Bagdi lineage, the Baiti, a member of the lineage who plays drum in the Jogadya temple, and a Malakar who works in the Jogadya temple.

The lineages of the Baiti and the Malakar are the same in the ritual of the Jogadya temple. These three members are given posts by the Maharaja and conduct occasional rituals in the Manasa temple. Moreover, they have equal rights to shares in the offerings after the ritual.

DASHAHARA

On the 10th of Jaishta, the people of the locality of the Manasa temple worship the earthen pot (*manasa-ghat*) enshrined in the temple. In the morning, people come to the temple and dedicate offerings at the altar. The Baiti comes to play his drum announcing the beginning of the Manasapuja in the morning. The Malakar prepares a basket of flowers to dedicate to the goddess. The Malakar and the Baiti are of the same lineages who have duties for the ritual services at the Jogadya temple. At the altar of the temple Manasa, the *deyasin* prepares for offerings, water of the Ganga, and the ritual utensils for the goddess. He lives in the house next to the temple in the Manasa-para.

The *deyasin* at the Manasa temple prepares the votive lights and incense. First, he purifies himself with sacred water of the Ganga, and sprinkles the water and the flowers over the altar. The next step is the ritual proclamation (*sankalpa*), in which the priest declares the beginning of Manasapuja at the altar in the name of the Maharaja Bardhaman. Then, he invokes the goddess Manasa at the altar, and dedicates through sacred verses and various offerings to the earthen pot of the goddess. In the same way as the Brahman priest in the Jogadya temple, the *deyasin* holds lights, flowers, and offerings in his hand, and performs the reception rites to the goddess. After the rituals at the temple, he leads the procession of the earthen pot of the goddess to the bank of a pond. With the sound of the drum, the *deyasin* holds the pot of the goddess in his hand, and brings it to the bank nearby. At first, he himself bathes in the waist-deep pond and then gives the pot an ablution. He puts the pot down on the ground, and performs again the rituals with flowers and sacred water with the recitation of sacred verses. The Baiti stands beside him and plays the drum in a specified rhythm for the goddess Manasa. Then they return to the temple and the priest enshrines the pot at the altar of the temple. Next is the sacrifice of an uncastrated goat and a few geese at the square in front of the temple. People of the locality gather around the square of the temple. The *deyasin* donates the goat, and the people of the locality offer the geese. After purification of the animals with sacred verses, they set up a block for sacrifices in front of the temple, and hold down the body of the goat. With the sounds of the drum, a Bagdi youth cuts the head of the goat with a sword. They pour the blood from the beheaded body to the wall of the Manasa temple and the head is dedicated on the altar. They then sacrifice the geese to the goddess one after another. Finally, the Baiti plays the drum announcing the end of the ritual.

After a series of rituals, the *deyasin* priest prepares a big earthenware pot outside his house. In ten days, he prepares local liquor fermented from rice in the pot. He performs the same ritual associated with the pot on the veranda in the afternoon and then treats the men of the locality with drinks. The *deyasin,* the participants in the ritual of the day, and the women who dedicated offerings to the goddess are required to observe a fast from the morning until the end of the ritual. After that, they can eat *cire* (flattened rice) soaked in the water, but do not eat boiled rice or food made from flour.

THE DISTRIBUTION OF THE OFFERINGS

There are two occasions to dedicate offerings to the Manasa temple, direct dedication and collections by the wife of the Bagdi priest (*deyasini*). The first is the dedication by the worshippers who came to the temple from the locality of Manasa-para and the neighbouring localities such as Chaudhuri, Samant, and Brahman. Most of the devotees are the housewives of each locality. From the early morning until the start of the ritual, they bring plates of offerings to the temple on behalf of their family. The main items to offer to the goddess are fruits, vegetables, rice, molasses (*gur*), mustard oil (*sarse-tel*), milk, and vermilion. They hand over the plates to the *deyasin* of the temple and make a deep bow to the goddess. The priest adds the offerings to those already in a basket on the altar. Then he picks up a little amount of them from the basket and returns the plates to the dedicators as *prasad* of the goddess. The major part of the offering is left in the basket on the altar. The piles of offerings are then shared equally among the Malakar, the Baiti, and the *deyasin* once the ritual is over.

A collection is made from every house in the village by the *deyasini.* She visits mainly the households of the upper castes of the village such in the localities of Samant-para, Datta-para, Josh-para, and Ghosh-para. The circuit she makes around the village covers nearly the whole upper-class locality except for that of the Chaudhuris. The main items of offerings are more or less the same as at the temple. She goes round every house of the localities carrying a big basket under her arm. At the houses, she sits down on the ground in the courtyard, and the housewife puts into her basket, offerings prepared in the household altar in the early morning. The wife of the priest only receives the offerings but does not return anything as *prasad.* Her basket gets heaped with offerings soon. The total amount of offerings after the making collection of the village is equivalent to several baskets. These offerings are dedicated to the temple Manasa once and become their share afterwards. Like the *deyasin*, his wife also got initiation with the sacred verses for the goddess Manasa from their spiritual master from a remote village. She also could perform the ritual service on behalf of her husband at the Manasa temple.

THE RITUAL IN EACH DAY OF *PANCHAMI*

The rituals on each day of *panchami* are performed in the 5th of both the bright and the dark fortnights in the months of Asar and Sraban. The ritual sequence is almost the same as the ritual in the day of *dashahara* in Jaishta. In these rituals, however, there is no ablution of the pot, or sacrifice. The villagers only visit the temple to dedicate their offerings for Manasa. The quantity of the offerings is not much on the day of *dashahara.* The Malakar, the Baiti, and the *deyasin* share them equally after the rituals. The *deyasini* also goes round the village to collect the offerings among the households in the same way as before.

BHADRA-SANKRANTI

The rituals in the Manasa temple are performed for three days, beginning from two days before the end of the lunar month of Bhadra (*bhadra-sankranti*). During the three days, the *deyasin* of the Manasa temple carries the pot of Manasa in his arms and makes a round of the village. On the final day, he calls at the Jogadya temple and on the *rajkachari* who makes a bow to the pot of the goddess Manasa.

On the two days before the end of Bhadra, the Baiti plays his drum in front of the temple of Manasa once in the morning announcing the beginning of the first day of the Manasapuja. In the evening, the *deyasin* starts his ritual in the name of the Maharaja at the altar of the temple and performs the ritual reception to the pot of the goddess. He carries the pot in his arms and goes round the temple once, and then he starts to go round the village accompanying the Baiti. This procession of the pot of the goddess proceeds across the village up to an altar at the foot of the Manasa plant (*manasa-tala*) in the locality of Kshirdighi-para in the western side of the village. The villagers on both sides of the streets hold flaming torches in their hands to illuminate the path of the procession. At each lane, they make a bonfire and light torches over them, particularly in the localities of the lower castes. In the light and deep smoke of the fire, the pot of the goddess in the arms of the *deyasin* moves. This procession of the pot repeats three times during three days. On the last day, they have more elaborated sequence of rituals than in the other days including the sacrifice. Let us examine in detail the process of the ritual on the day of the end of Bhadra (*bhadra-sankranti*).

The Baiti plays his drum five times on the day of the end of Bhadra. After the first play in the early morning announcing the beginning of the ritual, the people of the locality come to the Manasa temple to dedicate offerings. At the signal of the drum for the second time in the early afternoon, the people of every locality gather around the temple carrying the goose severally in their hands. The *deyasin* begins his ritual at the temple altar in the same way as in *dashahara*. The youth in the locality of Manasa-para set up a block for sacrifice in the square of the temple. The priest purifies the sword at the altar. The square is filled with a large crowd surrounding the temple. The villagers bring the goose to the altar of the temple for purification. The priest dedicates gooses at the altar, and sprinkles sacred water over it, with chanting sacred verses.

The ritual of sacrifice begins. At first, they sacrifice an uncastrated male goat dedicated by the family of the *deyasin* with drumbeats by the Baiti. The youth of the Bagdi lineage hold down the body of the goat to the block and hold up the sword. After sacrifice, the blood of the goat is poured on the wall of the temple. The body and the head are then dedicated at the altar. The next sacrifice is of rams, offered by private devotees. Finally, they sacrifice the goose. The youth of the locality sacrifice them one after another. At the altar of the temple, the priest performs the ritual to dedicate the heads of the geese, bringing them from the block immediately after their sacrifice. As almost every household in the locality dedicates a goose for the ritual, it takes nearly an hour to complete this sacrifice. The donors receive the beheaded bodies of the goose and carry them home as offerings of the goddess Manasa. After the sacrifice of all goose brought there, they perform the ritual sacrifice to a few wax gourds and sugar canes in the end. They put a wax gourd on a sheaf of straw on the ground. Just the same way as the sacrifice to the animals, they hold up the sword and cut down the gourd into two pieces. Immediately after that, the pieces of the gourd are thrown over the head of the sacrificer to the people gathering around. They rush to catch and scramble for a piece. After the sacrifice of wax gourds, they put a stalk of sugar cane on the straw. After its sacrifice, the people scramble for pieces again. People take pieces of wax gourd and the stalks of sugar cane to their respective house and put them in the manure pit. After all the sacrifices, the people around receive some offerings from the hand of the Bagdi priest as blessings of the goddess.

The Baiti plays his drum for the fourth time in the day a little while after the sacrifice. With the sound of the drum, the priest carries the pot in his arms and goes round the temple building once. He makes a temporary altar for the pot outside veranda of his house. It is situated next to the temple. He dedicates a basket piled up with the offerings and places the ritual utensils aside. He enshrines the pot at the centre of the altar. Many floral garlands dedicated by the villagers are put on the pot. Besides it, he dedicates three flat baskets with covers. Inside of these baskets, three poisonous snakes are put severally. The medicine man of the Bagdi (*ojha*) in the locality catches these snakes alive. He extractes the venom of the snakes and keeps them inside the baskets. These snakes are necessary for the ritual songs called *jhapan-gan*. Nobody is allowed to open the baskets with snakes inside to the public before the performance of the songs.

In the evening, people of the locality gather in the square of the temple. When it gets dark, they light torches of straw and the Palmyra leaves in their hands and make bonfires in the square. Being thick with the white smoke of the fires, the Baiti plays his drum for the fifth time in the day. This signals start of the procession to the Jogadya temple. The *deyasin* carries the pot to the veranda in his arms and sets out for the procession. Many followers such as persons sprinkling the sacred water over the pot, making the smoke by the incense burner, holding the ritual utensils in their hands, playing the drum and so forth, attend the priest. The fire of the torches in the hands of the villagers illuminates all members of the procession. The procession proceeds through the dense smoke of torches, bonfires, and incense.

At first, they pass through the locality of the Chaudhuris and turn to the Jogadya temple. The people on both sides of the streets to watch the procession passing off. They go through the locality of the Brahman and enter the ground of the Jogadya temple at the gate on the north-eastern side of the temple. Many villagers are already assembled there and also hold torches in their hands. At the centre of the square in front of the *rajkachari* office, they set up a small altar to enshrine the pot of the goddess for a while. The *rajkachari*, who supervises the organization of the Jogadya temple, stands at the middle of a row in front of the altar. The *deyasin* carrying the pot in his arms proceeds to the *rajkachari* and puts it down at the altar. The *rajkachari* lights a flaming torch in his hand over the pot. The *deyasin* sits down there and begins his rituals to the pot.

Afterwards, the Bagdi priest puts a sacred mark of vermilion (*phonta*) on the forehead of the *rajkachari*. The priest picks up one of the floral garlands from the pot, and puts it around the neck of the *rajkachari*. The *rajkachari*, who belongs of course to the Brahman in the village caste hierarchy, makes a deep bow to the pot of the goddess, where the *deyasin* is sitting before it. Then, the priest carries the pot again in his arms and leads the procession to the locality of Kshirdighi-para, where is on the opposite side of the village to the locality of Manasa-para. The route is from the gate, through the locality of the Brahmans, the branch street beside the Kshireshwari temple, the locality of Josh-para, and again through the main street of the village to the small altar of Manasa in the locality of Kshirdighi-para. On either side of the street and corners of the village, the people throng to see the procession and hold up the torches in their hands over them. Those present are almost choked by the smoke of the fire and congestion. At the altar of the

Manasa tree in the locality of Kshirdighi-para, the people of the locality gather and dedicate offerings in front of the Manasa plant. The priest in this locality (*deyasin*) is already prepared for the ritual. They all belong to the sub-caste of Tetuliya-Bagdi, while the people in the locality of Manasa-para belong to the Kusmethi-Bagdi. The Bagdi caste in the village is divided into these two sub-castes. When the procession arrives at the altar, the priest of Manasa-para puts down the pot on the middle of the altar and sits down. The priest of Kshirdighi-para also sits down aside him. They make ritual offerings to the pot and dedicate the offerings on the altar. The priest of Manasa-para picks up one of the garlands on the pot, and puts it around the neck of the priest beside him. He also gives a *phonta* of vermilion on the forehead of the priest of Kshirdighi-para, and then to the forehead of every member of the locality surrounding there one after another.

After the ritual at the altar of Kshirdighi-para, they go to another altar of Manasa at the neighbouring house of a family of the Bauri caste in the locality of Pashcim-para. The priest performs the ritual to the pot again in the same way as in the locality of Kshirdighi-para. He offers a garland and a *phonta* to the head of the family of the Bauri sitting beside him. Then the procession returns to the streets inside the village by way of the locality of Datta-para and the main street facing the Jogadya temple. They pass along the locality of Samant-para, and returns to the Manasa temple in the locality of Manasa-para. It is customary for the villagers who see the procession off on the streets to say the following phrase to their family at the gate of the house when they enter:

> *Ghare kena alo?*
> Why is a light burning in the house?

The family answer:

> *Ginni gechen ban berate. Sabai ache bhalo.*
> The housewife has gone out to the woods. Everybody is fine.

After recitation of these phrases, they enter the house. It is said that the housewife (*ginni*) in this sentence means the goddess Manasa and her going out to the woods means the procession of the goddess going round the village. The ritual of Manasapuja comes to an end at this point. The villagers add the ashes of the torches and the bonfires to the manure for their agricultural fields.

The Small Altars of the Goddess Manasa (*Manasa-tala*)

In the village, there are eight shrines with Manasa plants (*manasa-gach*) to worship the goddess, which are generally called *manasa-tala*. Each shrine of *manasa-tala* has its own priest (usually called *ojha*), who establishes the altar for the goddess. The *ojha* of the goddess is a non-Brahman priest who engaged in the rituals to protect the people from the calamity of snakes. He has a small altar to perform the ritual in front of the Manasa plants, but most of them are only simple trees without shrine buildings. During the days of the ritual, the people of the locality decorate the tree with garlands, enshrine a pot for rituals, and dedicate many plates of offerings. Table 7.3 shows the list of the ritual occasions at each altar of the goddess Manasa observed in the village.

The first line of location on table is the Manasa temple, and from (a) to (h) are the altars of *manasa-tala*. The lines of ① to ③ are the household rituals for the goddess Manasa in each locality, which will be discussed later. All the locations indicate the ritual occasions following the ritual cycle of Manasapuja as was examined in Table 7.2, and whether sacrifice is practised. The comparison among the localities in the village will make clear the contrasting attitudes towards the folk cult in Bengal among the different caste groups.

TABLE 7.3: RITUAL OCCASIONS OBSERVED AT EACH ALTAR OF THE GODDESS MANASA

Location	*Dashahara*	*Panchami*	*Sesi-panchami*	*Bhadra-sankranti*	*Bijaydasami*
Manasa Temple	◎	O	O	◎	
(a) Gyan Kundu	O	O	O	◎	
(b) Chaudhuri	O	O	◎		
(c) Kshirdighi-para	O	O	O	◎	
(d) Purba-para	O	O	O	◎	
(e) Das-para	O	O	O	◎	
(f) Bauri-para		O	O	O	◎
(g) Paschim-para	O	O	O	◎	
(h) Dom-para	O	O	◎		
① Brahman	O	O	O		O
② Muci	O	O	◎		O
③ Ugra-Kshatriya		O	O		

Note: Ordinary Ritual: O, Ritual with Sacrifice: ◎.

THE ALTAR OF GYAN KUNDU IN HIS YARD

Gyan Kundu is a well-known *ojha* in the village. He belonged to a Kayastha caste family, but he trained many disciples from various castes in the village and made them *ojhas.* After his death, there are three others who are considered experts in the technique of *ojha.* The villagers believe that an *ojha* can cure snakebites and other diseases by supplying various herbs and amulets. Especially, he can counteract the venomous snakebites, which otherwise may cause instant death, and it is not unusual thing at the rainy season in the fields. The *ojhas,* sometimes the ordinary villagers also, plant Manasa trees in their gardens for use in treatment in case of snakebites. It is the Manasa tree that is regarded as an effective antidote to the snakebite in the folk-belief, and also it is believed as an incarnation of the goddess Manasa.

In the garden of the house of Gyan Kundu, a fine Manasa tree was planted. He offered a prayer to the goddess Manasa in the Manasa temple at the locality of the Kusmethi-Bagdi and brought the spirit of the deity to the tree so as to build the Manasa altar anew in his garden. Then, he started to perform the ritual to the Manasa tree. After the emigration of his family the *ojha* of Das-para, who is one of his disciples, has succeeded him. The neighbouring people dedicate offerings everyday to propitiate the deity. However, on the special occasions, such as *dashahara,* each *pnachami,* and *bhadra-sankranti,* a priest of the lineage of the Brahman comes to perform the rituals to the tree.

THE HOUSEHOLD ALTAR OF THE FAMILY OF CHAUDHURI

In the locality of the Chaudhuri (Uttar-para), who belong to the Ugra-Kshatriya, in the northern part of the village, there is a small altar of Manasa by the side of street. It is said that at the time of marriage of the former head of a family in the locality, the bride brought a branch of the Manasa tree along with her trousseau from her native house in the village Kaicaur. She planted the tree and began the daily service to the goddess Manasa. The ritual at the foot of the tree is, therefore, connected with the ritual in the village Kaicaur. For example, the Brahman priest who is invited for the special occasions is their family priest, and performs the rituals of the goddess Manasa on the days of *dashahara* and each *panchami.* Above all, the day of *sesi-panchami* (the last *panchami*) is the biggest occasion for them along with the sacrifice of a unacastrated goat for the goddess. While, they have no rituals on the day of *bhadra-sankrati*, which is the biggest occasion in the Manasa temple of the village.

KSHIRDIGHI-PARA

Beside the square of the Kshirdighi-para, where is the dwellings of the Tetuliya-Bagdi, they have an altar of Manasa. Usually, women of the locality make offerings to Manasa at the altar everyday. The head of the family of Bhuniya who resides in front of the altar succeeds to the post of the priest of Manasa for generations. It is on the days of *dashahara*, each *panchami*, and *bhadra-sankranti* that he practises the rituals. The family of Bhuniya also offers the sacrifice of an uncastrated goat on the day of *bhadra-sankranti*. Each household of the locality dedicates a goose for sacrifice to the goddess. The Brahman priest, who is the family priest of the Bhuniya, comes to perform the ritual. In the evening, the people in the locality with flaming torches in their hands await the arrival of the procession from the Manasa temple. The *deyasin* who belongs to the Kusmethi-Bagdi of Manasa-para sits down and performs the ritual in front of the altar. The *deyasin* of the locality of Kshirdighi-para sits beside him. As a representative of the locality, the *deyasin* puts a garland for the goddess on the pot.

PURBA-PARA

The locality of Purba-para situated in the south-eastern fringe of the village, is inhabited by the Kusmethi-Bagdi. It is said that the people in Purba-para migrated from Manasa-para. They used to come to the temple Manasa in the locality of Manasa-para so as to dedicate offerings to the goddess on the days of Manasa rituals. Nowadays, they perform their rituals at the own altar at the foot of Manasa tree in the corner of the locality. After some disputes with the people of Manasa-para, they planted a Manasa tree for the altar and separated their rituals. They have no priest of their own so far. Usually, the women in the locality come to worship and dedicate some offerings to the altar in the morning and evening. On special occasions (*dashahara*, each *panchami*, and *bhadra-sankranti*), they invite a Brahman priest in the village for the ritual.

DAS-PARA

The locality of Das-para is a large area situated in the northern fringe of the village. The people here belong to the Muci caste. The *ojha* in the locality of Das-para used to assist Gyan Kundu. He learned much of the skills of *ojha* from Gyan Kundu and took even an initiation of the sacred verses from him. Then he became an *ojha* in Das-para. The people in the locality of Das-para used to come to worship Manasa at the place of Gyan Kundu. After migration of the family of Gyan Kundu, the *ojha* brought a branch of the plant from the yard of the house, and planted it by the side of the neighbouring road as an altar of Manasa. Now, he performs daily services to Manasa at the altar in the locality of Das-para.

The rituals of the goddess Manasa are performed on the days of *dashahara*, each *panchami*, and *bhadra-sankranti*. In all these days, the *ojha* of Das-para practices the rituals himself, but on the day of *bhadra-sankranti*, the Brahman priest of the village is invited to the altar. The *ojha* performs his rituals in the same way as the Brahman priests do in other rituals. On each day of the rituals people of the locality dedicate offerings such as sweets, flowers, and fruits to the goddess from early in the morning. Many of the housewives observe fast until the end of the ritual in the afternoon. They can, however, eat soaked (*cire*) and parched rice *muri* afterwards, but not boiled rice. They only dedicate the goose to the goddess on the day of *sesi-panchami* at their yard of the house. On the day of *bhadra-sankranti*, the people dedicate snakes at the altar for the goddess. These snakes are used in the ritual songs called *jhapan-gan* held afterwards.

DAMACIPUKUR-PARA (THE BAURI CASTE)

The locality of Damacipukuru-para is situated on the outskirts of the village toward the south. It is the locality of the Bauri caste. There the people have an altar of Manasa beside an altar of Kali. The *ojha* of the locality of Das-para used to come here to perform the ritual of Manasa. After the foundation of the altar at Das-para, he transferred his right to perform the ritual to a man of the Bauri caste of this locality. The latter is a head of the family, whose house is located in front of the altar of the Manasa tree. He performs the rituals at the foot of the tree on the days of *dashahara*, each *panchami*, and *bhadra-sankranti*. Usually he dedicates the sacred water, vermilion, and flowers to the tree and chants sacred verses. But, he is not engaged in the medicine rites. Only on the day of *bhadra-sankranti*, every family of the locality dedicates a goose to sacrifice to the goddess along with many other offerings. They have no Brahman priest so far.

THE HOUSEHOLD ALTAR IN PASHCIM-PARA

In the yard of a house of the Bauri caste in the eastern side of the village, that is called Pashcim-para. They have an altar beside their household of *tulsi-gach* (Ocimum tenuiflorum). The head housewife of the family usually dedicates offerings to the altars everyday. Only on the day of *bhadra-sankranti,* they invite a Brahman priest to perform the ritual of the goddess Manasa. They offered the sacrifice of an uncastrated goat for the goddess and the neighbouring people dedicate a goose. In the evening of *bhadra-sankranti,* the *deyasin* of the Manasa temple visits the altar on the way back to the Manasa temple carrying the pot of the goddess in his arms. He performs the ritual at the altar in company with the head of the family.

THE LOCALITY OF DOM

The biggest Manasa bush in the village is in the locality of the Dom at the eastern fringe of the village. This locality is called Bagal-para. Many villagers even from the locality of the Brahman and the Ugra-Kshatriya come to fetch the twigs from the thickly grown branches of Manasa in case of need for their rituals. Some other families belonging to the Kusmethi-Bagdi came afterward into the locality and made up now a mixed community with them. At the foot of the Manasa tree, they have the ritual for the goddess on the days of *dashahara,* each *panchami,* and *bhadra-sankranti.* The ritual process is not so complicated as in the Manasa temple. Except for the day of *sesi-panchami,* a priest of the locality performs a ritual, which consists of dedications of flowers, sweets, fruits, and the sacred water to the foot of the bush. The people of the locality prepare these offerings to the goddess. None of the priests of the Brahman caste come to perform the ritual to the tree. The *deyasin* of the Manasa temple and the Baiti playing the drum drop in at the time of their procession at *dashahara,* but never perform the ritual there. They have their own hereditary priest within the lineage of the Dom. At present, an old widow of the locality has taken over and continues to perform the ritual. She performs the daily service in the morning and evening and on special occasions for the goddess.

The most important occasion of rituals of the year is on the last day of *panchami.* Only this time every household of the locality offers a goose for sacrifice to the goddess at the foot of the tree. They can also offer something else for the fulfilment of personal prayers, but it is the only day to perform the sacrifice by all the households in the locality.

They prepare some special dishes for the goddess and for themselves. Nowadays, they arrange loudspeakers for music. They enjoy it for a whole day. In other localities, the rituals of the last *panchami* are almost the same as in other days of *panchami*. Hence, only this locality has a special arrangement to celebrate the Manasapuja in the village on this day.

The Household Altars

THE HOUSEHOLDS OF THE BRAHMAN

On the day before *dashahara*, every household of the Brahman fetches a twig of Manasa tree from the field and plant at the courtyard of their own houses. They ordinarily plant the twig beside the household shrine of *tulsi-gach*. On the day of *dashahara*, they invite their family priest for the ritual in their yards. At the beginning, the housewives prepare for the ritual utensils and dedicate offerings such as sweets, rice, *cire*, flowers, vermilion, mustard oil, turmeric, milk, and a little money on the plates in front of the Manasa tree. The priest lights incense and dedicates a votive light. After purification of his body and the ritual place with the sacred water, he puts mustard oil, turmeric, and vermilion on the tree and offers *cire* soaked in milk. With chanting the sacred verses, he pours sacred water to the tree. He sprinkles milk, flowers, and rice on the tree, blows a conch-shell, and makes a deep bow in the end. From in the morning, the housewives of the Brahman family observe fast. After the end of the ritual, they have *cire* soaked in water, milk, sweets, and fruits once a day, but they would not eat boiled rice or products of flour for the whole day.

After making a small altar of Manasa tree in their courtyards, they continue to perform the daily service in the morning and evening in the same way as to the altar of *tulsi-gach*. On each day of *panchami*, they invite the priest for the ritual of the goddess Manasa. However, the day of the last *panchami* is the final day to invite the Brahman priest, and they have no ritual on the day of *bhadra-sankranti*. In case of some diseases and accidents by the snakes, they would make use of the leaves of the tree for their herbal medicines. On the day of *bijay-dasami* in the lunar month of Aswin, they pick it up from their courtyard. Along with the procession of *naba-patrika*, which consists of the farewell rituals to the goddess Durga, they place the Manasa plant and throw it into the pond of Kshirdighi.

MUCI

On the day of *dashahara*, the people of the locality of Das-para (they belong to the Muci caste) fetch a twig of Manasa from the fields, and plant it beside the altar of *tulsi-gach* in the courtyard of their own houses. The housewives perform the daily service to the altar from this day. On special occasions such as *dashahara* and each *panchami*, they never invite the Brahman priest or *ojha* of their locality. Each head of the household performs the ritual at the altar for the goddess Manasa by himself. They dedicate to the goddess vermilion, turmeric, mustard oil and other items as the offerings. It is nearly the same things as dedicated in the households of the Brahman. They repeat the rituals to the altar on the days of each *panchami*. On the day of the last *panchami*, it is the most pompous festivity, and they dedicate one sacrificed goose per household. At the time of the farewell ritual on the last day of Durgapuja, they pick up the Manasa plant and throw into the pond along with *naba-patrika*. In these rituals, they have no relation with the temple Manasa in the locality of Manasa-para.

KITCHENS OF THE UGRA-KSHATRIYA

In the localities of *jana-aguri* (they are one of the sub-castes of the Ugra-Kshatriya in the village having the titles of Samant and Datta), is held a ritual for the goddess Manasa at the hearths of their households only once in a year on the day of the last *panchami* (*sesi-panchami*) in the lunar month of Sraban. The day before the last *panchami*, they prepare the twigs of Manasa in their kitchens. They perform the ritual at the hearths made of soil on the earthen floor of their kitchen. In the early morning, housewives cleanse the kitchen and draw various kinds of auspicious designs (*alpana*) with powder of rice on the hearth and the ground. They put a twig of Manasa into the hearth. It looks like a twig grown up through the opening of the hearth. They dedicate various kinds of offerings on a few plates in front of the hearth. Someone puts paste of vermilion on the twig, and waits for arrival of their family priest. The housewives must keep their fast for the day. After the end of the ritual, they can eat *cire* soaked in water and *muri*, but not boiled rice or flour for the whole day.

In the morning, the priests visit each family of their *jajmans*. They sit down in the kitchen, and perform ritual to the twig in the hearth just the same way as the ritual at the altar of Manasa tree. They bring offerings back to their house and leave a little bit for the family. Some priests in the village perform the ritual for the goddess in small temples in the locality where he is in charge of the services. After the ritual is over, they keep the twig in the hearth for the whole day. Throughout the day, they are forbidden to fight the hearth for cooking. Thus, nobody eats cooked food that day. The next morning, the housewives go to the ablution bank along with the twig and throw it into the pond while bathing.

DISCUSSION

As is discussed so far, the rituals regarding the goddess Manasa are diverse in the village. The caste distribution involving the Manasa rituals is very diverse and includes from the Brahman and the Ugra-Kshatriya to the untouchables such as the Bagdi, Muci, and Dom. And, each caste group practices the ritual courses separately according to their respective schedules. The participation patterns are also varied, from a simple devotee dedicating offerings to a full-time priest for the goddess (*deyasin*). Particularly, the people of the Bagdi caste regard that the Manasa rituals primarily belongs to them and in fact only the priest from the Bagdi lineage in the locality of Manasa-para can perform the rituals at the Manasa temple. The historical legitimacy endowed by the Maharaja to the Manasa temple and the service lands ensures in their opinion the primacy of the *deyasin* in the Manasa rituals. This is supported by the fact that even the director of the Jogadya temple, belonging to the Brahman caste accepts the ritual relations with the Bagdi by showing deference to the *deyasin* and his rituals.

Now, we will discuss the following three topics regarding the formation of the Manasa rituals based on the historical transition of the altars and the participation patterns in the rituals. First is the genealogy of the altars of the goddess Manasa in the village. Table 7.4 shows that many altars in the village originated from the Manasa temple of the Bagdi community where the *deyasin* and other medicine men (*ojha*) took lead. In general, it is very rare for the ordinary annual rituals such as Jogadyapuja and Durgapuja in the village to branch off from the original one. This is, therefore, in striking contrast to the annual rituals, organized by the village upper castes and where the Brahman priests officiate, and the rituals of Manasa which are mainly held by the lower castes, in which the *deyasin* plays a leading part. To use anthropological terms, it is understood as a contrast between the

TABLE 7.4: THE GENEALOGICAL TREE OF THE ALTARS OF THE GODDESS MANASA

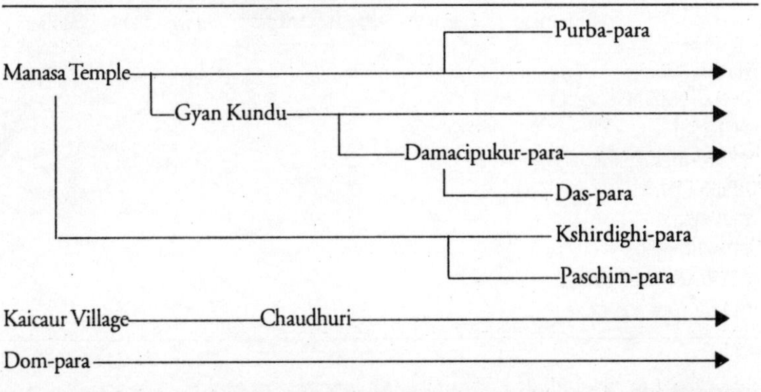

'great tradition' and the 'little tradition'; the former is the Sanskrit culture, which ensures the universality of the Hindu culture on the basis of the classical texts in Sanskrit, and the latter is the non-Sanskrit cultures, which contain the various indigenous cultures in South Asia, and secure the diversity of the regional cultures. But, we should rather understand this contrast as between mode of participation between the rituals dominated by the upper castes and ones amongst the lower castes; the former always emphasize the hierarchical relationships in the formation of rituals, and the latter allows all castes, lineages and localities to participate in the rituals spontaneously. In this respect, we need further examination of the pattern of ritual participations at the altars.

Second is the participation patterns of the village castes at the altar of Manasa. Manasapuja is the biggest occasion for the locality of Manasa-para, but the other castes and localities are also engaged in the rituals separately. Table 7.5 shows the caste wise participation patterns at the Manasa temple and each altar. The main caste groups in the village arranges on the horizontal axis. The mark of ◎ means full scale participation by the member, and O is partial participation. Table indicates clearly that in terms of participation the ritual of the Manasa temple is important for most of the caste groups in the village, while the other altars are rather held by respective caste groups.

The belief in the goddess Manasa is associated with the symbolism of the snake, that the snake is a menace to the human for its ferocious nature, and at the same time, preserves strong vitality and a unique

TABLE 7.5: CASTE WISE PARTICIPATION PATTERNS AT EACH ALTAR

	Brahman	Kshatriya	Bagdi	Muci	Bauri	Dom	Others
Manasa Temple	◎	◎	◎	◎	◎	◎	◎
①Gyan Kundu	O	O	O				O
②Chaudhuri		O					
③Kishrdighi-para			O				
④Purba-para			O				
⑤Das-para				◎			
⑥Paschim-para					◎		
⑦Damacipukur-para					◎		
⑧Dom-para						◎	

mode of life. The snake can harm people any time, but it is a belief that the goddess controls this dangerous power of the snake, and changes it into a blessing of nature. This ambiguity of the symbolism of the snake attracts many people in rural area to the Manasa cult. In fact, it is the most popular folk deity in rural Bengal cutting across caste and classe borders. As any one can suffer from snakebite in the rainy season, it is natural for the people to appease the serpent goddess, and participate in the rituals for the sake of her blessings. In other words, the people in the rural Bengal commonly share belief in the Manasa goddess because of the widespread menace of snakes, and it is consequently an autonomous folk deity free from the value system of the Brahman caste. In this sense, The Table indicates the clear contrast of the participation patterns between the Brahman and the lower castes. But, the problem regarding the middle castes such as the Ugra-Kshatriya, the Goera still remains.

Table 7.6 shows the caste belongings of the priests who are in charge of the Manasa rituals at each altar. The pattern of the caste distributions of priests seems to indicate the same pattern as the participations of castes in Table 7.6. But, it is noteworthy that the caste belongings of the participation groups and the priest do not always correspond, but rather we can classify broadly into two groups; the lower caste priests hired by their own communities, and the Brahman priests hired by the patrons belonging to other castes. In other words, the priests belonging to their own community are all from the lower castes and the other castes, namely the village upper and middle castes, hire their priests from the Brahaman caste as a *kula-purohit.* For example, the family of

TABLE 7.6: CASTE BELONGINGS OF ·THE PRIESTS AT EACH ALTAR

	Brahma	Kshatriya	Bagdi	Muci	Bauri	Dom
Manasa Temple			◎/O/Δ			
①Gyan Kundu	O	Δ				
②Chaudhuri	O		Δ			
③Kishrdighi-para	O		Δ			
④Purba-para	O					
⑤Das-para	O			◎/Δ		
⑥Paschim-para	O					◎
⑦Damacipukur-para				Δ	◎/O	
⑧Dom-para			◎			◎/O/Δ

Note: ◎: Daily rituals, O: Annual ritual, Δ: Medicine man.

Gyan Kundu and Chaudhuri belonging to the Ugra-Kshatriya and hire their priests from the neighbouring Brahman families. On the other hand, the Manasa temple, the locality of Damacipukur-para and the Dom have own priests. This means evidently the difference between the variety of participation patterns in the rituals and the exclusiveness of priestly occupations by specific castes in the village.

The appointment of the Brahman priests by the upper castes for their rituals looks like the so-called '*jajman–purohit* relation', which is sometime understood as the basis of the division of labour in the caste society. In contrast, it is interesting that the priests hired by the lower castes do not fit the slot of the *jajman–purohit* relation. The initiative of the *deyasin* in the Manasa temple shows rather a different dimension of the ritual relations with the other castes. For example, although most of the upper castes such as the Brahman and the Ugra-Kshatriya eagerly participate in the annual rituals and dedicate the offerings to the Manasa temple, it is rare to separate the altars from the temple and organize another set of rituals at their own place. As an annual ritual of the goddess Manasa, they prefer keeping their ritual relations with the Manasa temple. On the other hand, the conflict of the locality of Manasa-para with the Purba-para leads easily to the separation of their altar from the temple. As a result, the people of the Purba-para organize another set of rituals at their own place in spite of their kinship relation as a same clan. The separation of the altar from the Manasa temple naturally threatens the very basis of the temple organization. It is an interesting contrast between the upper castes and the lower castes towards the formation of the Manasa rituals; the former in general prefer participating in the rituals through the Brahman priests, and the latter keep an initiative to organize their rituals at their own place. This is the reason which explains the division between the Brahman and the lower caste priests in the village.

The initiative in the Manasa rituals by the lower castes of the village is due to its peculiar character as a snake goddess in rural Bengal. As a folk deity in Bengal, any one can ask her blessings, and certainly there is no distinction among the caste members. Simultaneously, the people who work in the fields are constantly under the threat of an attack from the ferocious snakes. Particularly in the rainy season, the snakes in Bengal hide in the bushes and appear on footpaths in the night. The agricultural labours, mostly belonging to the lower castes, are easily exposed to danger of the snakes in the fields. The *ojhas* are exclusively skilled in catching the snakes and taking out the poisons from them. It is, therefore, easy to point out a close relation between the threats of snakes in the fields and the monopoly in the rituals of the goddess Manasa by the lower castes such as the Bagdi.

The goddess Manasa is regarded as a popular folk deity in rural Bengal, and it has became one of the favourite addresses in popular Hinduism. However, as we have seen, irrespective of the popularity of the goddess Manasa beyond the difference of castes, Manasa rituals have a close connection with the idea of untouchability, which restricts the ritual practices essentially to the lower castes. The Bagdi priest at the Manasa temple takes particularly the initiative in organizing the Manasa rituals with the various castes, as the Brahman priests engage in the rituals with their patrons. It seems to be an another pattern of ritual relationship consisting of the Bagdi priests, patrons, and devotees, and the ritual exchanges over offerings and sacrifices among them. Dumont (1970: 43) emphasizes that the 'one fundamental conception', which is the opposition of the pure and the impure represented by the Brahamanical values 'underlies hierarchy' of the caste system in Hindu society. But, the village rituals having roots deep in the concepts of destructive as well as divine power of the folk deities are an important factor to construct the caste relations initiated by the marginal castes, which is evidently different to the way of hierarchical relation embodied by the Brahman caste.

The nature of the goddess Manasa represents an ambiguity of the folk deity, in which she can easily harm the people by her fatal venom, and at the same time she can become so benevolent that the people are saved from the attacks by snakes. The lower castes in the village hand down the folk knowledge of the skills in capturing the snakes and saving victims of snake bites. This corresponds to the fact that the marginal castes in the village transform the dangerous power of snakes into the power of fertility for everyone. The Maharaja Bardhaman lays the foundations of such dynamism of the multiplicity of caste relations in the village through the allotments of the service lands to the folk deities and the untouchables.

NOTE

1. However, it does not include the aggregate number of the household rituals held in the locality, but counts as a ritual occasion.

Conclusion

As is evident from the details discussed so far, our village has a close relationship with the Hindu kingship through various ritual processes. It is obvious that the dominant landholders of the village were connected with the zamindars in term of the tenurial relationship. Besides, the villagers had a strong relationship with the kingship on the basis of the temple ritual system. Each caste group has an indispensable role and associated duties to perform during the temple rituals. The village social life is systematically integrated into the kingship through the annual ritual cycle of the Jogadya temple. The supreme authority of the temple is the Maharaja of Bardhaman, and it is always reaffirmed through the ritual process in the temple. This relationship between the villagers and the king is demonstrated and strengthened through the ritual processes in the Jogadya temple. On the other hand, the rituals of the localities in the village are held on the basis of the kinship relations and cooperation. In particular, the rituals of the Brahman and the dominant caste have the stratified order with the other service castes in the village society. This ritual authority of the dominant caste seems to be an important element in keeping with their solidarity and hegemony over the other villagers. What we have tried to show can be summarized in the followings three points: (a) the ritual of kingship, (b) the organization of caste and untouchability, and (c) the sacrifice and kingship.

The Ritual of Kingship

The Maharaja of Bardhaman occupies an important role in the temple rituals. He is the prime servant of the temple. At the beginning of every ritual process observed in the temple, the Brahman-sebaits declare the beginning of the ritual in his name. It is not only in the big religious occasions such as Jogadyapuja, but also in the daily service (*nityaseba*) to the goddess when the priests announce the name of the Maharaja. The Maharaja himself usually never appears at the site of the temple. But the office in charge for the management for the rituals sends a representative to the village to supervise the sacrificial ritual every year at the end of the Jogadyapuja. Every service tenure of the temple was granted to the villagers in the name of the Maharaja and it is regarded as the source of the honour and the authority, by which every member is assured his exclusive ritual roles.

The temple priests are the servants to whom the Maharaja entrusted service of the goddess. In this sense, every service caste of the ritual is allotted a role in relation with the Maharaja and not in relation to the Brahman. Therefore, the ritual ranking of the temple ritual organization is not always parallel with the caste hierarchy in the village. The representative of the Datta lineage occupies the seat for the *jajman* in front of the Vedic altar. The seat could actually be regarded as the place for the Maharaja. The Datta occupies the highest rank among the nine lineages of the Ugra-Kshatriya of the village and they are one of the dominant landholders of the village. This means that the Datta represents the dominant force of the village in the ritual. At the same time, he plays the role of the delegation of the Maharaja in the rituals. The untouchables of the village are assigned definite ritual roles in the same manner as the other service castes. This gives them a certain ritual authority in the village. For example, in the Manasapuja (the ritual to the goddess Manasa), even the Brahman priests pay their respects to the Bagdi priest.

It thus appears that ritual organization of the local temple provides an important opportunity for the kingship to legitimize its rule and involve the local society. The superiority of the Maharaja in the village is beyond question. This provides evidence disproving the concept of secularized king of L. Dumont. We can point following three features regarding the ritual process of kingship, namely (1) ritual ranking and ritual time, (2) initiation for sacrifice, and (3) fertility and sacrifice.

RITUAL RANKING AND TIME

Ritual ranking is always emphasized in the ritual of kinghsip. The order of the *phonta*-giving will provide a good example. The priests address each title of the representatives of the Ugra-Kshatriya and the other ritual posts at the a Jagyakund. Then, they go in procession through the village from the Jagyakund to the temple. The ranking of the participants in this ritual is (i) Brahman, (ii) Datta and Samant, (iii) other lineages of the Ugra-Kshatriya, (iv) Malakar, (v) other service castes, and (vi) other villagers. All participants including the untouchables receive *phonta* on their foreheads. Similar ranking is observed in the ritual of offering the garlands in Durgapuja and offering food at the *nabanna-utsab*, and so on. It is the ritual ranking classified by the ritual posts which is emphasized in these ritual processes.

Another element is the control over the ritual time by the court of the Raj. The ritual of *lagna-utsab* on the fifteenth of Baishakh is a good example. Before the *lagna-utsab* every year, the deb-seba-office sends a Bengali almanac to the villagers, which gives a list of every ritual occasion. The yearly cycle of annual ritual, rites of passage, and daily life of the villagers are based on the ritual cycle of the Jogadya temple. It is, therefore, clear that village life was synchronized with the ritual in the court of the Raj through the temple calendar. In those days, it is possible to suppose that the royal almanacs ensured unified and synchronized ritual cycle in various temples all over the kingdom. It leads towards the assumption that the regional variation of the folk culture of Bengal, such as Rarh area and Barendra area, is based not on the geographical difference, but rather on the former political composition of various indigenous kingships of the state. For example, the spring ritual of *doljatra* (Holi), is commonly observed on the day of full moon of Chaitra, but in Bardhaman it is celebrated a day later in accordance with the Vaishnava traditions of the royal family. In addition, the styles of *kirtan*, which is a folk musical performance, are broadly different between eastern and western Bengal. Due to increased migration of Hindu families from the eastern side, their 'traditional' style of *kirtan*, accompanying various instruments, dominates over the simple style in West Bengal, and has now become quite popular as a 'new' style of *kirtan*.

At any rate, it seems to be an efficient way for kingship to regulate the ritual time of the kingdom through the almanac, which is regarded by the local priests as a fundamental authority to find out the auspicious occasions to perform the various rituals for their *jajmans*. In other words, the permeation of the printed almanac from Kolkata all over Bengal ushers the beginning of formation of the so-called 'popular Hinduism', in which the modern Bengali almanacs give a uniformity of ritual cycle and style beyond regional differences over rural Bengal.

INITIATION FOR SACRIFICE

The next point is about symbolism regarding death and initiation observed in the ritual sacrifices, especially in *ugalpuja*. It is an important matter for the patron of the ritual to have enough members to allot them appropriate posts in the ritual and to make them carry out their duties. In the ritual of *ugalpuja*, the descent of the jati or the lineage belonging to the specified ritual family is not a sufficient condition as the membership to participate in the sacrificial ritual. It is only after his initiation that a youth of the family is admitted to place of the altar of the sacrifice on the bank of Kshirdighi. The young man must offer a goat to the goddess when he participates in *ugalpuja* for the first time. After the sacrifice of the goat, which means a substitute for him, he becomes a full-fledged member of the ritual organization. The symbolism of death of a scapegoat and its regeneration is a necessary condition to qualify them to participate in the rituals of *ugalpuja*, and this is commonly observed in the rituals of initiation (see Bloch 1991; Turner 1969; van Gennep 1960). All the participants must acquire eligibility for the ritual, no matter whether they belong to the Brahman or the Bagdi caste.

FERTILITY AND SACRIFICE

The third point is about the ritual of fertility and sacrifice. As already discussed in Chapter 1, the fertility of crops, control of sexuality, and sacrificial ritual are interrelated in the ritual complex. Among the plentiful ritual traditions, the ritual of fertility is always observed in various stages of ritual processes. In rural Bengal, every stratum of the society depends on agricultural production, and the native farming techniques have been handed down for generations along with the ritual traditions. It is natural that various rituals of agricultural affairs are associated with the sacrificial rituals through the idea of fertility.

One example will be illustrated here. The story in the first part of the *jogadya-bandana* tells about human sacrifice to the goddess. The legendary king, Hari Datta, had seven sons and he had to offer them to propitiate the goddess one after another for seven years. After sacrifice of all his sons, the king allotted the responsibility for supplying a child for sacrifice every year to the families of the village by turn. This story suggests the logic of killing of a king (regicide) presented by J. Frazer: the fertility of the kingdom is ensured by the sacrificial rituals performed by the king, who is an embodiment of the cosmological order of the kingdom. The condition of the king's health is identified with the order and prosperity of the kingdom. In the case of a crisis in the kingdom, even the king is sacrificed to regenerate the fertility of the kingdom. This concept provides a next topic regarding the formation of the social organization in the rural society through the rituals of sacrifice based on caste and untouchability.

Organization of Caste and Untouchability

There are two topics to be discussed here regarding the formation of caste organization through the rituals, namely the hierarchical order and its relation with untouchability. The Durgapujas among the Ugra-Kshatriyas are organized through a rotation system called *sola-ana-puja* by each lineage. This idea enables us to recognize easily the kinship relation of each member to his *bangsha.* In this ritual organization, every head of the family is regarded as a joint patron of his lineage rituals. Hence, Durgapujas among the village Ugra-Kshatriyas strengthen the unity of the lineages. On the other hand, each Durgapuja in the village is integrated into the Durgapuja at the Jogadya temple through every ritual step. The Durgapuja at the Jogadya temple controls all the other Durgapujas, which are organized by the village dominant castes. The Maharaja of Bardhaman is the main patron of the Jogadya temple. It is, therefore, clear that the supreme authority of the Maharaja over the villagers is embodied in the ritual process of Durgapuja. The Durgapuja in the village intensifies the stratified order of the village social structure as well as the egalitarian unity of the kinship relation.

Of the lineages of the Ugra-Kshatriya, the Datta enjoys the highest ritual status. The legendary story of the goddess recited by the villagers adds legitimacy as the prime Kshatriya in the village. It is a belief that the king from the Datta ruled the village in the legendary period of the *treta.* Another name of the Raja Bharat Datta is also addressed in the ritual of *guya-dak* on every end of the months. These ensure the ritual post of the Datta as the chief representative among the Ugra-Kshatriya. This ritual status might reflect his former status as a regional chief, in which he ruled over the territory. It is quite important to suggest the existence of a little kingdom in this region, a concept of presented by Cohn (1962).

In this connection, it is further important to notice the ritual roles of the Dom, especially in the ritual of *domacoyarikhela.* In this ritual, the Dom is considered as the original worshipper of the goddess. Besides, the name called first in the ritual of *guya-dak* is *Phopal mashay,* who is thought as the chief of the Dom at one time. These rituals correspond to village lore that the people of the Dom caste were the original residents of the village but later gave away to the rule of the Datta and the Brahman. In this respect, it is possible to suppose that the ritual course of *domacoyarikhela* reflects certain historical facts. The villagers regard these ritual performances as a basis of authority, which paradoxically ensures their legitimacy regarding the origin of specific posts in the rituals.

The rituals in the Jogadya temple have the character of well-regulated organization and affect the ranking order in the ritual course. There is, however, another important point to be discussed regarding ritual performances. It is well known that Turner (1969) proposes to analyse a ritual in two aspects; structure and anti-structure, and it seems to be useful to analyse the rituals performed by the Bagdi caste, because the rituals such as boisterousness in the procession of buffalo in Jogadyapuja and Durgapuja stand as contrasts to the usual orderly and decently observed temple rituals. The character of anti-structure appears in the rituals mainly performed by the Bagdi youth, while the structural aspect is characterized by a normative behaviour in the rituals led by the Brahman, and consequently reinforce the order of existing social relations.

Kingship and Sacrifice

It is clear that the ritual system of the temple has been controlled by a stratified organization based on granted lands, the assignment of roles, and the allotment of offerings and sacrifices. Although this organization is ultimately grounded on the authority of the Maharaja, the lineages of the Ugra-Kshatriya hold their own legendary origin, which provides legitimacy to their ritual roles. The Dom caste also has own legendary history in relation to the temple ritual. This ritual system of the temple, therefore, includes these castes and lineages having their own legendary origin and the legitimacy of the ritual roles, in which each caste and lineage has been ensured its peculiar status in the organization. But the rituals of the temple as a whole put them into a classified organization in terms of relations with other castes and with the kingship.

As Quigley (1993: Ch. 6) suggests, the theory of Hocart provides the potential to view Hindu society from the vantage of a combination between kingship and caste. His stand enables us to explain Hindu society as a process of interaction between the kingship and the village society, which is based on caste and kinship. In opposition to the attempt to legitimation by kingship, the dominant caste always tries to establish its hegemony over the service castes in the village through rituals within the locality. This interactional process could appear again between the dominant caste and the lower castes.

On the other hand, the buffalo procession by the Bagdi towards the altar of Jagyakund is in marked contrast with the procession of the pot of the goddess by the Datta towards the Jogadya temple. The excited youths of the Bagdi drag the buffalo to the altar of sacrifice with a furious roll of the drums. Most of them get drunk before they start from the Jogadya temple and some get too drunk to follow the procession. They dance and romp around the buffalos to the beats of the drums. Over-excited, some even lose consciousness. It is obvious that the Bagdi youths lead the procession in contrast with the procession of the pot, which the Brahman-sebait and the Datta lead. It is an egalitarian order, which is emphasized in the procession of the Bagdi, while a hierarchical order is stressed in the procession of the pot. In the egalitarian order, every member participates equally as an individual in the chaotic ritual, which is a state beyond the ordinal social relation and even transcending self. The rituals such as boisterousness in the procession of buffalo in Jogadyapuja and Durgapuja stand as contrasts to the usual orderly and decently observed temple rituals.

The rural society of Bengal has retained rich agricultural traditions, often associated with the rituals of fertility. This is a reason that the kingship attempts to establish its legitimacy through sacrificial rituals in the rural areas. This sacrificial ritual, further, appears from every stratum of the rural society. The dominant caste organizes its own rituals of sacrifice showing its authority and power over the other castes in the village. Yet the lower castes have the own rituals of sacrifice through interaction with other castes, though these rituals are ultimately integrated into the rituals held by the dominant caste and the kingship. These sacrificial rituals, therefore, suggest the continual rising rivalries in rural society. It is the sacrificial rituals which are performed always within the dynamism of powers and symbols between the kingship and the local dominant forces, the landlords and the tenants, the village dominant caste and the service castes, the Brahmán and the untouchables, and so on. In other words, the formation of sacrificial organization can be understood as a consequence of interaction of power and authority in Hindu society.

APPENDIX 1

The Phases of the Moon in the Bengal Lunar Calendar

New moon	Amabasya	অমাবস্যা
Full moon	Purnima	পূর্ণিমা
Bright fortnight	Shuklopaksha	শুক্লপক্ষ
Dark fortnight	Krshnapaksha	কৃষ্ণপক্ষ
The phases:		
The first	pratipada	প্রতিপদ
The second	dwitiya	দ্বিতীয়া
The third	tritiya	তৃতীয়া
The fourth	caturthi	চতুর্থী
The fifth	panchami	পঞ্চমী
The sixth	sasthi	ষষ্ঠী
The seventh	saptami	সপ্তমী
The eighth	astami	অষ্টমী
The ninth	nabami	নবমী
The tenth	dashami	দশমী
The eleventh	ekadashi	একাদশী
The twelfth	dwadashi	দ্বাদশী
The thirteenth	troyodashi	ত্রয়োদশী
The fourteenth	caturdashi	চতুর্দশী

APPENDIX 2

Bengali Lunar Months and the Six Seasons

Six Seasons	Bengali Month		Western Calendar
Grishma kal	Baishakh	বৈশাখ	April-May
গ্রীষ্মকাল	Jaishta	জ্যৈষ্ঠ	
Barsha kal	Asar	আষাঢ়	June-July
বর্ষাকাল	Sraban	শ্রাবন	
Sarata kal	Bhadra	ভাদ্র	August-September
শরৎকাল	Aswin	আশ্বিন	
Hemant kal	Kartik	কার্ত্তিক	October-November
হেমন্তকাল	Agrahayan	অগ্রহায়ন	
Sheet kal	Poush	পৌষ	December-January
শীতকাল	Magh	মাঘ	
Basant kal	Phalgun	ফাল্গুন	February-March
বসন্তকাল	Chaitra	চৈত্র	

APPENDIX 3

The 51 Sakta-Pithas

Sakta-Pitha	Body's part	Goddess	Location
1 Hingula Hingulata	Brahmarandhra	Kottari Koṭṭavi Kottarisha	Pakistan
2 Karavira Sarkarara	Trinetra	Mahishamardini	Pakistan
3 Sugandha	Nasika	Sunanda Sugandha	Bangladesh
4 Kashmira	Kantha	Mahamaya	Kashmir
5 Jvalamukhi	Jihva	Siddhida Ambika	Dharamsala, Pathankot
6 Jalandhara	Stana	Tripuramalini Tripuranashini	–
7 Vaidyanatha	Hridaya	Jayadurga	Santal Pargana, Deoghar
8 Nepala	Janu	Mahamaya	–
9 Manasa Malava	Dakshina-hasta	Dakshayani	Tibet, Manas Sarobar
10 Virajakshetra in Utkala	Nabhi	Vimala Vijaya	Puri
11 Gandaki Gandaka	Ganda	Gandaki Candi	Bihar
12 Bahula	Vama-bahu	Bahula	Bardhaman, Ketugram
13 Ujjayini Ujani Ujjani Urjani Urjayini	Kurpara	Mangala Mangalacandi	Guskara, Kogram
14 Cattala (Candrashekhara)	Dakshina-bahu	Bhavani	Bangladesh, Sitakund
15 Tripura	Dakshina-pada	Tripura Tripurasundari	Agartala, Udaipur

Sakta-Pitha	Body's part	Goddess	Location
16 Trisrota (Sans. Trisrotas) Tirota	Vama-pada	Bhramari Amari	Jalpaiguri, Salbari
17 Kamagiri in Kamarupa (ten pithas were originally located here)	Mahamudra (Yoni)	Kamakhya	Assam, Guwahati
18 Yugadya (Kshiragrama)	Dakshina-padan- gustha	Yugadya (Yogadya)	Bardhaman
19 Kalipitha Kalapitha (Kalighat)	Dakshina-padan- guli	Kali	Calcutta
20 Prayaga	Hast-anguli	Lalita	Uttar Pradesh
21 Jayanti Jayanta	Vama-jangha	Jayanti	Bangladesh, Jayanti Pargana
22 Kirita Kiritakona	Kirita	Bhuvaneshi Vimala	Elahiganj
23 Manikarnika at Varanasi	Kundala	Vishalakshi	Varanasi
24 Kanyashrama	Prishtha Drishti	Sarvani	–
25 Kurukshetra	(Dakshina)-gulpha	Savitri	Haryana
26 Maniveda Manivedika Manavedaka	Manibandha	Gayatri	–
27 Shrishaila Shrihatta	Griva	Mahalakshmi Mahamaya	Bangladesh
28 Kanei	Kankala	Devagarbha	Birbhum
29 Kalamadhava	Nitamba	Kali	–
30 Narmada Shona Shaila	Nitamba	Sona Narmada	–
31 Ramagiri Rajagiri Ramakini	Stana Nasa Nala	Shivani	Bilaspur
32 Vrindavana (Umavana) Keshajala	Kesha	Uma Katyayani	Uttar Pradesh
33 Shuci Anala	Urdhva-danta	Narayani	–

Sakta-Pitha	Body's part	Goddess	Location
34 Pancasagara	Adhodanta	Varahi	–
35 Karatoyatata	Vama-karna Talpa Gulpha	Aparna	Bangladesh
36 Shriparvata	Dakshina-karna Talpa (Dakshina)-gulpha	Sundari	–
37 Vibhasa	Vama-gulpha	Bhimarupa Kapalini	Medinipur
38 Prahbasa	Udara Adhara	Candrabhaga	Mathura
39 Bhairavaparvata Bhiruparvata	Urdhvoshtha Oshtha Tunda	Avanti	Ujjain
40 Janasthana Jala-sthala	Civuka	Bhramari	–
41 Godavaritira	(Vama)-ganda	Vishveshi Rakini	–
42 Ratnavali	Dakshina- skandha	Kumari Shiva	–
43 Mithila	Vama-skandha	Uma Mahadevi	Bihar
44 Nalahati	Nala	Kali	Birbhum
45 Kalighata (Kalipitha)	Munda	Jayadurga	–
46 Vakreshvara	Manas	Mahishamardini	Birbhum
47 Yashora	Pani	Yashoreshvari	Bangladesh
48 Attahasa	Oshtha	Phullara	Birbhum
49 Nandipura	Hara	Nandini	Birbhum
50 Lanka	Nupura	Indrashi	Sri Lanka
51 Virata	Padanguli	Ambika	–

Source: The list of pitha, body's part, and goddess is quoted from D.C. Sircar, *The Sakta Pithas*, Delhi: Motilal Banarsidass, 1973, pp. 35–7. The locations follow the list on *P.M. Bagcir Dairektari Panjika: Puja Paddhati*, Kolkata, by P.M. Bagchi and Co., pp. 37–8, there is, however, scope for regional differences of the places in Bengal and elsewhere.

APPENDIX 4

The Temples Founded by the Raj Family of Bardhaman

Temple	Place	Year	Founder
Jogadya	Kshiragram	1730	Kirticand
Gopeshwar Sib	Baikunthapur	1732	Kirticand
Sarbamangala	Bardhaman	–	Kirticand
Barduyari	Kanchannagar	–	Kirticand
Barduyari Ghat	Danihat	–	Brajkishori
Lalji	Kalna	1740	Brajkishori
Siddheshwari	Kalna	1741	Citrasen
Sib	Kalna	1746	Ramdeb Nag
Gopinath	Bharatpur	1747	Rajrajeshwari
Krishnacandra	Kalna	1751	Lakshmikumari
Rameshwar	Kalna	1753	Changakumari
Candreshwar	Bardhaman	–	Changakumari
Mitreshwar	Bardhaman	–	Indrakumari
Anantabasudeb	Kalna	1754	Trilokacand
Baikunthanath-sib	Kalna	1754	Brajkishori
Giridhari	Kalna	1758	Brajkishori
Rupeshwar-sib	Kalna	1761	Rupakumari
Bijay-baidyanath	Kalna	1763	Lakshmikumari
Sib	Kalna	1763	Bisankumari
Laksminarayan	Bardhaman	–	Trilokcand
Sib	Kalna	1764	–
Kasinath-sib	Kalna	1765	Tulasi Debi
Gopal	Kalna	1766	Krishnacandra
Kishor Kishori	Danihat	–	Trilokcand
Bardhamaneshwar-sib	Danihat	–	Trilokcand
Rajrajeshwar-sib	Danihat	–	Trilokcand
Karpureshwar-sib	Danihat	–	Trilokcand
Gangadhar-sib	Danihat	–	Bisankumari
Trilokeshwar	Khasahabheli	–	Trilokcand
Rameshwar-sib	Kalna	1783	Bisankumari
108-sib	Nababhat	1789	Bisankumari

Temple	Place	Year	Founder
Sib	Sundarbag	1800	Maharani of Tejcandra
Sib	Sundarbag	–	Maharani of Tejcandra
Sib	Anandabag	1801	Maharani of Tejcandra
Sib	Anandabag	1810	Maharani of Tejcandra
108 Sib	Kalna	1810	Tejcandra
Rameshwar	Bardhaman	1812	Tejcandra
Kamaleshwar	Bardhaman	1812	Kamalkumari
Kali	Tejganj	–	Tejcandra
Kali	Borahat	–	Tejcandra
Sib	Kalna	1842	Ganga Dasi
Kasinath-sib	Kalna	1845	Debaki Debi
Pratapeshwar-sib	Kalna	1849	Pyarikumari
Baikunthanat	Kalna	1850	Pyarikumari
Radhaballabh	Sankatigar	1860	Pyatikumari
Bhubaneshwari	Bardhaman	1899	Narayankumari
Narayaneshwar	Bardhaman	1899	Narayankumari
Kshireshwar	Kshiragram	1900	Bijaycand

Source: Jogeshwar Caudhuri, *Bardhaman: Itihas o Sanskriti*, Dwitiya Khanda, Calcutta: Pustak Bipani, 1991, pp. 213–14.

Glossary

adhibas	অধিবাস	preliminary ritual to any ceremony
aguri	আগুরি	another name of the Ugra-Kshatriya
ahban	আহ্বান	invitation, invocation
aman	আমন	winter rice crop
angsha	অংশ	quota of ritual duty and right allotted on the basis of the calculation system of *sola-ana*
angshidar	অংশীদার	holder of *angsha*
ana	আনা	one-sixteenth of a rupee
annabhog	অন্ন ভোগ	offering of boiled rice
annapurna	অন্নপূর্ণা	the goddess Annapurna
arati	আরতি	offering with lamp to the deity
atop-caul	আতপ চাউল	sun-dried rice
Baiti	বাইতি	the village drummer caste
baidik-hom	বৈদিক হোম	the Vedic fire ritual
baidik-purohit	বৈদিক পুরোহিত	the priest eligible for the Vedic fire ritual
bangsha	বংশ	lineage
baran	বরণ	ritual reception, invocation
baroyaripuja	বারোয়ারী পূজা	community ritual
bel	বেল	stone-apple tree (Aegle marmelos)
bhandari	ভাণ্ডারী	storekeeper
bhog	ভোগ	food offering for the deity

bisarjan	বিসর্জন	farewell ritual
cakran-sampatti	চাক্রান সম্পত্তি	service land
Candi	চণ্ডী	another name of Durga, or sacred literature of Candi, which consist a part of the *Devimahatmya*
candipath	চণ্ডীপাঠ	recitation of the Candi
caukidar	চৌকিদার	village watchman
caturthi-patrika	চতুর্থি পত্রিকা	*patrika* of four kinds of plants
cire (cinra)	চিড়ে	rice flattened after boiling and threshing
danda	দণ্ড	measure of time equal to twenty-four minutes
dasahara	দশহরা	the tenth day of bright fortnight of Jaishta
debottar	দেবোত্তর	rent-free or revenue free land granted to temples
deyasin	দেয়াশিন	priest of non-Brahman origin, votary versed in mantra
diksha-guru	দীক্ষা-গুরু	spiritual master who gives initiation and mantra
domacoyarikhela	ডোমচোয়াড়ী খেলা	ritual fight between the Dom and the Brahman
durba	দূর্ব্বা	grass (Cynodon dactylon)
gajan	গাজন	ritual of Siva in the end of the month of Chaitra
gosthi	গোষ্ঠী	agnates
ghat	ঘট	ritual pot for the deity
ghatsthapan	ঘটস্থাপন	ritual placing of *ghat* filled with sacred water on the altar at commencement of ritual

gamastha	গমস্তা	village agent of landholders, rent collector in the local office
gamcha	গামছা	washcloth, towel
ganesmund	গনেশ মুণ্ড	stone plinth at the foot of the eastern wall of the Jogadya temple
gotra	গোত্র	clan
Grahacarya	গ্রহাচার্য	priest for almanac
guyabedi	গুয়া বেদি	stone plinth for *guyadak* in the Jogadya temple
guyadak	গুয়া ডাক	ritual of the Jogadya temple on every *sankranti*
hal-nagal	হাল নাগল (হাল লাঙল)	ritual tilling on the 30th of Baishakh
hom	হোম	oblation of fire
jajman	যজমান	client on whose behalf priest performs ritual
jhapan-gan	ঝাপান-গান	ritual song with snake's dance
Jagyakund	যজ্ঞ কুণ্ড	the ritual stage for the Vedic fire at the western side of the village
kachari-bari	কাছাড়ি বাড়ি	the superintendent office of the Jogadya temple
khai	খই	roasted rice
khatiyan	খতিয়ান	land register
kshir	ক্ষীর	milk condensed by boiling
kshirkalasi	ক্ষীরকলসী	ritual on the first day of Jogadyapuja, or the ritual pot used on the day
kula-purohit	কুল পুরোহিত	family priest
kul	কুল	nut, Zizyphus jujuba

lagna-utsab	লগ্ন উৎসব	ritual of the Bengali almanac in the New Year
lakheraj	লাখেরাজ	revenue-free or rent free-land
luci	লুচি	flour-puff fried in *ghi*
madal	মাদল	a pair of drums used in Jogadyapuja
mahalay	মহালয়	new-moon day before the autumnal Durgapuja
Maharaja	মহারাজা	great king
mahisbali	মহিষ বলি	sacrifice of buffalo
makari-saptami	মাকরী সপ্তমী	ritual on the seventh of Magh
manasa-gach	মনসাগাছ	Manasa tree, Euphorbia neriifolia
Manasapuja	মনসাপূজা	ritual to the goddess Manasa
manasa-tala	মনসা তলা	altar of the Manasa tree
Mangalkabya	মঙ্গলকাব্য	Bengali folk literatures
mansik	মানসিক	offering or sacrifice promised and dedicated to the deity if the vow is fulfilled
mantra	মন্ত্র	sacred verse
mauza	মৌজা	revenue village
mayurnac	ময়ূর নাচ	dance of peacock, ritual dance performed in Jogadyapuja
mela	মেলা	fair
merya-khata	মেরয়া কাটা	sacrifice in the end of Jogadyapuja performed by the Dom
mula-paik	মূল পাইক	chief-servants of the Bagdi in the Jogadya temple
murki	মুড়কি	parched rice coated with molasses

naba-patrika	নবপত্রিকা	*patrika* of nine kinds of plants
naba-shakh	নবশাখ	nine artisan castes of Bengal
nabanna	নবান্ন	new rice
nabanna-utsab	নবান্ন উৎসব	ritual for the new rice
naibedya	নৈবেদ্য	offering to the deity, in which *atop-caul* is a main item
nishidhambal	নিশিধম্বল	ritual of drum playing at the Jogadya temple of midnight in Magh month
nityaseba	নিত্য সেবা	daily service to the deity
naru	নাড়ু	sweet ball made of parched rice, coconut and molasses
Natmandir	নাটমন্দির	dance hall
ojha	ওঝা	medicine man
paik	পাইক	temple servants
paita	পৈতা	sacred thread put on the shoulder by the Brahman and other upper castes
pan	পান	betel leaf
pancha-pradip	পঞ্চপ্রদীপ	votive light having five wicks
panjika	পঞ্জিকা	almanac
pala	পালা	turn to ritual duty or right
paladar	পালাদার	a person in the turn of ritual
para	পাড়া	locality
pargana	পরগনা	revenue unit of the medieval Bengal
patakadhari	পতাকাধারী	holder of the Maharaja's red flag
pat-naran	পাট নড়ান	ritual of pulling up the goddess's image on the 29th of Baishakh
pathabali	পাঁঠাবলি	sacrifice of goat

patrika	পত্রিকা	bundle of plants as a symbol of the goddess
pattanidar	পত্তনীদার	intermediary under a zamindar
phonta	ফোঁটা	sacred mark put on the forehead of devotees
pitha-sthan	পীঠ স্থান	sacred place of the sakta-cult, where the goddess Sati's limb is believed to have fallen
Pradhan-purohit	প্রধান পুরোহিত	chief priest
pradakshin	প্রদক্ষিণ	act of going around the altar of deity in clockwise
pradip	প্রদীপ	votive light
pranam	প্রণাম	making a deep bow
prasad	প্রসাদ	food offering given to devotees after the ritual
pujari	পূজারী	Brahman priest employed in ritual
purohit	পুরোহিত	Brahman priest who serves for his *jajman*
puspanjali	পুষ্পাঞ্জলি	offering of flower
raiyat	রাইয়ত	tenant farmer
rajkachari	রাজ কাছাড়ি	superintendent of the Jogadya temple
ruti	রুটি	bread made of flour
Sabha-pandit	সভা পণ্ডিত	director of the ritual organization
shola	শোলা	sponge wood tree, Aeschynomene spera
sakta-pitha	শাক্ত পীঠ	general term of *pitha-sthans*
shal	শাল	Shorea robusta tree
sandhipuja	সন্ধি পুজা	ritual at the liminal moment between the eighth and the ninth

		of the bright fortnight in Durgapuja
sandhya	সন্ধ্যা	evening
sandhyarati	সন্ধ্যা আরতী	evening service to the deity with fire
sankalpa	সংকল্প	announcement of the name of patron at the begging of ritual
sankranti	সংক্রান্তি	the last day of any lunar month
sannyasi	সন্ন্যাসী	ascetic
saraswati	সরস্বতী	the goddess Saraswati
sarbajanin-puja	সার্বজনীন পূজা	community ritual, everybody's ritual
sarse-tel	সর্ষে তেল	mustard oil
sebait	সেবাইত	temple servant
ser (seer)	সের	an Indian measure of weight, = 1/40 *man*
siddhi	সিদ্ধি	leaves and shoots of hemp
sindur	সিঁদুর	vermilion
sital-bhog	শীতলভোগ	evening food offerings to the deity
sorashopacar-puja	ষোড়শোপচার পূজা	sixteen steps of ritual
sola-ana	ষোলআনা	one rupee, traditional calculation unit, symbolically it means totality
sola-ana-puja	ষোলআনা পূজা	a ritual organization based on the rotation rule of *sola-ana*
sraddha	শ্রাদ্ধ	funeral rite
supari	সুপারি	betel-nut
taka	টাকা	Bengali currency unit
tala	তাল	rhythm

tantra	তন্ত্র	scripture, ritual system, sacred book of the cult of sakta and also other sects
tantradharak	তন্ত্রধারক	assistant priest who chants sacred verses
tarpan	তর্পণ	ritual form of ancestor worship
tengai	টেঙ্গাই	notification of the time of ritual by drum playing
thana	থানা	police station, jurisdiction under the police station
tulsi-gach	তুলসী-গাছ	plant, sacred basil, Ocimum sanctum
Ugra-Kshatriya	উগ্র ক্ষত্রিয়	Aguri, a Kshatriya caste in Bengal
ugalpuja	উগল পূজা	ritual of pulling up the goddess's image from the Kshirdighi pond
ulu (uluddhani)	উলুধ্বনি	sound by women made by moving their tongues within the mouth on any ritual occasion
unun	উনুন	hearth
upos (upabas)	উপোস	abstinence from food
zamindar	জমিদার	landowner

Bibliography

Adhikari, Anand Gopal, 1991, *Pith Dedi Jogyada: Kshiragram* (Bengali), Katwa: Janata Printing Works.

Ahmed, Wakil, 1968, *Banglay Bideshi Parjatak* (Bengali), Dhaka: Globe Library.

Ahmed, Rafiuddin, 1981, *Bengal Muslims 1871–1906: A quest for identity*, Delhi: Oxford University Press.

Appadurai, Arjun, 1977, 'Kings, sects and temples in south India', *The Indian Economic and Social History Review*, 14(1): 47–73.

———, 1981, *Worship and Conflict under Colonial Rule: A South Indian case*, Cambridge: Cambridge University Press.

Appadurai, Arjun, 1983, 'Puzzling status of Brahman temple priests in Hindu India', *South Asian Anthropologist*, 4(1): 43–52.

Appadurai, Arjun and Carol Breckenridge, 1976, 'The south Indian temple: authority, honour and redistribution' *Contributions to Indian Sociology*, n.s. 10(2): 187–211.

Asad, T., 1973, *Anthropology and the Colonial Encounter*, New York: Humanities Press.

ASI (Anthropological Survey of India), 1981 *Directory of Anthropologists in India*, Calcutta: ASI.

Babb, Lawrence, 1975, *The Divine Hierarchy: Popular Hinduism in Central India*, New York: Columbia University Press.

Baden-Powell, B.H., 1892, *Land Systems of British India*, 3 vols., Oxford: Clarendon Press.

Bagchi, Subhendugopal, 1980, *Eminent Indian Sakta Centres in Eastern India*, Calcutta: Punthi Pustak.

Bailey, F.G., 1957, *Caste and the Economic Frontier: A Village in Highland Orissa*, Manchester: Manchester University Press.

Bandhu, Sanjib, 1986, *Ugrakshatriya Pariciti* (Bengali), Bardhaman: Bijaytoran Prakasani.

Banerjee, Biswanath, 1973, 'Sarbojonin Durgotsab in Calcutta: A Preliminary Report of the Puja', *Folklore* 14: 347–53.

Barth, Fredrik, 1959, *Political Leadership Among the Swat Pathans*, London: The Athlone Press.

Basak, Shila, 1995, 'Meyeli Brate Lokacar', in *Meyeli Brata Bisaye* (Bengali), Sanat Kumar Mitra, ed., Calcutta: Pustak Bipani.

———, 1998, *Banglar Brataparban* (Bengali), Calcutta: Pustak Bipani.

Basu, Arabinda, Mahadeb P. Basu, and Ashim Adhikary (eds.), 1981, *Directory of Anthropologists in India*, Calcutta: Anthropological Survey of India.

Bayly, C.A., 1983, *Rulers, Townsmen and Bazaars: North Indian Society in the Age of British Expansion, 1770–1812*, Cambridge: Cambridge University Press.

Bayly, Susan, 1984, 'Hindu kingship and the origins of community: religion, state and society in Kerala, 1750–1850', *Modern Asian Studies*, 18(2): 177–214.

Bennett, Lynn, 1983, *Dangerous Wives and Sacred Sisters, Social and Symbolic Roles of High-Caste Women in Nepal*, New York: Columbia University Press.

Beteille, Andre, 1976, 'Hindu transactions: Diversity without dualism', in *Transactions and Meaning*, ed. B. Kapferer, Philadelphia: Institute for the Study of Human Issues.

———, 1971, *Caste, Class and Power: Changing Patterns of Stratification in a Tanjore Village*, Berkeley: University of California Press.

———, 1992, *Society and Politics in India: Essays in a comparative Perspective*, Delhi: Oxford University Press.

Bhattacharjee, Binay, 1980, *Cultural Oscillation: A Study on Patua Culture*, Calcutta: Naya Prokash.

Bhattacharyya, Asutosh, 1998(1958) *Bangla Mangalkabyer Itihas* (Bengali), Calcutta: A. Mukherji.

———, 1948, 'The Cult of Sasthi in Bengal', *Man in India*, 28: 153–65.

———, 1977, *The Sun and Serpent Lore of Bengal*, Calcutta: Firma K.L.M.

———, 1982, *Banglar Loksanskriti* (Bengali), New Delhi: National Book Trust.

Bhattacharyya, Deborah P., 1986, *Pagalami: Ethnopsychiatric Knowledge in Bengal*, Maxwell School of Citizenship and Public Affairs, Syracuse, N.Y.: Syracuse Univeristy.

Bhattacharya, N.C. and L.A. Natesan (eds.), 1932, *Some Bengal Villages: An Economic Survey*, Calcutta: Calcutta University.

Bhattacharyya, N.N., 1968, *Indian Puberty Rites*, Calcutta: Indian Studies: Past and Present.

Bhattacaryya, Surendramohan, 1986, *Purohita-darpan: Sam, Jaju, Rik, Ei Tribidh Bedokta Satkarnmanusthan Paddhati* (Bengali), Calcutta: Styanarayan Library.

Bhowmick, Prabodh Kumar, 1963, *Lodhas of West Bengal: A Socio-Economic Study*, Calcutta: Punthi Pustak.

Biardeau, M., 1989 (1981), *Hinduism: The Anthropology of a Civilization*, trans. by R. Nice, Delhi: Oxford University Press.

Bloch, Maurice, 1977, *From Blessing to Violence: History and Ideology in the Circumcision, Ritual of the Merina of Madagascar*, Cambridge: Cambridge University Press.

———, 1989, *Ritual, History and Power: Selected Papers in Anthropology*. London: The Athlone Press.

———, 1991, *Prey into Hunter: The Politics of Religious Experience*, Cambridge: Cambridge University Press.

Bloch, Maurice and Parry Jonathan (eds.), 1982, *Death and the Regeneration of Life*, Cambridge: Cambridge University Press.

Bock, Philip K., 1974, *Modern Cultural Anthropology: an Introduction*, New York: Alfred A. Knopf.

Bose, Nirmal Kumar, 1949, *Hindu Samajer Gadan*, Calcutta: Visva-Bharati Granthalaya.

———, 1975, *The Structure of Hindu Society*, trans. A. Beteille, from *Hindu Samajer Gadan*, Delhi: Orient Longman.

Bose, Nirmal Kumar (ed.), 1961, *Peasant Life in India: A Study in Indian Unity & Diversity*, Memoir No. 8, Calcutta: Anthropological Survey of India.

Bradford, N.J., 1985, 'The Indian renouncer: Structure and transformation in a Lingayat community', in *Indian Religion*, ed. R. Burghart and A. Cantlie. London: Curzon Press.

Breckenridge, Carol, 1978, 'From protector to litigant-changing relations between Hindu temples and the Raja of Ramnad', in *South Indian Temples*, ed. B. Stein, New Delhi: Vikas Publishing House.

Breckenridge, Carol and Peter van der Veer (ed.), 1993, *Orientalism and the Postcolonial Predicament*, Philadelphia: University of Pennsylvania Press.

Burghart, Richard, 1978, 'Hierarchical Models of the Hindu Social System', *Man*, n.s. 13: 519–36.

———, 1983, 'Renunciation in the religious traditions of south Asia', *Man*, n.s. 18: 635–53.

———, 1990, 'Ethnographers and their local counterparts in India', in *Localizing Strategies: Regional Traditions of Ethnographic Writing*, ed. R. Fardon, Edinburgh: Scottish Academic Press.

Buchanan, Francis, 1928, *An Account of the District of Purnea in 1809–10*, Districts Gazetteers in India.

Cakrabartty, Sanat Kumar, 1988, *Saktimahapitha Rarer Kshiragram o Debi Jogadya* (Bengali). Bardhaman: Jalpaiguri Book Binding.

Capwell, Charles, 1986, *The Music of the Bauls of Bengal*, The Kent State University Press.

Chakrabarti, Kunal, 2001, *Religious Process: The Puranas and the Making of a Regional Tradition*, Delhi: Oxford University Press.

Chaudhuri, Abul Ahasan, 1988 *Kangal Harinath Majumdar: 1833--96*, Bangla Academy.

Chaudhuri, Jogeshwar, 1991 *Bardhaman: Itihas o Sanskriti* (Bengali). Dwitiya Khanda, Calcutta: Pustak Bipani.

Chaudhuri, Narayan and Anukulacandra Sen, 1966, *Bardhaman Pariciti* (Bengali), Calcutta: Book Syndicate Private Ltd.

Chatterjee, T.M., 1948, *Alpona: Ritual Decoration in Bengal*, Calcutta: Orient Longmans.

Chattopadhyay, Bankimcandra, 1974 (1873) *Bangadesher Krishak: Bangadarshan*, vol. 1, Calcutta: Rifhlekt Publishing.

Chattopadhyay, Gouranga, 1964, *Ranjana: A Village in West Bengal*, Calcutta: Bookland Private Limited.

Choudhury, N.C. (ed.), 1976, *Bibliography of Anthropology of India: 1960–64*, Calcutta: Anthropological Survey of India.

Clark, T.W., 1955, 'Evolution of Hinduism in Medieval Bengali Literature: Siva, Candi, Manasa', *Bulletin of the School of Oriental and African Studies*, vol. 17: 503–18.

Clifford, J. and G.E. Marcus, 1986, *Writing Culture: The Poetics and Politics of Ethnography*, Berkeley: University of California Press.

Cohn, Bernard S., 1962, 'Political systems in eighteenth century India: the Banaras region', *Journal of the American Oriental Society*, 82: 312–20.

———, 1963, 'Comments on papers on land tenure', *The Indian Economic and Social History Review*, 1(2).

———, 1987(1968) 'Note of the history of the study of Indian society and culture', in *Structure and Change in Indian Society*, ed. Milton Singer and B.S. Cohn, New York: Wenner-Gren Foundation for Anthropological Research.

———, 1987, *An Anthropologist among the Historians and Other Essays*, Delhi: Oxford University Press.

Dalton, Edward Tuite, 1960 (1872) *Descriptive Ethnology of Bengal*, Calcutta: Indian Studies, Past and Present.

Danda, Ajit Kumar and G. Dipali, 1971, *Development and Change in Basudha: Study of a West Bengal Village*, Hyderabad.

Daniel, E. Valentine, 1984, *Fluid Signs: Being a Person the Tamil Way*, Berkeley: University of California Press.

Das, Sudhir Kumar, 1951, 'Vratya and Vrata', *Man in India*, 31(3–4): 172–84.

Das, Sudhir Ranjan, 1953, *Folk Religion of Bengal*, Part 1–I, Calcutta: S.C. Kar.

———, 1958, 'Folk religious rites: A study in origins', *Journal of the Department of Letters*, University of Calcutta, vol. II-2: 79–196.

Das, Sunil Kumar, 1995, 'Meyeli Brata-Anushthan', in *Meyeli Brata Bisaye* (Bengali), ed. Sanat Kumar Mitra, Calcutta: Pustak Bipani.

Das, Veena, 1977, *Structure and Cognition: Aspects of Hindu Caste and Rituals*, Delhi: Oxford University Press.

———, 1983, 'Language of sacrifice', *Man*, n.s. 18–3: 445–62.

Dasgupta, Birendramohan (ed.), 1982, *Bengali-English Dictionary* (Bengali), Calcutta: Sahitya Samsad.

Dasgupta, Shashibhusan, 1976 (1946), *Obscure Religious Cults*, Calcutta: Firma KLM.

Davis, Marvin, 1983, *Rank and Rivalry: The Politics of Inequality in Rural West Bengal*, Cambridge: Cambridge University Press.

Day, Lal Behari, 1874, *Govinda Samanta*, vols. I–II, London: Macmillan.

———, 1878, *Bengal Peasant Life*, London: Macmillan.

Derrett, J.D.M., 1976, 'Rajadharma', *Journal of Asian Studies*, 35: 597–609.

Dimock, Edward C., 1966, *The Place of the Hidden Moon: Erotic Mythsticism in the Vaisnava-sahajiya Cult of Bengal*, Chicago: University Press.

Dirks, Nicholas B. 1976, 'Political authority and structural change in early south Indian history', *The Indian Economic and Social History Review*, 13(2): 125–57.

———, 1982, 'The pasts of a Palaiyakar: the ethnohistory of a South Indian little king', *Journal of Asian Studies*, 41: 655–83.

———, 1986, 'From little king to landlord: property, law, and the gift under the Madras permanent settlement', *Comparative Studies in Society and History*, 28(2): 307–33.

———, 1987, *The Hollow Crown: Ethnohistory of an Indian Kingdom*, Cambridge: Cambridge University Press.

———, 1989a, 'The original caste: power, history and hierarchy in South Asia', *Contributions to Indian Sociology* (n.s.), 23(1): 59–77.

———, 1989b, 'The invention of caste: civil society in colonial India', *Social Analysis*, 25: 42–52.

Dirks, Nicholas B. (ed.), 1992, *Colonialism and Culture*, Michigan: University of Michigan Press.

Dube, Leela, 1988, 'On the construction of gender: Hindu girls in patrilineal India', in *Socialisation, Education and Women: Explorations in Gender Identity*, ed. C. Karuna, Delhi: Orient Longman.

Dumont, Luis, 1959, 'A structural definition of a folk-deity', *Contributions to Indian Sociology*, 3: 75–87.

———, 1962, 'The conception of kingship in ancient India', *Contributions to Indian Sociology*, 6: 48–77.

———, 1980 (1970), *Homo Hierarchicus: The Caste System and its Implications*, Chicago: University of Chicago Press.

———, 1983, *Affinity as a Value: Marriage Alliance in South India, with Comparative Essays on Australia*, Chicago: University of Chicago Press.

———, 1986 (1957), *A South Indian Subcaste: Social Organization and Religion of the Pramalai Kallar*, Delhi: Oxford University Press.

Durkheim, E., 1915 (1912) *The Elementary Forms of the Religious Life*, London: Allen and Unwin. (*Les formes elementaires de la vie religieuse.*)

Dutta, Nripendra Kumar, 1965, *Origin and Growth of Caste in India*, vol. II, Calcutta: Firma KLM.

Eaton, Richard, 1994 *The Rise of Islam and the Bengal Frontier, 1204–1760*, Delhi: Oxford University Press.

Famine Inquiry Commission, 1945, *Famine Inquiry Commission: Report on Bengal*, Calcutta: Government of India Press.

Field, C.D., 1875, *The Regulations of the Bengal Code*, Calcutta: Thacker, Spink and Co.

———, *1940, Final Reports on the Survey and Settlement Operations in the District of Burdwan: 1927–34*, Alipore: Bengal Government Press.

Firminger, W.K., 1962 (1917), *Historical Introduction to the Bengal Portion of 'The Fifth Report'*, Calcutta: Indian Studies, Past and Present.

Fox, Richard G., 1971, *Kin, Clan, Raja, and Rule: State-hinterland Relations in Preindustrial India*, Berkeley: University of California Press.

Frazer, James George, 1911–36, *The Golden Bough: A Study in Magic and Religion*, 13 vols., London: Macmillan and Co. Limited.

Freeman, James, 1980, 'The ladies of Lord Krishna: Rituals of middle-aged women in eastern India', in *Unspoken World: Women's Religious Lives in North-Western Cultures*, ed. N. Falk and R. Gross, San Francisco: Harper & Row, pp. 110–26.

Fruzzetti, Lina M., 1990 (1982), *The Gift of a Virgin: Women, Marriage, and Ritual in a Bengali Society*, Delhi: Oxford University Press.

———, 1989, 'Women in Hindu society', in *Gender and Anthropology*, ed. Sandra Morgan, Washington: AAA, pp. 268–93.

Fruzzetti, Lina M. and Akos Ostor, 1976, 'Seed and earth: a cultural analysis of kinship in a Bengali town', *Contributions to Indian Sociology*, n.s. 10(1).

Fuller, C.J., 1977, 'British India or traditional India? An anthropological problem', *Ethnos*, 3–4: 95–121.

———, 1979, 'Gods, priests and purity: on the relation between Hinduism and the caste system', *Man*, n.s. 14: 459–76.

———, 1984, *The Servants of Goddess: The Priests of a South Indian Temple*, London: Cambridge University Press.

———, 1988, 'Misconceiving the Grain Heap: A Critique of the Concept of the Indian, Jajmini System', in *Money and the Morality of Exchange*, ed. J. Parry and M. Bloch, Cambridge: Cambridge University Press.

———, 1992, *The Camphor Flame: Popular Hinduism and Society in India* Princeton: Princeton University Press.

Fuller, C.J. and J. Spencer, 1990, 'South Asian Anthropology in the 1980s', *South Asia Research*, 10: 85–105.

Gait, Edward, 1933 (1905), *A History of Assam*, Calcutta: Thacker Spink & Co.

———, 1913, *Census of India 1911*, Part I, *Report*, Calcutta: Superintendent Government Printing.

Galey, J.C., 1984, 'Reconsidering kingship in India: an ethnological perspective', *History and Anthropology*, 4: 123–87.

Gatwood, Lynn E., 1985, *Devi and the Spouse Goddess*, Delhi: Manohar.

Geertz, Cliford, 1973, *The Interpretation of Cultures*, New York: Basic Books.

———, 1980, *Negara: The Theatre State in Nineteenth-century Bali*, Princeton: Princeton University Press.

Ghosh, Binay, 1976, *Pashcimbanger Sanskriti* (Bengali), vols. 1–5, Calcutta: Prakas Bhaban.

Ghurye, G.S. 1932, *Caste and Race in India*, New York: Alfred A. Knopf.

Gonda, J., 1956, *Ancient Indian Kingship from the Religious Point of View, Numen*, vol. III, Lieden: E.J. Brill.

———, 1985, *Change and Continuity in Indian Religion*, Delhi: Munshiram Manoharlal.

Gordon, Stewart, 1978, 'Legitimacy and loyalty in some successor states of the eighteenth century', in *Kingship and Authority in South Asia*, ed. J.F. Richards, Madison: University of Wisconsin.

Grant, James, 1917 (1812), 'Historical and Comparative Analysis of the Finances of Bengal', *The Fifth Report from the Select Committee of the House of Commons on the Affairs of the East Indian Company*, ed. W.K. Firminger, Calcutta: R. Company.

Greenough, Paul, 1982, *Prosperity and Misery in Modern Bengal: the Famine of 1943–44*, New York: Oxford University Press.

Guha, Ranajit, 1963, *A Rule of Property for Bengal: An Essay on the Idea of the Permanent Settlement*, Paris: Mouton.

Guha, Ranajit (ed.), 1982–9, *Subaltern Studies: Writings on South Asian History and Society*, vols. I-IV, Delhi: Oxford University Press.

Guide and Glossary to Survey and Settlement Records in Bengal, 1938 (1917), Alipore: Bengal Government Press.

Gunasekara, Alex, 1978, 'Rajakariya or the duty to the king in the Kandyan kingdom of Sri Lanka', in *The Concept of Duty in south Asia*, ed. W.D. O' Flaherty and J.D.M. Derrett, New Delhi: Vikas.

Gupta, Eva Maria, 1983, *Brata und Alpana in Bengalen*, Wiesbaden: Franz Steiner Verlag.

Heesterman, J.C., 1978, 'The conundrum of the king's authority', in *Kingship and Authority in South Asia*, ed. J.F. Richards, Madison: University of Wisconsin.

———, 1985, *The Inner Conflict of Tradition*, Chicago: University of Chicago Press.

Hirst, Captain F.C., 1912, *Notes on the Old Revenue Surveys of Bengal, Bihar, Orissa and Assam*, Calcutta: Thacker, Spink & Co.

Hirst, R.J., 1910, 'The early collectorate records of Burdwan, 1786–90', *Bengal Past and Present*, vol. 6, 228–42.

Hobsbawm, Eric and Ranger Terence, eds., 1983, *The Invention of Tradition*, Cambridge: Cambridge University Press.

Hocart, Arthur M., 1927, *Kingship*, London: Oxford University Press.

———, 1968 (1950), *Caste: A Comparative Study*, London: Methuen and Co.

———, 1970, *Kings and Councillors: An Essay in the Comparative Anatomy of Human Society*, Chicago: The University of Chicago Press.

Hubert, H. and M. Mauss, 1964 (1899), *Sacrifice: Its Nature and Function*, trans, W.D. Halls, London: Cohen and West (*Essai sur la nature et la function du sacrifice*).

Hunter, William Wilson, 1868, *The Annals of Rural Bengal*, London: Smith, Elder and Co.

———, 1875–77, *A Statistical Account of Bengal*, London: (Indian Council of Social Science Research (ICSSR).

———, 1974, *A Survey of Research in Sociology and Social Anthropology*, vols. I–III, Bombay: Popular Prakashan.

Inden, Ronald B., 1976, *Marriage and Rank in Bengali Culture: A History of Caste and Clan in Middle-period Bengal*, Berkeley: University of California Press.

———, 1978, 'Ritual, authority and cyclic time in Hindu kingship', in *Kingship and Authority in South Asia*, ed. J.F. Richards, Madison: University of Wisconsin.

———, 1986, 'Orientalist Constructions of India', *Modern Asian Studies*, 20–3: 401–46.

———, 1990, *Imagining India*, Oxford: Basil Blackwell.

Inden, Ronald and Ralph Nicholas, 1977, *Kinship in Bengali Culture*, Chicago: The University of Chicago Press.

ISI (Indian Statistical Institution), 1948, *Reports Submitted to the Government of Bengal on the Rural Indebtedness Inquiry and the Agricultural Labour Enquiry*, Calcutta: ISI.

Jack, J.C., 1916, *The Economic Life of a Bengal District* (*Faridpur*), Oxford: Clarendon Press.

Kamilya, Mihir Caudhuri, 1992, *Anchalik Debata: Loksanskriti* (Bengali). Bardhaman: Bardhaman Vishwavidyalay.

Kane, P.V., 1974, *History of Dharmasastra*, vols. 1–5, Poona: Bhandarkar Oriental Research Institute.

Karkar, Sudhir, ed., 1981, *The Inner World: A Psycho-analytic Study if Childhood and Society in India*, Delhi: Oxford University Press.

Kawai, Akinobu, 1986, '*Landlords' and Imperial Rule: Change in Bengal Agrarian Society, c. 1885–1940*, Tokyo: Institution for the Study of Languages and Cultures of Asia and Africa.

Keesing, Roger M., 1981, *Cultural Anthropology: A Contemporary Perspective*, Holt, Rinehart and Winston.

Khare, R.S., 1976, *The Hindu Hearth and Home*, Durham: Carolina Academic Press.

Kinsley, D.R., 1987, *Hindu Goddess: Vision of the Divine Feminine in the Hindu Religious Tradition*, Delhi: Motilal Banarsidass.

Konar, Gopi Kant, *Bardhaman Jelar Mela: Smajtattvik Parjalocana*, (Bengali), Calcutta: College Street Publication.

Kopf, David, 1969, *British Orientalism and the Bengal Renaissance: The Dynamics of Indian Modernization 1773–1835*, California: University of California Press.

Kopf, David, ed., 1969, *Bengal Regional Identity*, Michigan: Michigan State University.

Korom, Erank J., 1992, 'To Be Happy': Narrative, Ritual Play and Leisure in An Annual Bengali Religious Festival, Ph.D. thesis in Folklore and Folklife, Faculties of the University of Pennsylvania.

Kshiragram Srijogadya Banipitha, 1969, *Kshiragram Srijogadya Banipitha Patrika, Platinam Jayanti Sangkhya* (Bengali).

Kulke, Hermann, 2001, *Kings and Cults: State Formation and Legitimation in India and Southeast Asia*, New Delhi, Manohar.

Levi-Strauss, Claude, 1966 (1962), *The Savage Mind*, London: Weidenfeld and Nicolson (*La pensee sauvage*).

———, 1967 (1958), *Structural Anthropology*, trans. Claire Jacobson and Brooke Grundfest, Schoepf, Garden City, NY: Doubleday (*Anthropology Structurale*).

Lieten, G.K., 1992, *Continuity and Change in Rural West Bengal*, New Delhi: Sage.

Long, J., ed., 1868, *Adam's Three Reports on Vernacular Education in Bengal and Behar*, Calcutta: Home Secretariat Press.

Mackay, E.J.H., 1948, *Early Indus Civilization*, 2nd edn., London: Luzac.

Madan, T.N. and Sarana Gopala (eds.), 1962, *Indian Anthropology: Essays in Memory of D.N. Majumdar*, London: Asia Publishing House.

Mahapatra, L.K., 1977, 'Gods, Kings, and Caste System in India', in *The New Wind: Changing Identities in South Asia*, ed. Kenneth David, Chicago: Mouton.

Maine, Henry, 1980, *Village Communities in the East and West*, London: John Murray.

Maity, Pradyot Kumar, 1966, *Historical Studies in the Cult of the Goddess Manasa*, Calcutta: Punthi Pustak.

———, 1988, *Folk-Rituals of Eastern India*, Delhi: Abhinav Publications.

———, 1989, *Human Fertility Cults and Rituals of Bengal*, Delhi: Abhinav Publications.

———, 1995, *Samaj o Sanskritir Ruparekha* (Bengali), Calcutta: Purbadri-Prakasani.

Majumdar, Amiya Kumar, 1984, *Satipitha Parikrama*, Calcutta: Gangotri.

Majumdar, Asutosh (ed.), 1992, *Meyeder Brata-katha* (Bengali), Calcutta: Deb Sahitya Kutir.

Majumdar, D.N., 1947, *Progress of Anthropology in India* (*1911–46*), Delhi: Indian Science Congress Association and Council of Scientific & Industrial Research.

Majumdar, Dakshinaronjyan Mitra, 1992 (1907), *Thakurmar Jhuli: Banglar Rupa-katha*, Calcutta: Mitra & Ghosh Publishers.

Majumdar, R.C., 1973, *History of Mediaeval of Bengal*, Calcutta: G. Bhardwaj & Co.

Marglin, Freederi, 1985, *Wives of the God-King: The Rituals of the Devadasis of Puri*, Delhi: Oxford University Press.

Marriott, Mckim, 1965, 'Caste ranking and food transactions, a matrix analysis', in *Structure and Change in Indian Society*, ed. Milton Singer et al. Chicago: Aldine Pub.

———, 1966, 'The feast of love', in *Krishna: Myths, Rites and Attitudes*, ed. M. Singer, Honolulu: East-West Center.

Marriott, Mckim (ed.), 1955, *Village India*, Chicago: University of Chicago.

Marriott, McKim and Ronald Inden, 1977, 'Toward an ethnosociology of the caste system', in *The New Wind: Changing Identities in South Asia*, ed. Keneth David, The Hague and Paris: Mouton.

Mauss, M., 1967, *The Gift: Forms and Functions of Exchange in Archaic Societies*, trans. Ian Cunnison, New York: Norton.

Mayer, A.C., 1960, *Caste and Kinship in Central India*, London: Routledge.

———, 1981, 'Perceptions of Princely Rule: Perspective from a Biography' *Contributions to Indian Sociology* (n.s.), 15: 127–54.

Mazumdar, Sucheta, 1981, 'Socialization of Hindu middle class Bengali women', in *UCLA South Asia Bulletin* 1 (Winter): 30–37.

McCutchion, David J., 1972, *Late Medieval Temples of Bengal: Origins and Classification*, Calcutta: The Asiatic Society.

McDaniel, 1989, *The Madness of the Saints: Ecstatic Religion in Bengal*, Chicago: University of Chicago Press.

McGee, Mary, 1991, 'Desired fruits: motive and intention in the votive rites of Hindu women', in *Roles and Rituals for Hindu Women*, ed. Julia Leslie, London: Pinter Publishers, pp. 71–88.

McGilvray, Dennis B., 1982, 'Mukkuvar Vannimai: Tamil caste and matriclan ideology in Batticaloa, Sri Lanka', in *Caste Ideology and Interaction*, ed. Dennis B. McGilvray, Cambridge: Cambridge University Press.

———, 1983, 'Paraiyar Drummers of Sri Lanka: Consensus and Constraint in an Untouchable Caste', *American Ethnologist*, 10: 97–115.

McLane, John R., 1993, *Land and Local Kingship in Eighteenth-century Bengal*, Cambridge: Cambridge University Press.

M'Crindle, J.W., 1987 (1901), *Ancient India: As Described in Classical Literature*, Patna: Eastern Book House.

Mencher, J.P., 1974, 'The caste system upside down, or the not-so-mysterious east', *Current Anthropology*, 15, 4: 469–78.

Mitra, Ashok (ed.), 1953, *The Tribes and Castes of West Bengal*, Calcutta: West Bengal Government Press.

———, 1961, *Pashcinbangerpuja-Parban o Mela* (Bengali), Panchamkhandu, Bharaterjanaganana.

Mitra, Sanat Kumar (ed.), 1995, *Meyeli Brat Bisaye* (Bengali), Calcutta: Pustak Bipani.

Mitra, Sarada Charan, 1898, *The Land-Law of Bengal*, Calcutta: Thacker, Spink & Co.

Moffatt, Michael, 1979, *An Untouchable Community in South India: Structure and Consensus*, Princeton University Press.

Monier-Williams, M., 1979, *A Sanskrit-English Dictionary*, Delhi: Motilal Banarsidass.

Mookerjee, Radharomon, 1919, *Occupancy Right: Its History and Incidents*, Calcutta: University of Calcutta.

Morinis, E. Alan, 1984, *Pilgrimage in the Hindu Tradition: A Case Study of West Bengal*, Delhi: Oxford University Press.

Mukherjea, Charulal, 1946, 'Bratas in Bengal', *Man in India*, vol. 26, nos. 3–4, pp. 202–6.

Mukherjee, Ramkrishna, 1956, *The Dynamics of a Rural Society: A Study of the Economic Structure in Bengal Villages*, Berlin: Akademi-Verlag.

———, 1971, *Six Villages of Bengal*, Bombay: Popular Prakashan.

Mukhopadhyay, Rakhal-Das, 1913, *Bardhaman-rajbangsnucarita* (Bengali), Calcutta.

Mukhopadhyay, Satyanarayan, 1961, *Kshiragramerpracinaitijja, Pashcinbanger-puja-parban o mela* (Bengali), Panchamkhandu, Bharaterjanaganana.

Murase, Satoru, 1991, Patchwork Jacket and Loincloth: An Ethnographic Study of the Bauls of Bengal, Ph.D. thesis, University of Illinois.

Nicholas, R.W., 1962, Villages of the Bengal Delta: A Study of Ecology and Peasant Society, Ph.D. thesis, Chicago University.

———, 1967, 'Ritual hierarchy and social relations in rural Bengal', *Contributions to Indian Sociology*, n.s. 1: 56–83.

Nigurananda, 1984, *Mahatirth Ekannapither Sandhane* (Bengali), Calcutta: Srat Publishing House.

Oldham, W.B., 1894, *Some Historical and Ethnical Aspects of the Burdwan District,* Calcutta.

Ostor, Akos, 1978, 'On the ethnographic study of complex Bengali puja and Festivals', *Journal of the Indian Anthropological Society*, 13: 3.

———, 1980, *The Play of the Gods: Locality, Ideology, Structure, and Time in the Festivals of a Bengali Town*, Chicago: University of Chicago Press.

———, 1982, *Puja in Society*, Lucknow: Ethnographic and Folk Culture Society.

———, 1984, *Culture and Power*, Delhi: Sage.

O'Malley, L.S.S., 1913, *Bengal, Bihar, and Orissa and Sikkim, Census of India. 1911*, vol. V, Calcutta: Bengal Secretariat Book Dept.

———, 1935, *Popular Hinduism: The Religion of the Masses*, Cambridge: Cambridge University Press.

P.M. Bagucir Dairektari Panjitka (Bengali), Calcutta, 1994 (1401).

Padel, Felix, 1995, *The Sacrifice of Human Being: British Rule and the Konds of Orissa*, Delhi: Oxford University Press.

Palit, Chittabrata, 1975, *Tensions in Bengal Rural Society: Landlords, Planters and Colonial Rule, 1830–60*, Calcutta: Progressive Publishers.

Pandey, Rajbali, 1969, *Hindu Samskaras: Socio-Religious Study of the Hindu Sacraments.* Delhi: Motilal Banarsidass.

Parry, J., 1974, 'Egalitarian values in a hierarchical Society', *South Asian Review*, 7, 2: 95–121.

———, 1979, *Caste and Kinship in Kangra*, London: Routledge & Kegan Paul.

———, 1980, 'Ghosts, greed and sin: The occupational identity of the Benares funeral priests', *Man* (n.s.), 15: 88–111.

Pearson, Anne Mackenzie, 1996, '*Because It Gives Me Peace of Mind': Ritual Fasts in the Religious Lives of Hindu Women*, New York: State University of New York Press.

Porter, A.E., 1987 (1933), *Census of India, 1931*, vol. V: *Bengal and Sikkim*, Part 1: *Report*, Delhi: Usha Publication.

Preston, James J., 1980, *Cult of the Goddess: Social and Religious Change in a Hindu Temple*, Delhi: Vikas Publishing House.

Price, P.G., 1979, 'Rajadharma in Ramnad, land litigation, and largess', *Contributions to Indian Sociology*, n.s. 13(2): 207–40.

Quigley, Declan, 1993, *The Interpretation of Caste*, Oxford: Oxford University Press.

Raheja, G.G., 1988a, *The Poison in the Gift: Ritual, Prestation, and the Dominant Caste in a North Indian Village*, Chicago and London: University of Chicago Press.

———, 1988b, 'India: Caste, Kinship, and Dominance Reconsidered, *Annual Review of Anthropology*, 17: 497–522.

———, 1989, 'Centrality, Mutuality and Hierarchy: Shifting Aspects of Intercaste Relationships in North India', *Contributions to Indian Sociology* (n.s.), 23(1): 79–101.

Ray, Niharranjan, 1949, *Bangalir Itihas: Adiparban* (Bengali), Calcutta: Dey's Publishing. English translation, *History of the Bengali People: Ancient Period* by John W. Hood, 1994, Calcutta: Orient Longman.

Ray, Ratnalekha, 1979, *Change in Bengal Agrarian Society: c. 1760–1850*, Delhi: Manohar.

Ray, Shyamal Kumar, 1974, *Bibliographies of Eminent Indian Anthropologists*, Calcutta: Anthropological Survey of India.

Ray, Sudhansu Kumar, 1961, *The Ritual Art of the Bratas of Bengal*, Calcutta: Firma K.L.M.

Risley, H.H., 1881 (1891), *The Tribes and Castes of Bengal: Ethnographical Glossary*, 2 vols, Calcutta: Firma K.L.M.

———, 1915, *The People of India*, London: W. Thacker & Co.

Rivers, W.H.R., 1907, *The Todas*, London: Macmillan.

Robinson, Sandra P., 1980, The Dharmapuja: A Study of Rites and Symbols: Association with the Bengali Deity Dharmaraj, Ph.D. thesis, University of Chicago.

———, 1983, 'Hindu Paradigms of Women: Images and Values', in *Women, Religion and Social Change*, ed. Y.Y. Haddad and E.B. Findly, Albany: Suny Press, pp. 181–215.

Rowlands, J. Helen, 1930, *La Femme Bengalie dans la Litterature du Moyen Age*, Paris: Librairie d'Amerique et d'Orient.

Roy, Asim, 1983, *The Islamic Syncretistic Tradition in Bengal*, Princeton: Princeton University Press.

Roy, Atul Chandra, 1977, *History of Bengal: Mughal Period* (*1526–1765 A.D.*), Calcutta: Nababharat Publishers.

Roy, Indrani Basu, 1993, *Kalighat: Its Impact on Socio-Cultural Life of Hindus*, Calcutta: Gyan Publishing House.

Roy, Sarat Chandra, 1966, *Studies in Indian Anthropology*, Calcutta: Indian Studies.

Rudolph, L. and S. Rudolph, 1967, *The Modernity of Tradition: Political Development in India*, Chicago: University of Chicago Press.

Sachuau, Edward C., 1993 (1888), *Alberuni's India*, New Delhi: Asian Educational Service.

Sahlins, M., 1985, *Islands of History*, Chicago: University of Chicago Press.

Said, Edward W., 1979, *Orientalism*, New York: Vintage.

Saiyad, 1991, *Bardhaman Jelay Kamiunist Andokaner Atit Prasang* (Bengali), Bardhaman: Natun Cithi Prakashana.

Sanyal, N.B., 1961, 'A Tale of a Pilgrimage', *Kalna College Magazine*, Kalna: Kalna College.

Sanyal, Hitesranjan, 1971, 'Continuities of social mobility in traditional and modern society in India: Two case studies of caste mobility in Bengal', *The Journal of Asian Studies*, 30(2).

Sarana, Gopala, 1971–2, *Anthropological Method and Indian Anthropology*, Madras: University of Madras.

Sarkar, R.M., 1995, 'Meyeli brat-anushthaner sarbajaninta', in *Meyeli Brata Bisaye* (Bengali), ed. Sanat Kumar Mitra, Calcutta: Pustak Bipani.

Sarma, Jotirmoye, 1980, *Caste Dynamics among the Bengali Hindus*, Calcutta: Firma K.L.M.

Sarma, Jotirmoye, 1957, 'Changes in Durga Puja festival', *Study of Change in Traditional Culture*, Calcutta: University of Calcutta.

Sastri, Haraprasad, 1897, *Discovering Living Buddhism in Bengal*, Calcutta: Hare Press.

Schendel, Willem van (ed.), 1992, *Francis Buchanan in Southeast Bengal (1798): His Journey to Chittagong, the Chittagon Hill Tracts, Noakhali and Comilla*, Dhaka: University Press Limited.

Sekine, Yasumasa, 1989, *Theories of Pollution: Theoretical Perspective in a South Indian Tamil Village*, Tokyo: Institute for the Study of Language and Culture of Asia and Africa.

Sen, Dinesh Candra, 1920, *The Folk-Literature of Bengal*, Calcutta: University of Calcutta.

Sen, Nabendu, 1995, 'Meyeli brata: kodal-kata dhan', in *Meyeli Brata Bisaye* (Bengali), ed. Sanat Kumar Mitra, Calcutta: Pustak Bipani.

Sen, Sukumar, 1940, *Bangla Sahityer Itihas* (Bengali) Calcutta: Anand Pablishars.

Sengupta, Purba, 1997, *Satir Dehacched Ekanna Pitha* (Bengali), Calcutta: Mitra o Ghosh Publishers.

Sengupta, Sankar, 1970, *A Study of Women of Bengal*, Calcutta: Indian Publications.

———, 1972, *Banglar Mukh Ami Dekhiyachi* (Bengali), Calcutta: Indian Publications.

Sengupta, Syamalkanti, 1973, *The Social System in a Bengal Village*, Calcutta: Edition Indian.

Shulman, David Dean, 1980, *Tamil Temple Myths*, Princeton: Princeton University Press.

Singer, Milton, 1972, *When a Great Tradition Modernizes: An Anthropological Approach to Indian Civilization*, New Delhi: Praeger.

Sinha, Ranajit, 1911, *Law of Service Tenures in Bengal*, Madras: Law Printing House.

Sirkar, D.C., 1973, *The Sakta Pithas*, Delhi: Motilal Banarsidass.

Sirkar, D.C., ed., 1967, *The Sakti Cult and Tara*, Calcutta: University of Calcutta.

Srinivas, M.N., 1952, *Religion and Society among the Coorgs of South India*, Bombay: Media Promoters & Publishers (rpt. 1978).

———, 1987, *The Dominant Caste and Other Essays*, Delhi: Oxford University Press.

Srinivas, M.N. (ed.), 1955, *India's Villages*, Calcutta: Government of West Bengal Publication.

Srinivas, M.N., M.S.A. Rao and A.M. Shah, 1972–4, *A Survey of Research in Sociology and Social Anthropology*, 3 vols., Bombay, India: Popular Prakashan.

Srinivas, M.N. and M.N. Panini, 1987, 'The development of sociology and social anthropology in India', in *Indian Sociology: Reflections and Introspections*, ed. T.K. Oommen and Partha N. Mukherji, Bombay: Popular Prakashan.

Stein, Burton, 1980, *Peasant State and Society in Medieval South India*, Delhi: Oxford University Press.

Tagore, Rabindranath, 1931, *The Religion of Man, being the Hibbert Lectures for 1930*, London: George Allen & Unwin Ltd.

Tambiah, Stanley J., 1976, *World Conqueror and World Renouncer: A Study of Buddhism and Polity in Thailand against a Historical Background*, Cambridge: Cambridge University Press.

Tanabe, Akio, 1999, 'Kingship and Caste: The Relationship between King/ Dominant Caste and the Brahman Reconsidered', in *Rituals as Popular Cultures: Towards Historico-Anthropological Understanding of Modern Indian Society*, ed. Steering Committee of the Research Project: Institutions, Networks and Forces of Changes in Contemporary South Asia.

Tanaka, Masakazu, 1991, *Patrons, Devotees and Goddesses: Ritual and Power among the Tamil Fishermen of Sri Lanka*, Kyoto: Kyoto University, Institute for Reseach in Humanities.

———, 1993, 'Why are Brahman temple priests highest in the caste hierarchy? The Case of Chidambaram Nataraja Temple, South India', *From Vedic Altar to Village Shrine*, Senri Ethnological Studies, 36, Osaka: National Museum of Ethnology.

Thakur, Abanindranath, 1943 (1919), *Banglar Brata* (Bengali), Santiniketan: bishwa-Bharati University.

Tod, James, 1972(1829), *Annals and Antiquities of Rajasthan or the Central and Western Rajpot States of India*, Delhi: Motilal Banarsidass.

Togawa, Masahiko, 1992, From Court Ritual to Popular Riwal: An Ethnohistorical study of Durgapuja in Bengal (Japanese), *Japanese Jaurnal of Ethnology*, 57: 2, pp. 174–96.

———, 1997, 'Untouchable or Scheduled Castes?—a Gram Panchayat Election in West Bengal in 1993', in *Untouchability and the Depressed in the Caste System: Japanese Studies on South Asia*, no. 1, ed. Hiroyuki Kotani, Delhi: Manohar, pp. 275–339.

———, 1999, 'Ritual towards totality: *Sola-ana-puja*, the ritual organization of *durgapuja* in rural Bengal', in *Rituals as Popular Culture: towards Historico-Anthropological Understanding of Modern Indian Society*, ed. Hiroyunki Kotani, Tokyo. Steering Committee of the Research Project: Institutions, Networks and Forces of Changes in Contemporary South Asia.

———, 2001, 'Women within the hierarchy: The *jajmani-purohitani* relationship in the *brata* ritual of Bengal', *Journal of the Japanese Association for South Asian Studies*, no. 13.

———, 2002, 'Caste, kingship and village studies: a theoretical prospect of anthropology in South Asia', in *Contemporary Anthroplogy: Theory and Practice*, ed. S.M. Nurul Alam, Dhaka: University Press Limited.

Turner, Victor, 1967, *The Forest of Symbols: Aspects of Ndembu Ritual*, Ithaca: Cornell University Press.

———, 1976(1969), *The Ritual Process: Structure and Anti-structure*, Chicago: Aldine.

———, 1974 *Dramas, Fields, and Metaphors*, Ithaca: Cornell University Press.

Usuda, Masayuki, 1992, 'Historical evolution of a Talukdari village in southern Bangladesh', *The Bulletin of the Faculty of Letters*, Tokai University, nos. 51, 52, 55, 1989–91.

Van der Veer, Peter, 1989, *Gods on Earth: The Management of Religious Experience and Identity in a North Indian Pilgrimage Center*, Delhi: Oxford University Press.

van Gennep, Arnold, 1960, *The Rites of Passage*, trans. Monika B. Vizedom and G.L. Caffee, London: Routledge & Kegan Paul.

Vidyarthi, L.P., 1961, *The Sacred Complex in Hindu Gaya*, Bombay: Asia Publishing House.

———, 1977, 'Rise of social anthropology in India (1774–1972): a Historical Appraisal', in *The New Wind: Changing Identities in South Asia*, ed. Kenneth David, Chicago: Mouton Publishers.

Wadley, S.S., 1976, 'Brothers, husbands and sometimes sons: kinsmen', *Eastern Anthropologist* 29, no. 1: 149–70.

———, 1977, 'Power in Hindu ideology and practice', *The New Wind: Changing Identities of South Asia*, The Hague: Mouton Publishers.

———, 1980, 'Hindu Women's Family and Household Rites', in *Unspoken Worlds Women's Religious Lives in Non-Western Cultures*, ed. N. Falk and R. Gross, pp. 94–109.

———, 1983, 'The rains of estrangement', *Contributions to Indian Sociology*, vol. 17, no. 1.

———, 1984, 'Vrats: transformers of destiny', in *Karma: An Anthropological Inquiry*, ed. Charles Keyes and E.V. Daniel, Berkeley: University of California.

———, 1992, 'The village Indra', in *Balancing Acts: Women and the Process of Social Change*, ed. P.L. Johnson, Boulder: Wetviesw Press, pp. 65–87.

Weber, Max, 1958, *The Religion of India (Hinduismus und Buddhismus)*, trans. H. Gerth and D. Martindale, Glencoe: The Free Press, Tubingen.

Whitehead, Henry, 1921, *The Village Gods of South India*, Delhi: Sumit Publications.

Wiser, Willam Henricks, 1936 (1958), *The Hindu Jajmani System: A Socio-Economic System Interrelating Members of a Hindu Village Community in Services*, Lucknow: Lucknow Publication House.

Zbavitel, Dusan, 1961, 'The Development of the Baromasin Bengali literature', *Archiv Orientali*, 29: 582–619.

———, 1961, 'Songs of the twelve months in Bengal', *New Orient*, 3: 109–12.

———, 1976, *Bengali Literature*, Wiesbaden: Otto Harrassowitz.

OFFICIAL DOCUMENTS

Bengal District Gazetteers, Calcutta, 1910–24.

Bengal Tenancy Act, 5th edn., Rai Surendra Chandra Sen Bahadur, Calcutta: M.C. Sarkar & Sons, 1925.

Census 1951: West Bengal, Alipore, 1953.

Final Reports on the Survey and Settlement Operations in the District of Burdwan: 1927–34, Alipore, 1940.

Guide and Glossary to Survey and Settlement Records in Bengal, 1938 (1917).

Indian Land-System: Ancient, Medieval and Modern (With Special Reference to Bengal), Alipore, 1958.

Pascimbanger Puja-Parban o Mela, vols. 1–5, ed. A. Mitra, in *Census 1951*.

Report of the Land Revenue Commission, Bengal, vol. 1, 1940.

Some Historical and Ethnical Aspects of the Burdwan District, by W.B. Oldham, Calcutta, 1894.

The Tribes and Castes of West Bengal, ed. A. Mitra, in *Census 1951*.

West Bengal District Gazetteers, Calcutta, 1968.

West Bengal District Records (n.s.), Calcutta, 1954.

Index